REMINISCENCES

OF

REAR ADMIRAL JOSEPH MUSE WORTHINGTON

U. S. Navy (Retired)

U. S. NAVAL INSTITUTE

ANNAPOLIS, MARYLAND

1975

Preface

This volume contains the transcript of seven taped interviews with Rear Admiral Joseph Muse Worthington, USN (Ret.) at his home on Gibson Island, Maryland in 1972 (April to August). The interviews were obtained by John T. Mason, Jr. for the Oral History project of the U.S. Naval Institute.

Admiral Worthington corrected the original transcript. It was then re-typed and indexed. The Admiral has added an appendix of various documents. A list of these documents is incorporated in this volume. It will be found immediately preceding the documents themselves at the back of the book.

The researcher will be interested especially in Admiral Worthington's account of the Battle of Midway and in several other battles that followed in the South Pacific. He participated in these as skipper of the USS BENHAM. Other sections of note are those dealing with the Naval War College and the Industrial College of the Armed Forces.

John T. Mason, Jr.,
Director of Oral History
U.S. Naval Institute
Annapolis, Maryland
October, 1975

DECLARATION OF TRUST

The undersigned does hereby appoint and designate as his (her) Trustee herein, the Secretary-Treasurer and Publisher of the United States Naval Institute to perform and discharge the following duties, powers, and privileges in connection with the possession and use of a certain taped interview between the undersigned and the Oral History Department of the United States Naval Institute.

1. Classification of Transcript.

   (X)a. If classified OPEN, the transcript(s) may be read or the recording(s) audited by the qualified personnel upon presentation of proper credentials, as determined by the Secretary-Treasurer of the U. S. Naval Institute.

   ( )b. If classified PERMISSION REQUIRED TO CITE OR QUOTE, the user will be required to obtain permission in writing from the interviewee prior to quoting or citing from either the transcript(s) or the recording(s).

   ( )c. If classified PERMISSION REQUIRED, permission must be obtained in writing from the interviewee before the transcribed interview(s) can be examined or the tape recording(s) audited.

   ( )d. If classified CLOSED, the transcribed interview(s) and the tape recording(s) will be sealed until a time specified by the interviewee. This may be until the death of the interviewee or for any specified number of years.

   It is expressly understood that in giving this authorization, I am in no way precluded from placing such restrictions as I may desire upon use of the interview at any time during my lifetime, nor does this authorization in any way affect my rights to the copyright of my literary expressions that may be contained in the interview.

Witness my hand and seal this 14th day of May 1975

I hereby accept and consent to the foregoing Declaration of Trust and the powers therein conferred upon me as Trustee:

REAR ADMIRAL JOSEPH MUSE WORTHINGTON, U. S. NAVY, (RETIRED)

Joseph Muse Worthington was born in Annapolis, Maryland, on March 11, 1902, graduated from the Donaldson School, Howard County, Maryland, in 1919, and was appointed to the Naval Academy from that state, entering on June 9, 1920. He was graduated on June 4, 1924, and commissioned Ensign on June 5, 1924, promoted to Lieutenant (junior grade), June 5, 1927, and Lieutenant June 30, 1934. He was subsequently promoted as follows: to Lieutenant Commander, July 1, 1939; Commander (T), August 1942 and Captain June 1, 1943.

After graduation in 1924 and temporary duty in the Bureau of Ordnance, Rear Admiral (then Ensign) Worthington reported to the USS TEXAS, operating in the Atlantic, in which ship he was assigned to gunnery duty. The next year he reported to the USS NOKOMIS in which he served two years engaged in surveying the North Coast of Cuba. In September 1927 he joined the USS MEMPHIS, first serving as Anti-Aircraft Officer and later as Communications Officer. During this cruise the MEMPHIS operated successively in the Atlantic, Pacific and Asiatic Fleets. In March 1929, he reported to the USS TUTUILA of the Yangtze Patrol as Chief Engineer, Gunnery and Communications Officer, and served in that ship until December 1930.

Rear Admiral (then Lieutenant j. g.) Worthington reported for temporary duty as an instructor in the Seamanship Department of the Naval Academy in March 1931. He graduated from the Army Chemical Warfare School in Edgewood Arsenal in June, then was under instruction at the Postgraduate School, Annapolis, Maryland, General Line Course, graduating in May 1932. In that year he was a member of the winning Navy Leech Cup Tennis Team. He reported to the Chief of Naval Operations for temporary duty in June 1932; to the Army Industrial College in August, graduating in 1933 from that College.

In June 1933, Rear Admiral (then Lieutenant j. g.) Worthington joined the USS PENSACOLA, where he served three years in the Gunnery Department, the last year as Assistant Fire Control Officer. His next duty was in the Navy Department, Office of the Judge Advocate General, from June 1936 until August 1937. He was again a member of the winning Navy Leech Cup Tennis Team in 1937, and of the Navy Tennis Team which won the Bar Harbor Trophy from the British Navy. In August 1937 he reported for duty at the Naval Academy and served as an instructor in the Executive Department until May 1938.

In June 1938, Rear Admiral (then Lieutenant) Worthington reported for duty in the USS MINNEAPOLIS as Aide and Flag Secretary on the Staff of Commander Cruiser Division 6, Scouting Fleet, and served two years on that staff when Rear Admiral (later Admiral) R. E. Ingersoll was Commander Cruiser Division 6 and Commander Cruisers Hawaiian Detachment. In June 1940 he was ordered to duty as Gunnery Officer of the USS NORTHAMPTON, and in that capacity did considerable experimental work in the practical use of radar in cruiser gunfire control.

R. Adm. J. M. Worthington, USN, Ret.

Upon completion of the Okinawa operations, Rear Admiral (then Captain) Worthington with Destroyer Division 113 reported to Commander THIRD Fleet, Admiral Halsey, for operations off Japan. For his services in this command he was awarded a Gold Star in lieu of a second Legion of Merit, Combat "V," with the following citation:

Gold Star in lieu of Second Legion of Merit: "For exceptionally meritorious conduct in the performance of outstanding services to the Government of the United States as Commander of a Destroyer Division during operations against enemy Japanese Homeland from July 1 to August 22, 1945. During this period, Captain Worthington skillfully directed his division in carrier strikes against the Honshu, Tokyo and Hokkaido areas and, on several occasions, supervised the ships under his command while acting as a destroyer radar picket group for the carrier Task Force. On August 13, five enemy planes were destroyed by the combat air patrol controlled by this unit. His skill, leadership and devotion to duty were in keeping with the highest traditions of the United States Naval Service."

On November 5, 1945, Rear Admiral (then Captain) Worthington was detached from Command of Destroyer Squadron 57, then in the Eastern Japan Force, and returned to the United States, where he was on temporary duty in the Bureau of Naval Personnel, Navy Department, Washington, D. C., until reporting for duty on the Staff of the Army Industrial College as Director of Instruction on December 12, 1945. In August 1946, Rear Admiral (then Captain) Worthington became Deputy Commandant of the Industrial College of the Armed Forces and continued duty as Director of Instruction.

On December 16, 1948, at Boston, Massachusetts, Rear Admiral (then Captain) Worthington assumed command of the U.S.S. ROCHESTER, operating in the Atlantic. The ship placed second of the eleven cruisers in the Atlantic Fleet Battle Efficiency competition. Detached from this command on December 21, 1949, he reported for duty in the Office of the Chief of Naval Operations, International Affairs Division, where he served as Assistant for Joint Chiefs of Staff and Armed Forces Policy Council matters, and Assistant Director until August 1952. His final assignment was United States Planner, Standing Group, North Atlantic Treaty Organization, Office of the Secretary of Defense.

In addition to the Legion of Merit, Combat "Vs," and Gold Star; the Bronze Star Medal, Combat "V," and three Gold Stars; Rear Admiral Worthington has the Yangtze Service Medal; American Defense Service Medal (Fleet Clasp); American Campaign Medal; Asiatic-Pacific Campaign Medal with engagement stars for the following: Battle of Midway, Guadalcanal-Tulagi Landings, Capture and Defense of Guadalcanal, Eastern Solomons (Stewart Island), Okinawa Gunto Operations, THIRD Fleet Operations against Japan (July 10 - August 15, 1945), Kurile Island Operations (Kurabu Saki, Matsuwa.) He also has the World War II Victory Medal and Navy Occupation Service Medal (Asia Clasp).

R. Adm. J. M. Worthington, USN, Ret.

On June 30, 1954 he was relieved of all active duty in the Navy. Having been especially commended by the executive department for his performance of duty in actual combat, he was transferred to the retired list with the rank of Rear Admiral.

On July 1, 1954 Rear Admiral Worthington took a position with J. R. Greiner Company of Baltimore, Maryland, Consulting Engineers; and since that date has been assigned as Resident Engineer charged with carrying out the responsibilities of this Company under the terms of the Trust Agreement securing Ohio Turnpike Revenue Bonds.

He and his wife, the former Katharine Crem of Cambridge, Massachusetts, and two children, Joseph M., III, and Katharine Crem Worthington, Jr., live at 2631 Ashton Road, Cleveland 18, Ohio.

2 March 1962
Copied - 17 April 1967

Worthington #1 - 1

Interview No. 1 with Rear Admiral Joseph Muse Worthington,
U.S. Navy (Retired)

Place: His residence on Gibson Island, Maryland

Date: Wednesday morning, 5 April 1972

Subject: Biography

By: John T. Mason, Jr.

Q: Admiral, I've been looking forward to this series with you. I know that you have an understanding of the problem of the historian and therefore I expect that you will keep him in mind as you talk about the events in your naval career.

Would you begin in the proper way for a biography by giving me the date of your birth, the place of your birth, and a little something about your family background?

Adm. W.: I was born in Annapolis, Maryland, March 11, 1902, on Church Street, in the house which belonged to my grandfather from the time he retired from the Army. He was Surgeon Burton Randall, Brevet Lieutenant Colonel, U.S. Army.

My father was Joseph Muse Worthington, M.D., who practiced in Anne Arundel County and Annapolis for many years. I lived at this place on Church Street until I was eleven years old. During my school days, I attended the Holladay School . . .

Q: Was that a public school?

Adm. W.: A private school on Charles Street.

Q: Inasmuch as you were a resident of Annapolis, you, of course, were Navy-oriented, I suppose?

Adm. W.: Yes. My uncle was class of 1875, Walter F. Worthington. He retired in 1919 as a rear admiral. Another uncle was John L. Worthington, who died as a passed midshipman of the class of 1880.

I spent every summer on our farm on the Severn River, near Annapolis, Clements Creek. I went away to boarding school in Howard County, Maryland, in 1914, completing five years there and graduating in 1919.

Q: What kind of a school was that?

Adm. W.: It was a church school run by the rector of Mt. Calvary Church in Baltimore. Fr. William A. McClenthen D.D. and Fr. Herbert S. Hastings were headmasters. This was a small school but it had a splendid faculty. We had classes six days a week and plenty of sports. I was able to participate in football, baseball, basketball, and tennis.

In preparing for the Naval Academy I crammed at Knox Stallings preparatory school.

Q: You overlooked Bobby Werntz?

Worthington #1 - 3

Adm. W.: Yes. He was round the corner. Knox Stallings was on Prince George Street.

Q: Tell me first when you decided to go to the Academy. What influenced you, other than the atmosphere in Annapolis itself?

Adm. W.: My oldest brother, Ellicott Worthington, who built this house that I'm living in now, asked when I was still in the Donaldson School if I was interested in the Navy. I said I hadn't thought much about it, but I was. He said, "I will see what I can do about getting you an appointment." And this is rather interesting, I think, because I had waited a year for an appointment, until he encountered a business friend, O. E. Weller, later Secretary of War, head of the Army, and later senator, but the political boss in Maryland, the Republican Party. And he said, "I will write my friend, Congressman Mudd and he will send you the appointment." -- Sydney E. Mudd.

Q: Was he of the Annapolis district?

Adm. W.: The Annapolis district, but the thing that interested me was that all my family in Annapolis since the first one had voted the Democratic ticket.

I entered on June 9, 1920, was sworn in by the superintendent, Rear Admiral Archibald H. Scales, and spent a very busy summer in the practical workings of the Navy, not very much in the academic field in those days.

Q: Drilling.

Adm. W.: Drilling, sailing, rowing, working in the shops over in the machine shops.

Q: You had the benefit of knowing what you were in for, didn't you, that first year?

Adm. W.: Yes, I did, but the first year was really rugged when September came and the upper classmen returned, and we had an unusual happening that year. The hazing caused unfavorable publicity for the Naval Academy to such an extent that Admiral Scales segregated the plebes on the lower floor of Bancroft Hall, upper classmen on the upper floors, and stationed an upper classman with a fixed bayonet at each stairway connecting.

Q: What provoked this? You say it was hazing, but was there a specific incident?

Adm. W.: Well, it received publicity. Someone, I believe, wrote to a congressman or a senator, but it received publicity which you are familiar with in the Baltimore Sun and the Washington papers. The superintendent was called by the

Secretary and he had to take drastic action. This was cleared up before the Army-Navy game and I would say the rest of plebe year passed without incident.

Q: So the segregation didn't last very long?

Adm. W.: About a month, until they were willing to try again.

Q: It sounds like a rather unworkable system?

Adm. W.: It was a most undesirable system, frankly, but I think the superintendent felt it was justified. The rest of the year went off with hard work and the upper classmen more or less ignored the fourth class but saw that they did plenty of drilling, marched them to class.

Q: How did you adapt yourself to this discipline?

Adm. W.: The discipline did not bother me one iota for this reason. I made up my mind that plebe year was going to be tough and I was going to survive. The system did not bother me too much. I'd worked before, on the farm every summer, in a munition plant in 1918, the Bartlett Heyward Company plant in the summer of 1918, and on a peach farm in Belair in the summer of 1919. I was used to work.

Q: How about scholastically, how did you find the courses?

Adm. W.: Tough. I found the courses exceedingly hard. I do not know whether it was because I had majored in this particular type of school - I had Latin, French, English, Spanish and Greek, with lesser time devoted to mathematics, algebra, and geometry, and physics.

Q: The emphasis in your preparatory school was quite the opposite to what it was in the Academy then?

Adm. W.: Well, the preparatory school was excellent for one thing. They every day went over the previous examinations and naturally we went through a cycle and then would repeat it. There was nothing that I can recall that appeared on the Naval Academy entrance exam that we hadn't covered time and time again in class. I made excellent marks on the entrance exam, but it was not the kind of a course that you have now that prepares you for work.

Q: What I meant by the preparatory school was the private school that you attended that put an emphasis on cultural subjects.

Adm. W.: That's right.

Q: Languages, which was not what the Academy wanted.

Adm. W.: That's right. The graduates went to Princeton, Johns Hopkins, spread around the country, but that was the type of education, they did stress history, which I liked, among other things, church history particularly. They really went in for that.

We did complete plebe year, went off on my first cruise, which was a long journey for me, away from home, never having been that far before, having been brought up in Annapolis, Maryland. The _Kansas_, the battleship _Kansas_, a coal-burner, and the first thing that greeted me on boarding the ship was sacks of coal stacked in the waistline turrets, the barbette area, which indicated we were going to use some on the way!

The first cruise was twenty-one days from Annapolis to Christiana, now Oslo, Norway. The ship was fine. Captain Frank H. Brumby was as fine as you could find. He was later Commander, Battle Force. Commander Byron McCandless was the executive officer, the father of Bruce McCandless.

Q: Yes.

Adm. W.: All I can recall of that first twenty-one days is passing coal and trying to get clean between sessions of passing coal, which was impossible.

Q: Did you on such cruises have faculty from the Academy, and did you have classes?

Adm. W.: We had a couple of officers, in my recollection, no civilian faculty. Several officers were assigned to the ship and they tried to give a little instruction, but when you pass coal eight hours every day of the twenty-four there's not much energy left for absorbing instruction. It was a work cruise. I would say largely a work cruise. The visit in Christiana was delightful. We had two weeks to stay there and sightsee. We arrived on, I believe, the 21st of June, which is known as Midsummer's Day, and every house sitting up the fjord we passed had a Norwegian flag out in greeting, which made a very favorable impression.

We next sailed for Lisbon and on that part of the cruise completed the engineering assignment, that was the engine room and the ice machines and evaporators.

Q: You'd graduated from lifting coal?

Adm. W.: Yes. We had a more respectable job, and we learned considerably more.

Q: How many midshipmen were included on this tour?

Adm. W.: Well, there were five battleships.

Q: Oh, five battleships.

Adm. W.: Yes, the _Connecticut_, _Kansas_, _South Carolina_,

Minnesota, and Michigan.

We had a respectable cruise on to Lisbon and a nice visit in Lisbon, did some more sightseeing. The principal things in Lisbon that stick in my mind was, one, the fantastic Museum of Kings, where they keep their bodies preserved in alcohol and glass so you could see them. And the next thing I remember was the Museum of Carriages, which was extremely interesting to me, and the bull fight, which was quite spectacular. I did not care for bull fights but in comparison with one I'll mention later on this was a beautiful display of fine horses, fine performers, skilled performers, but, of course, they're bound to kill some bulls, and I don't think much of that what they call sport.

Well, to go on from Lisbon to Gibraltar. We stopped there long enough to coal, loaded with this horrible Welsh coal, and steaming westward, some of us tried to sleep on deck and we would be covered with coal dust in the morning. It would go up the stack, at the speed of the ship, with no wind it was just enough to bring the cinders up the stack and down on the decks. What a job, trying to keep the ship clean on that trip. We stopped at Guantanamo for a brief visit, then steamed northward and returned to Annapolis.

All together, it was a most worthwhile cruise.

Q: Did it serve, since it was difficult in terms of physical labor, to eliminate any of the midshipmen, discourage them from continuing to pursue a naval career?

Adm. W.: I really do not recall too many resigning as a result of the cruise itself, but I'll go into it a little bit later. We were in a peculiar period. For instance, my class, as I recall, had nearly a thousand enter. We graduated I think 525. We commissioned about 400, some in the Army, there wasn't room for them. So I don't know that that was a direct effect. We did lose some people after that cruise, but not very many that I can remember. But there was, I consider, very serious attrition to the class between entering and graduating.

You see, that was the first year I believe that they accepted without examination. That was the trial year on that, so they didn't have the well-thought-out, well-documented ratings of the schools throughout the country that first year. They tried to select and I think most of those did all right that they accepted, but they didn't have as much data as they did later on, when they accepted those that had a good record at school and they knew what they were getting.

Third-class year, as far as I can remember, was a very pleasant year. I was having less trouble with the academics. It seemed like I was able to keep up with them a reasonable amount. I did work hard to do it and we had some regular recreation. In those days a midshipman, third class, was allowed to attend the dances once a month and were glad to get out maybe one more weekend a month -- I mean out in town, not leave town, except on the very great holiday periods which, incidentally, were established that year by the new superintendent, Admiral Henry B. Wilson, who was really out to improve the Naval Academy and did, I think, a tremendous job. He started giving them vacations at Christmas and Easter, he started letting them go out more frequently, he changed the uniform so they had a jacket a bit more like the officers, we got away from the high collars and things like that. He did a lot to instill spirit in the midshipmen, and, as you know, those were grim years for the Navy. We're talking about 1921 - 1922.

Q: The limitation of armaments.

Adm. W.: I'll bring up the effect that had a little later. That was part of it. It was being discussed all the time. Another thing, we had many midshipmen who entered the Naval Academy to avoid the draft, quite a few, and also athletes that came in. And, after the war, they wanted other colleges. They didn't like the Navy. I don't believe they should keep anyone in the Navy that's not going through with it and you can't always tell that they will like it. I think Admiral Sims is the one who said it's worth paying $10,000 to get rid of them.

Q: I suppose these changes that were effected by Admiral Henry Wilson reflected in a sense the changes which took place in the country after World War I?

Adm. W.: Absolutely. I think they did.

Q: A liberating movement.

Adm. W.: He appreciated that and he was determined to have good naval officers regardless of what the country was doing. He was going to instill them, and he kept pushing that forward all the time.

Another incident - and I'll have to go back on this because it's affected my whole life in a way - in the middle of fall in my youngster year Hanson Baldwin, my classmate, asked me if I'd like to room with him. I said I'd be delighted to and I said, "I wonder it we can get it through the authorities." We both debated that and we didn't think so but it was worth a try. So we made our official request to be allowed to room together. We were within one company of each other, but we had the same friends in Baltimore and Annapolis and whatnot, and we felt that we'd like to try it. The request went up through channels and it got as far as the superintendent, or the commandant - I don't know whether it ever got to the superintendent. But it came back with the endorsement that it was not the policy of the Naval Academy to change roommates during the academic year. That sort of floored us for the moment, but Hanson Baldwin's father was the editor of the Baltimore Sun and he was a little bit annoyed by that, that two boys couldn't room together if they wanted to. So he called up Governor Ritchie, who called up Admiral Wilson, and the next week we were rooming together! It affected both of us. We had a very pleasant relationship going on from that day to this. It helped me a lot and I think probably I was some help to him. I don't know.

But the rest of youngster year went off very pleasantly, and the second-class cruise in the Delaware was unfortunate, in that that was when the Navy didn't have fuel enough to make a cruise really. So they took the North Dakota, Delaware, Olympia, and the Florida. We cruised to Panama. The cruise was very pleasant and interesting.

Q: These, again, were coal-burning ships, were they not?

Adm. W.: Oh, yes, but I'd been promoted. I was now a fireman and had to use an instrument known as a Johnson bar. I don't know whether you're familiar with it, but it weighed almost as much as I did. It's a great long steel bar that you stick in a hot fire and use it to break up the clinkers.

Q: That was a great promotion!

Adm. W.: That was a promotion! And, of course, part of the time I tended water, a watertender. At any rate, it was still in the fire room and this was the hot part of the cruise.

Then we went to Fort de France in Martinique, and one of the impressions of Fort de France that I received was that I had the morning, four to eight, watch in the fireroom stoking, the ship was anchored and, without getting breakfast, they decided to shift anchorage and we had to go back in the fireroom again, instead of putting the next watch on. And to top that off, we were scheduled for a tennis match that morning. So we went to the house of a friend in Fort de France for this tennis match and he gave us each a little order of vermouth, vermouth but no breakfast. Then the team we played was mixed, black and white and part each, male and female. So it was an interesting greeting from Fort de France!

Next we went on an all-day expedition to visit St. Pierre and climb Mount Pelee. I did not make the top. Some of my friends did, two or three of them, and I had very rough going up that mountain. If you've ever climbed volcano ash, it's pretty good going until you get near the top, and we had to rush back to reach the landing before our steamer was to sail back to Fort de France. We did, and that's been my last volcano.

The *Delaware* was the only ship to visit Fort de France. The others went to St. Lucia and St. Kitts and other places in the islands.

Then we went on for a three weeks' stay in Culebra. I don't know how much I learned there. I'm afraid not very much. The bow-hook of a motor launch that carried the garbage to sea every day. That was alternate days. The day I was off, we were on the tennis detail and we cleared the tennis court at Dewey Basin, which had been built by Dewey after the Spanish War. Of course, being led to believe that we would get tennis practice, but the admiral by the name of McCully and his staff occupied the tennis court!

Q: They were simply having their flunkeys clear the debris off!

Adm. W.: Clear the debris of the jungle. Any time a tennis court's been buried in the jungle for twenty years, it's quite a job.

We had a landing force there and a lot of it. Midshipmen never cared too much for landing force. But there were nice beaches there for swimming, and it was clean in those days.

Then we went on to Halifax, and Halifax was extremely pleasant, an all-out welcome to the American naval squadron. We had a reception, dances in the street. The North Dakota and Delaware tied together for a dance. The British cruiser Raleigh ran on the rocks in the Straits of Belle Isle during the visit, and Admiral McCully dashed off in the Olympia to see if he could help the Raleigh. He did not have to go all the way because the rescue had been made. The ship was lost, but the Halifax papers made a great display about the American admiral coming to the help of the British. They put it in the same category as an incident you must be familiar with, of Lord Chichester in Manila in 1898 when Dewey was there with his flagship and the German was seemingly not very friendly, so Lord Chichester moved his flagship between Dewey and the German. No incident took place, but he was indicating which side he was on at a very critical time there. This was all in the headlines of the Halifax papers.

Of course, steaming in those northern waters - now it's no problem with radar - but in those days it was pretty grim.

Q: Because of the fog?

Adm. W.: Navigating, yes, terrible fogs. We depended a lot on the deep-sea lead. It's quite a job pulling on the deep-sea lead, and you do that for four hours on end, and taking samples of the bottom and all that sort of thing.

At the completion of that cruise, we were again on the southern drill grounds and fired our guns. But, in comparison to the first cruise, I didn't think this was profitable from the viewpoint of giving you a little bit of the world picture rather than just local areas.

Q: A coastal cruise.

Adm. W.: The second-class year was a grim one to me at the Naval Academy. I got into difficulty in mechanics. I had to take a re-exam. The difference that kept me in the Naval Academy from going out was 200ths of a point - in other words, the passing grade was 2.50 and I got 2.42. If I had had 2.39 for an average I would not have been considered for a re-exam. I think those were the rules at the time, but anyway I was able to battle through that year.

I was getting into more practical subjects, which was

very helpful - navigation, ordnance, electrical engineering, seamanship, all those subjects which had something more for the future. And I think there was something else. I was thinking about it recently, about why I had such great difficulty in that second-class year and in that first semester. I think it was hovering over all of us as to how many of us were going to stay in the Navy, be allowed to stay. The disarmament business was on, they settled that, and all these ships were being scrapped. They did split a class, it was graduated in two parts - I think that was 1921 - they were getting half out in three years, you see, and half in four. There was still some doubt in a lot of people's minds as to would we have a job when we got through.

Q: So there was a morale factor?

Adm. W.: I think that might have had considerable bearing on it, because to me I thought it was very important to get through and I liked what I found about it.

Q: Your incentive was a little bit dulled.

Adm. W.: A little bit blunted. I don't know. I never looked at it from that angle until recently when I've been going over all this, revealing what was going on at various times. But the rest of the year went off pretty well. Then we had what I considered a great break, first-class cruise.

To begin with, I got assigned to the North Dakota and the captain was Joseph Mason Reeves, who I thought and still believe was one of the finest people we ever had for leadership, courage, and just thinking ahead, thinking of the Navy of the future. He gave us talks. He would take the report sheets and tear them up and give us a sermon, and a good one. He'd make you feel so bad! But he did so many things. He was a beautiful shiphandler. He spoke without notes. You could hear him from one end of the ship almost to the other, with his booming voice. We had a funeral on board and he gave the funeral oration, and the way he presented that was so beautiful. I'll say more about him later because I encountered him a few times.

Q: He really associated with the midshipmen and had contact with them?

Adm. W.: Yes. He was around all the time. He saw us and he was trying to make first-class midshipmen officers. He'd give them responsibility with the ship and with various jobs.

That cruise went to Copenhagen, first stop, and then something happened and they decided they wanted a ship to go to Sweden and the North Dakota, I believe, was the senior ship beside a flagship and was sent. So we had about ten days in Goteborg. It was a very interesting visit, and the Swedes went all out to receive us.

Q: Was that the Swedish naval base?

Adm. W.: I cannot remember that it was the Swedish naval base. I think it was nearby. We went up a long channel that went from our anchorage to Goteborg, where we landed. It was a tremendous shipping center and the principal port of Sweden, and a big city.

Our next port of call was Greenock, the seaport of Glasgow. We had a very pleasant visit there. I visited relatives over in Edinburgh, only a short way across. As a tennis group, we were invited up to Lord McClay's estate, up in the hills. He was minister of shipping for Great Britain in World War I and a fascinating personality. He had tennis courts, grass courts, clay courts, covered courts. He was then, I suppose, an old man. He must have been in his seventies, and he played croquet-golf with us. He had a tremendous estate, and he was just as nice and cordial to us as anyone could be.

From Greenock, the next port was Cadiz, which was very discouraging to me. Nothing like Lisbon. The worst thing I can remember about Cadiz was a terrible bullfight they had, which was just horrible. I left after one round or something. It was just so crude and awful, bestial and crowded. Fortunately, it was only a short visit, and we again went on to Gibraltar for our coaling.

Q: Would you complete that thought that you had. You went to -

Adm. W.: . . . Hampton Roads where we coaled ship then stood out to the southern drill grounds for firing and upon completion sailed up the Chesapeake to the Naval Academy.

First-class year was delightful in every respect that I can think of. In the first place we were given more responsibility, we were treated more like officers, and Admiral Wilson insisted on us being that.

Q: Did you have greater assurance of a future naval career?

Adm. W.: I think we did, yes. Well, we knew pretty soon. I can't recall exactly when they told how many were going to be commissioned, but by that time we'd lost quite a number and I know of some requests for the Army and all but one went in the Coast Artillery. One went in the Cavalry. His father, Malin Craig, was chief of Cavalry. 522 graduated and 422 wound up in the Navy and Marine Corps.

I believe that covers the Naval Academy.

Q: So you graduated.

Adm. W.: Now, can we go to the next ship?

Q: Yes, and your first tour of duty was in the Bureau of Ordnance, wasn't it?

Adm. W.: That's right. My orders were to the battleship

Texas, then on the midshipmen's cruise, and we were ordered to temporary duty under the chief of the Bureau of Ordnance, then Rear Admiral Claude Bloch. He very wisely, in my opinion, sent us first to the Naval Powder Factory at Indian Head, where we observed at firsthand the manufacture of powder and had particular indoctrination as how to keep powder safe and the danger of explosives.

Next, we spent three weeks at Dahlgren, Virginia, at the Naval Proving Ground. We saw all types of guns proved down there on the range and calculations for making various tests, armorplate tests, and it, I think, among other things gave me tremendous respect for the power of big guns.

Q: How big an establishment was Dahlgren at that time?

Adm. W.: Captain A. C. Pickins was the inspector of ordnance in charge at that time and the executive officer was Oliver Bagby, who was killed in a freak accident when they were testing one of the guns there, shortly after we left. His son in 1938 graduated from the Naval Academy. They had a proof officer, E. P. Sauer, who I served with several times in later years. There were not many officers. I don't believe they would have over a dozen officers, all told, and three or four civilians.

I'd like to go into this a little bit. They had one of the most interesting things to me at Dahlgren, and that was the first Navy plane that was controlled by radio in the air by another Navy plane. And this was a thing that didn't really come into the fleet until six or eight years later because they were afraid of it. But the only target thing we've had, radar-controlled now, they were radio-controlled at first. J. J. Ballentine was the proof officer and, as you know, he got to be quite famous - I served under him later on, but he worked with us. A civilian scientist and I think his name was Hayes was developing this beginning - he specialized in radio-controlled planes. It was fascinating.

Next after Dahlgren we finished the remaining part of all this at the Naval Gun Factory in Washington, part of the time observing the manufacture of guns, particularly large-caliber guns, the relining of guns, and a very important item was the naval optical school, where we received very good instruction on the care and use of and calibrating a rangefinder, which was then exceedingly important to our gunnery until radar arrived.

Q: It was kind of a Cook's tour for graduates of the Academy?

Adm. W.: Yes, it was a Cook's tour, but we made the maximum use out of what we were going into.

Then we reported aboard the *Texas* in Annapolis Roads in late August of 1924. The captain was Ivan C. Wettengel, the executive officer Herbert H. Michael, whom I'll say more about later. The gunnery officer was Miles P. Refo, Jr. I could not have been more fortunate in being assigned to this ship on graduation.

Q: And this is of paramount importance in getting a good experience.

Adm. W.: The officers had spirit, from the top down, and they were enthusiastic. It was considered an old ship. We knew she was going in for modernization at the end of the year, but people were full of interest. My division officer was Ensign Halstead S. Covington, class of 1922, and I couldn't have had a finer officer to break me in on the duties of a junior watch and division officer.

We coaled ship the first day. The next week we were on the southern drill grounds. We had two weeks to get ready for short-range battle practice, and we were able to get an "E" turret, which boosted our morale considerably, my first turret I was associated with. The ship did very well in the practice. Then we had some other exercises in the fall. As I'm speaking mostly of the Texas, we operated with the other ships in the Scouting Fleet. The Wyoming was the flagship, the Utah and the Florida.

Q: This was all in the Atlantic?

Adm. W.: The Atlantic.

Then an interesting thing happened. We were assigned special duty to observe certain exercises taking place off - well, actually, at the 47-fathom curve. The battleship Washington, BB-47, to be destroyed by the terms of the Disarmament Treaty of 1922, was the subject of the experiments. At that time there was a tremendous controversy going on about how the Army Air Force could destroy any ships afloat and we did not need them. This was 1924.

Q: When General Mitchell was in it.

Adm. W.: This was Mitchell's gang. So we anchored the battleship Washington, two anchors, off the 47-fathom curve, and Billy Mitchell's bombers started bombing from 10,000 feet. They finally got down to 3,000 feet, over a period of weeks, and during these bombings, believe it or not, the Chief of Naval Operations, Admiral Charles F. Hughes, observed them from the conning tower of the Washington, which fact helped considerably in the testimony before Congress next spring. They finally got two hits -

Q: From what altitude?

Adm. W.: 3,000 feet - and they penetrated the upper decks but didn't go all the way through. Then the Navy wanted to test her hull a little bit, they didn't think she'd been hurt, and they placed depth charges at verying distances from the side of the hull, at varying depths. I forget the number, but roughly maybe a dozen depth charges were exploded, and a party from the Texas went over after each explosion and examined the ship to see what the effect was. Finally, it was getting near time for the exercise to end and the Washington was still afloat, so the Texas was told to sink her. Should I read that little procedure in here? It's rather short and I think it might interest you.

Q: This is an excerpt from what?

Adm. W.: The following is taken from the USS Texas procedure for main battery firing on battleship 47, ex-Washington, at sea, 21 November 1924:

> "This vessel will fire at battleship 47 with the main battery in director fire to determine certain data required by the Department. Battleship 47 will be anchored with both bow anchors for the firing. The Texas will be under way with only steerageway. All firings against battleship 47 will be directed against her starboard side. Antares will act as fall-of-shot observing vessel and will radio the error of the mean point of impact of each salvo to Texas after each salvo. The firing against battleship 47 will be at two ranges, 6,000 yards and about 18,000 yards."

I don't think you want the rest of this but I'll tell you briefly.

The Texas was allowed forty rounds of drill shells to sink the Washington.

Q: Drill shells? How do they differ?

Adm. W.: They're unloaded, they're dummies, no powder in them, no explosive.

These shells, the last salvo, the 10-gun salvo, directed at the waterline of the Washington put in ten 14-inch gun holes, which let in enough water to give the coup de grace to the ship.

The next part of the Texas will be after the Christmas holiday season in the Norfolk Navy Yard, when she proceeded south with the Scouting Force again for two months' exercises in the Guantanamo Bay area. These were splendid tactical exercises, training exercises, firings, landing force, and the culmination of this whole thing is the long-range battle practice fired by the Texas, which made a fantastic score. After that we returned to Norfolk. Commander Michael was relieved by Commander Charles A. Blakeley as executive officer. I was given additional duty as aide to Commander Blakeley, which was a tremendous privilege.

Our next exercises were off the Atlantic coast, doing anti-aircraft firings with our ancient batteries, and with very successful results. The anti-aircraft officer we had at that time was then Lieutenant E. P. Sauer - you'll hear of him later on from me - and he did a very fine job with these anti-aircraft firings. One of the interesting firings was against the target towed by the Shenandoah. At that time, the Shenandoah was flying the flag of Rear Admiral Moffett, then Chief of the Bureau of Aeronautics. Incidentally, I believe this was the first time at sea that a surface ship fired a salute to an admiral's flag in the air.

Q: She was a lighter-than-air ship?

Adm. W.: CRS, yes, the same as the Macon. I can't remember her number. The Macon was CRS-5, and the Shenandoah was CRS-3, I think. The Akron was 2.

Q: May I ask you about the anti-aircraft guns that were in use at that time?

Adm. W.: 3-inch/50s.

Q: Were they U.S. made?

Adm. W.: Oh, yes. We didn't have any foreign makes on our ships in those days, as I recall.

Another interesting exercise with the Shenandoah was to moor to the USS Patoka, fitted with a mooring mast - I believe our only ship so fitted. Fortunately, I was invited to observe that operation. A complete mooring required 12 minutes. It was a beautiful, smooth operation.

Our next and last exercise with the Shenandoah was a long-range search, the object being to locate the battleship Texas. The Texas arrived safely in Hampton Roads without being discovered by the airship, which was a great shock to a lot of people.

This was the _Texas'_ last cruise before modernization. We arrived in Norfolk Navy Yard to be converted from coal to oil. We had two oilburners but the other power was all coal. To have extra 5-inch armor plates in the decks against horizontal bombing, to improve the fire control of the anti-aircraft battery, and they put on 5-inch guns instead of 3-inch guns. She was completely modernized. This was a very interesting operation for me because I soon found myself one of twelve remaining officers and we reduced the crew from 1,400 to 300. I was still aide to the executive officer and was made division officer of the 3rd, 4th, and 5th divisions with regular drills and safety instructions, was ship's secretary, then became communication officer when Commander Blakeley became commanding officer. It was a fascinating experience.

Q: Almost like being on a destroyer, wasn't it?

Adm. W.: Well, it was, and this was a battleship. I can still see those three tremendous safes of registered publications. One of the other officers still surviving among the twelve was Hanson Baldwin, and we were still rooming together. To show you how much on his toes he was, when I was on leave when my orders came in detaching me he had already signed the registered publications and taken over the communications, the things that had to be done, he'd already taken the inventory and when I got back Commander Blakeley said, "You're extremely fortunate." I said, "Why, Sir?" He said, "You have orders to the USS Nokomis and her commanding officer is Commander R. E. Ingersoll. In case you don't know it, he will be a future commander-in-chief." I thought this was pretty straightforward, but Commander Blakeley was that way, and that was wonderful.

I detached in a hurry, arrived in Philadelphia, reported to the Nokomis, a survey yacht in the Philadelphia Navy Yard, and we sailed shortly for the southern surveying areas. Lieutenant Commander F. L. Lowe was the executive officer. I served with him later on, too. He had the Pensacola at Midway and later became an admiral. I'm not sure what his later commands were.

We sailed south, to Key West, coaled ship - Nokomis was a coal-burner. We took aboard all the supplies we possibly could, steel parts for the 100-foot towers, lumber for the tripod towers, all the stores we could get plus a deckload of gasoline, which was extremely dangerous, and took the houseboat Aramis in tow, escorting our 36-foot motor launches to Cardenas, Cuba, strictly Cardenas Bay. We resumed surveying in Cardenas Bay, where the expedition had left off the previous year.

Q: This was something for the Hydrographic Office?

Adm. W.: For the Hydrographic Office. We were now working directly under the Hydrographer of the Navy. That year it was Crosley, I believe. Kempff was one year and Crosley was the other.

I was assigned to the houseboat *Aramis* in rather primitive living conditions, you might say, but I was in charge of what we called a shoreline party. I had a dinghy, two bluejackets, and a Johnson motor, and a sail. My work in the field was taking aerial photographs that had been taken the previous year from 5,000 feet altitude and plotting the shoreline, the objects I could find, on these photographs. By taking horizontal sextant angles and cutting them in with our towers and our signals.

Then, returning to the ship - I'll have to explain that operation a little later I believe, how we translated that data to the boat sheets and from the boat sheets to the charts. This was a new development in surveying which the then Commander Ingersoll personally performed himself and he showed me how to do it. He traced these photographs in ink, the shoreline shows very clearly on them, and then we plotted these fixes - I plotted the fixes on the boat chart - then we used a pantograph to translate the exact line from a tracing cloth to the boatsheet, so we had accurate delineation of the shoreline on the boat sheet which was later inked in on the smooth chart at Philadelphia Navy Yard in the summer.

Q: I take it this was a job that had never been done before?

Adm. W.: This was the first year we did it in this manner. That's my understanding. They'd taken the photographs the previous year, but they had not used them. All this winter

Worthington #1 -31

Ingersoll worked in the plotting room himself. He'd work all night, he'd get engrossed in this thing.

Q: Was this detailed surveying on the part of the U. S. Navy confined to our own areas of the oceans, or was it worldwide?

Adm. W.: No, as I recall it, the Army Engineers had the U. S. continental waters, the Coast and Geodetic Survey then had the Philippine area and certain other areas, the Ocean and Lake Survey operated at that time one expedition off the north coast of Cuba, they had another one off the south coast of Cuba in the Hannibal, and we had another one off Venezuela in the Niagara. We had three at that time. The Ocean and Lake surveys under the Hydrographic Office were a separate appropriation. I'll mention that later because it was very handy.

Q: And we were principally interested in the Caribbean and Latin American waters?

Adm. W.: Yes. We were interested in waters not handled by anybody else that we wanted charted. The charts from Cuba were perfectly fantastic.

Q: I take it then we had an adequate interchange with the Royal Navy?

Adm. W.: On Admiralty charts, yes. But the Admiralty charts of Cuba that we used I think were maybe fifty years old or something like that when we went down there. Oh, yes, we've been exchanging with the Admiralty all over the world, but they were no longer spending money on Cuba as long as we were doing it, I suppose. That survey work, to me, was very valuable help to the United States, and I trust the Russians aren't using them but they probably are.

Incidentally, on one of our expeditions back and forth, I used to go back to the Nokomis and be the officer of the deck when we went to Key West for supplies, and on one of the trips back we surveyed Matanzas Harbor, that's the first big harbor to the east of Havana. I think it's 90 miles east, as I remember it. We spent some time in Matanzas Harbor and surveyed it. I did the shoreline and then I had to carry the transit ashore. It was a miserable assignment. I worked with the local people too at Matanzas. The governor there and his mayor were very helpful and asked to see the charts.

Q: I take it, then, that Spanish had been your language at the Academy?

Adm. W.: No, I didn't know any Spanish. I took French at the Naval Academy but Commander Lowe told me one day, "You talk to him. I don't know this language." One of these people up in the islands. But I made out all right. They had somebody with them who spoke English, one of the local people, and an engineer that worked with us spoke Spanish very well. But when I got the blueprints of Matanzas I was going to take those with a pantograph and get them onto that chart, you see, to make a finished product. So I took a transit up the main street and started cutting in points on this blueprint. That was fine and the blueprint was accurate, but there was one thing I didn't quite understand. I said, "These streets are all paved." "Oh," he said, "think nothing of it. That just means that money was appropriated and somebody stole it." Machado was the dictator then.

But to go on back to the field, I think I covered the activity of that year, except at the end of that year I was assigned to understudy for building these 100-foot steel towers and returning to Philadelphia I was made Ocean and Lake survey officer. So I did have sufficient money - we didn't have any in any other department. The Navy was so short, but we did have enough to buy the necessary survey equipment.

Q: Tell me about these steel towers. They were communication towers?

Adm. W.: They were triangulation towers, 100 feet high. Windmill towers is what they really are, only we didn't put the windmill on the top. We spent the summer in Philadelphia plotting up the smooth work.

Commander Benjamin Dutton - Commander Ingersoll was ordered to Naval War College and Commander Benjamin Dutton, Jr., was the new commanding officer. He, as you know, was the author of _Navigation and Nautical Astronomy_, which has gone through many editions and he was another perfectly marvelous captain. This year I was assigned to the _Nokomis_ and one other officer was assigned to the _Nokomis_, Lieutenant, junior grade, John Higgins, who I served under many times later on. He had a wonderful war record. But this year I was to take a group of twenty men in a 50-foot motor launch and when I could get it, when they could spare a 36-foot one, I'd take the two launches and be maybe ten or twenty miles ahead of where the ship was based erecting these towers. We tried to build them roughly in rectangles or in pentagons, in pentagonal shapes, every ten miles. So the hydrographic engineer we had with us, L. M. Samuels, who had spent his life in the business for the Hydrographic Office, did the transit triangulation work. I worked very closely with him because he could not take a transit triangulation with these towers at ten miles away unless it was pretty rigid, if they swayed in the wind it could be very unpleasant. But we were able to build a good tight tower and we put skirts near the top of the tower for the boat officers to do their triangulation from the boats, in cutting in their position on the sounding line. Then when he went to do his major triangulation work, we would take these skirts off to reduce vibration. The towers were successful that year.

Q: When the survey of a particular coastal area had been completed, were the towers dismantled?

Worthington #1 - 35

Adm. W.: Yes, and moved on to use again. Sometimes we left them from the end of one season to the beginning of the next, if they would be the base for the next quadrilateral or pentagonal. Others we took down and moved along and took back to Key West for storage in the summertime. We did not leave any in Cuba, except those that we could use the next year. Some of them we used certainly three years in succession. I mean take them down and put them up again. Sometimes they were hard to get together after a few times of being manhandled.

This operating away from the ship was quite rugged. Frequently, I'd be away ten days at a time. On the other hand, when we got back to the Nokomis it was much pleasanter living than the little houseboat Aramis. We had a little better food and refrigeration and water and everything.

At the end of that second season, we'd gone about 200 miles, as I recall, east of Havana when I left the expedition. Of course, they went on several years after my time.

We returned to Philadelphia, and I was getting worried about rejoining the Navy. Surveying was delightful duty but I was afraid I was spending too much time away.

Q: It was a tangent, wasn't it?

Adm. W.: It was not a good thing. Of course, Commander Dutton was perfectly fine. He said, "Of course, you get anything you can, you get what you want, and I'll approve it." So the Memphis returned from Europe with a great deal of fame for having brought Lindbergh home, and moored across the dock from the Nokomis. Stuart Blue of 1925, who later lost his life in the Atlanta, I think it was, a friend of mine, was aboard. He wanted to get to the survey ship; he'd had enough of this fancy business in Europe -- dress parades and all that business. So we made a straight swap. My request to the Bureau of Navigation came back by return mail. Commander Dutton said, "You must have friends over in the Navy Department." And I said, "No, Sir, they got both requests at the same time, so no problem."

Then I reported to the Memphis in New York. Captain Ralph E. Pope was the new commanding officer. Incidentally, I think he's still living, in his nineties, in San Diego. Commander W. H. Lee was the executive officer.

Q: Willis Lee?

Adm. W.: No. I served with him later. This was "Mandy" Lee. That was "Chink" Lee. Willis Lee was "Chink" Lee. J. K. Esler was gunnery officer and my good friend in Annapolis, Philip Welch, assistant. He was a tremendous help to get me indoctrinated in the Memphis gunnery department just as fast as he could, and I was assigned the second division, which was the antiaircraft division. I had also under jurisdiction the torpedo tubes and the searchlights, and the quarter deck division, the ceremonial division. So it was a fascinating tour for me. The ship was fine; the crew were fine.

We went right out of New York Harbor and started into night exercises and tactical exercises. Here I'd been in the survey ship and I had to learn fast, and it was most interesting. We did some firing in the fall and made out very well. My antiaircraft battery didn't do as well as I liked but I found out what happened and remedied that.

Q: May I ask about the night exercises, what did they comprise?

Adm. W.: Night firing. Some tactical exercises. We had tactical exercises quite frequently, but the night firing that I was speaking of in particular was shorter range in those days because we had to use the searchlights which, to my mind, were never any good -- star shells and searchlights. My antiaircraft battery had to fire the star shells and I was supposed to control the searchlights. But we did get some fairly good shooting in the fall, and then were suddenly ordered to the Washington Navy Yard on a protocol mission to transport the remains of the late ambassador from Guatemala to Washington, Latour, and his family.

We were in the Navy Yard two or three days and I made the most of them. An assistant in the gun factory had been in the Texas with me. This was E. P. Sauer, who had been serving in the Texas. He immediately came down to look over the Memphis and he said, "What can I do to help you?" I said, "If you can get me firing locks that work for twenty rounds, I would sincerely appreciate it."

He was a very rigid, tough, strict person, but he knew something ought to work and why it didn't. He said, "Well, I don't know what I can do, but you take those breech plugs off and send them up to my shop."

I said, "We may be sailing tomorrow." "That's all right, I'll see what we can do."

So I got them back on board and he said, "Those cams are made of too soft metal. You won't have any trouble with these."

Do you know, we never had another misfire or another cam failure while I was still in the Memphis. It was just a question of getting somebody to act and furthermore he never charged a dime for the work. He said, "Oh, no, just charge it off to profit and loss." We didn't have any money to pay for it. You had to go through requisitions in those days or you could swap material.

After that, we had this very peaceful funeral expedition to Puerto Barrios, Guatemala, transferred the remains and the family ashore with proper ceremony. They wanted us to pay calls in port. Of course, the funeral was to be in Guatemala City, which is about 200 miles inland, but we returned immediately to Philadelphia and were prepared to go south right after the holidays.

We sailed south with the Scouting Fleet, Cruiser Division Two - Light Cruiser Division Two: the Trenton, the Milwaukee, the Memphis, the Raleigh - and en route we were detached to Key West, Florida to embark the President of the United States and his party, proceeding to open the first Pan American Conference in Havana. The original plan was not too satisfactory. We embarked the President and his party, took them out to the Texas in Key West Roads. The Texas was this newly modernized battleship with everything beautiful and Admiral H. A. Wiley was the Fleet Commander-in-Chief aboard. Rear Admiral Butler was chief of staff. But transferring the presidential party, ladies and others -

Q: This was President Hoover?

Adm. W.: Coolidge - in Key West Roads when it was quite rough was not an easy matter, but we succeeded, and then escorted the party to Havana. Needless to say, in the delay of transfer, with these difficult waters, the Texas had to make a full-power run to Havana, to arrive in Havana for the conference opening with no paint on her stack. But Havana was never in more beautiful shape than on that occasion. The streets were clean - they'd been getting ready for it for months. It was Sunday afternoon and the crowds were out in that big esplanade to greet us. There must have been half the population to see the battleship and cruiser and destroyers. We stayed there for several days. The President opened the conference. But coming back he would have none of the Texas. He came aboard the Memphis in order that he would not have to transfer in the open roadstead again.

Q: Why, because she rode better?

Adm. W.: Well, we could take him right into the dock, he didn't have this transfer. Coolidge did not like the sea. We had quite a gathering there. Charles Evans Hughes was one of them that went down to the conference. Kellogg was the Secretary of State. Charles Evans Hughes was the Chief Justice. The Secretary of the Navy, Wilbur, and his wife. Mrs. Coolidge was along, who, incidentally, was most charming. Both Mrs. Coolidge and Secretary Wilbur wanted to be catapulted in a Memphis plane, but their respective spouses said nothing doing. Nothing happened on the trip back. It was very pleasant and we were glad to get everybody disembarked. We went right alongside the dock for the train. The last one to leave was H. A. Wiley.

We went on to Guantanamo for some more gunnery exercises, and incidentally with these improved gun cams we made a 100 percent practice on the antiaircraft firing. With the torpedo battery we made a 100 percent firing. So we were learning, with hard work. We had a wonderful crew and they really worked, and the officers were trying. The Memphis had both engineering "Es" that year. Of course, steaming alone in Europe made it relatively easy to do, I would say.

We proceeded down to Panama and we had joint exercises there with the Army and the defense forces of Panama, and then

Worthington #1 - 41

proceeded up the West Coast. We cruised at 8 knots. For the 36-knot light cruiser division to have to cruise and maneuver at 8 knots was pretty deadly.

Q: But why?

Adm. W.: Economy. They were trying to save up fuel for the fleet exercises. But we learned how to handle ships at slow speeds. There were lots of fish so we did lots of fishing on the way out.

Q: What does a slow speed do to -

Adm. W.: You don't have enough steerage control. When you get a little more speed on the ship, you can control the rudder. You see, it reacts on the rudder. The faster you're moving through the water, you act on the rudder, and you can turn awfully fast. And at higher speed, which you have to do in exercises and tactics - to me, this was almost wasted, this trip up. It was a pleasant cruise.

Q: As far as fishing went!

Adm. W.: Well, there wasn't too much work to do on board. Of course, we were keeping the ship clean and we were training people for the next exercise, but we'd finished our gunnery year and were going up to join the fleet on an exercise to Hawaii. So the Memphis worked in the Atlantic exercises, the exercises off Panama, then she went up the West Coast and joined the Pacific Fleet. This was all on one cruise out of Philadelphia. Home port Philadelphia and supposed to be back in two months.

We arrived at San Diego and I took advantage there of that still water, checking our directors and so forth, which was very useful. We then went on to San Pedro.

Q: This was your first tour in the Pacific, wasn't it?

Adm. W.: This was my first time west of Panama. I should say north of Panama, in the Pacific. I got in touch with my uncle who lived at Pasadena and this was very enlightening to me because a member of the class of 1924 discussing the Navy with the class of 1875 was quite an interesting contrast. He went to sea as chief engineer when ships didn't even turn over their engines in a month's cruise. They had sails. Saved their fuel and saved their engines. But I learned a great deal from him and a great deal about the old Navy. It was fascinating.

Four days later we sailed for the exercises. Cruiser Division Two was assigned a scouting problem, ships and planes, to locate the battle fleet, which sailed from San Francisco for Hawaii. To make a long story short, we missed the battleships and the reason was very simple. I think the admiral was Louis de Steiger, who hoisted sail on his slowest ships, so with following winds they made a couple of knots more speed and the search curves didn't work. That was quite a lesson.

Worthington #1 - 43

Q: This was by design on his part?

Adm. W.: Oh, sure. It was perfectly legitimate.

Q: To foil the potential enemy.

Adm. W.: It never occurred to anybody that he would do it. Ships of the train, our tugs and our slow ships would hoist sail.

We had a short stay in Hawaii, a very pleasant one, till suddenly Light Cruiser Division Two was ordered to China and the only ship that was ready to leave immediately was the Memphis. I think we sailed within twenty-four hours, and steamed independently for Chefoo. We encountered a typhoon en route, which we didn't avoid as much as we should have, and it did some damage to the ship. Cracked a plane up somewhat against the after stack and did some other damage.

Q: That causes me to ask about the weather reports available in that time.

Adm. W.: Not like they are now. Nothing like what they are now. We did receive, of course, typhoon warnings, but they came from either Manila or a place in Shanghai - Zickawei, I think, was Shanghai. We received two warnings, Zickawei Observatory and Manila Observatory. We hit the typhoon but, on the other hand, the captain had orders to get out there at good speed. We steamed across at about 18 knots, which was quite a contrast

Worthington #1 - 44

to the 8 knots up the California coast.

Q: What was your mission out there?

Adm. W.: The trouble brewing in north China again and Chin-wang-tao. We only stopped in Chefoo long enough to anchor there when we received orders from Admiral Mark Bristol in Shanghai to proceed immediately for Chin-wang-tao. This was the time Chang Tso-lin was assassinated. He was the great war lord of northern Manchuria. I have to be careful how I word this because historians disagree. I talked recently to Felix Morley - you've met him, haven't you? He was a reporter out there at the time, and he said his recollection was that the Japs did away with him. I told him that was quite possible, but my recollection, and this was my good authority on the golf course where you get it from the caddies, was that Chang Hsueh-liang, the young emperor, had invited Chang Tso-lin to a banquet to discuss their differences. There was fighting going on but this was an armistice. During that banquet he is supposed to have been assassinated. When they got around to the liqueurs they bumped him off.

I've never been able to pin that down in any history book, but that's the thing that we reported from our source. We do know he was assassinated. His train was blown up. We do know that this puppet, this guy Chang Hsueh-liang got to be a Japanese puppet. He never did anything very much after that. So he might have been in cahoots with the Japanese. That's just one of those

Worthington #1 - 45

things I don't know. Some day I might find out, talk to a real Japanese scholar.

We stayed there about ten days and ships of foreign navies all came in there. The Royal Navy had a cruiser, the Japs had a cruiser, the Italians had a cruiser. There was quite a military assembly there. We had really very little to do. We drilled feverishly all the way from Hawaii to Chefoo on landing force. We thought we were going to throw a landing force ashore somewhere. We didn't know where, we simply went over because there was this rush.

Oh, I must make one remark. In Hawaii I'd been promoted from the 3-inch battery to the forward 6-inch battery. I was extremely happy about it. It was a bigger division, bigger guns, and everything. After we'd crossed the date line, the captain called me in and said I was communication officer. I told him that I much preferred my gunnery job. I knew nothing about communications. He said, "You're still my communication officer." That was very fortunate for me in a way because we didn't do too much shooting for a while, but on the China Station I was mixed up in these codes all day and all night. A lot of them I didn't know about, but there were officers on the ship who helped me and I was able to do it and was fully able to make an intelligence report every day, intercepting the intelligence reports, and all that. So I was right on top of what was going on on the China Station. We had an armistice after about ten days and so they sent us back to Chefoo.

Then Admiral Mark Bristol really gave the _Memphis_ a tour. He sent us to Chefoo, Tsingtao - we never stayed more than a couple of days - Shanghai, I think he allowed us five days there, Manila, back to Shanghai, back to Tsingtao, back to Chefoo, to the point where Captain Pope got a little bit exasperated. He said the _Memphis_ seemed a rather large ship to use for the U. S. mail service. Why don't they try the Chinese, they always get the mail on time. Of course, I don't think his method was appreciated. We still had the mail run. But we got back to Chefoo in time, then the _Trenton_ and _Milwaukee_ arrived. They always had a war on in China for some reason.

Q: You spoke about the intelligence reports that were coming in on the shore situation. Were these forwarded to Washington?

Adm. W.: Oh, yes. We forwarded reports to Washington and to the commander-in-chief, Admiral Mark Bristol. We had several officers from the ship ashore. Those that played golf got it on the golf course. There was a club and anyone that they could contact ashore that they could talk to, the Americans ashore. That's why we were there. There were several American families, very nice families. There was the Standard Oil Company and others. And the foreign families, they were always glad to see us, any sign of an American ship. Foreigners had it rough in China that year. They were killing them right and left, without any warning.

And that's why we went there.

We had a battalion of the Fifteenth Infantry down at Pei tai ho, they were stationed there at Tsingtao, but were down for their summer training in Pei tai ho, which was near Ching wan tao.

Returning to Chefoo, we had some excellent tactical exercises, gunnery firings, another typhoon exercise, which I might dwell on a little bit here because it was rather unusual and I know of no other case of it happening in the Navy.

Our tug, Avocet, was blown in this typhoon up on the beach. There was considerable land between the waterline and the Avocet after the typhoon. So we tried all kinds of schemes to get that ship off, and one of them was to put the Memphis as far in as we could get because we didn't want to get in too-shallow water with a towline out and anchors out. Another fleet tug was anchored out with towline out. Then we steamed the destroyer division by at high speed to make waves and, inch by inch, we got the Avocet back into the water, with the help of Jason and two more tugs.

Q: That was a tedious task, wasn't it?

Adm. W.: A tedious task and our people were perfectly furious about it because they did not want to risk the sand getting into the condensers of a light cruiser. In any ship it's bad news.

Q: Did you have any responsibility or did you show any concern for American citizens who were missionaries ashore?

Adm. W.: Oh, yes.

Q: Were they in danger also?

Adm. W.: Oh, yes, all American civilians ashore were under the jurisdiction of the American consul, or whatever American representative was there. We had an American consul in Chefoo. We had an American mission in Chefoo. There was one in Tsingtao, I believe. I'm much more familiar with the missions up the Yangtze which we'll come to later. Our assignment there was to protect lives.

I remember taking a message down to the captain that came in under instructions as to how to perform. I read it and I was shaken up a little bit. It said, "You will protect the lives of American citizens in the area." The captain read it once, then he read it twice, and said, "I don't see anything about property."

I said, "I don't either, Captain, and I don't understand it. I thought it was always a function of the American Navy to protect lives and property of Americans abroad."

But these were the kind of things you got into when you were working - the Navy gets into some of these things. I thought it was extremely unfortunate. But in that area we had enough ships on the coast. The missionaries could come out if they wanted to, and I think after the Nanking affair a couple of years previous they were ready to get out. A lot of them had gone. My trouble up the river was with those who would not come out.

Q: I expect they would offer a particular problem.

Adm. W.: Yes, you felt responsible.

Q: You'd feel you had to care for them and yet they -

Adm. W.: All you can do is tell them, as I told them several times, I wasn't going to risk the lives of my bluejackets.

The Memphis was again ordered back to Chin wang tao for another incident, and this time we had at least a division of Destroyer Squadron 45 with us and we stayed about ten days, until a new armistice was signed and they agreed to stay on each side of the river. A lot of this China fighting - I don't want to go into it, it's been written up so much -- but the Russians were mixed up in all this, armored trains and so forth.

When this incident apparently settled and things quieted down, my ship was ordered to Taku Bar, which is the port of Tientsin. This, to me was one of the most interesting parts of the expedition. We embarked three Japanese code typewriters and three U. S. Marine operators in the ship, all bluejackets and naval officers, and they were immediately in my jurisdiction. We tried to mount a full-power run on the way to Yokohama. We made better than

Worthington #1 - 50

32 knots, a beautiful run, then through the inland sea; but as soon as these operators got aboard I locked them up in the radio direction-finder shack, with their typewriters and told them to keep out of sight as we passed through Japanese waters. They started copying. When we got into the inland sea and passed the anchorage of the Japanese fleet, I was hanging around this radio place all the time to see what they were getting. Of course, I didn't understand the Japanese, but I could see by the operator's expression that he had something good.

Q: They read Japanese?

Adm. W.: Oh, yes, they read it and they copied it. They got a battleship, so I said, "All right, we'll identify it." I put the radio direction-finder on the bearing of a transmission while the operator was copying the transmission, and then I took a visual bearing from the bridge and identified with what silhouettes we had. In that way we didn't positively identify the battleship and the transmissions with the code, but we gave them, I think, a good deal of useful information.

At any rate, we copied 120 pages of legal paper of Japanese code.

Q: This was in a code, it wasn't in clear Japanese?

Adm. W.: No, this was Japanese code, and I delivered it by hand. I'd signed my report. It covered only one page, in English, and

Worthington #1 - 51

I delivered it by hand to, I'm sure, Zacharias, who was the Fleet Intelligence Officer. It was either Zacharias or Davis, but I'm pretty sure this was Zacharias. Both of them were out there at the time I was there. To me, of course, this was all super secret, nothing was ever mentioned about it to anybody. I think the only person who knew anything about this was the captain; he knew what I was doing. I was so afraid these Marines would raise a question with the Japs, you see, instead of putting them in bluejackets uniform and be disguised. Anyway, they got the information, and I'm sure that all helped in the future.

Q: I take it that you were then reading some of the Japanese codes, in that early time?

Adm. W.: If you hear my talk on the Battle of Midway, we were reading - we swiped the Japanese code back in 1921, I think it is. That's another story. I got that from other sources.

Q: Was this a naval code or was it a diplomatic code?

Adm. W.: This was naval code, but originally we found out that the Japanese commercial code and the naval code were identical, so we borrowed the keys to the Japanese consular office in New York, which they rented in the RCA Building, the commercial attaché. We were able to get our people in there when they weren't working nights - get in there, get the combination to the safe, copy the code, and put it back. The Japanese never knew it. I'm sure this was 1921.

One other happening in Japan that was always of interest to me was the fact that we were caught in Yokohama Bay in a typhoon and the senior officer aboard was an aviator who had not served in ships in many years. He designated me as navigator and with an ensign officer of the deck we battled the typhoon. Fortunately, we were able to veer chain every yard we dared as the stern was on the breakwater, close to the breakwater, and were steaming with our engines. We were able to hold position until the storm veered. We were more fortunate than a fellow cruiser who had dropped a second anchor and had a considerable time getting disentangled.

Next, from Yokohama Bay, we sailed to Shanghai and to Guam for fleet exercises. On the approaches to Guam we had a shore bombardment, a landing of Marines, and a few days in the harbor. The fleet flagship returned to shanghai, Cruiser Division Two proceeded to the Philippines via San Bernardino Strait. This was an interesting exercise and I believe worthwhile. I will append here a report on that exercise. [Appendix 1.]

After we did some firing in the Philippines, in the Mariveles area for the long-range and Subic Bay for the shorter ranges, we were in Manila over the holidays. Following that, we had another cruise to the southern part of the Philippines, getting as far as Coron Bay.

I was detached from the <u>Memphis</u> in Manila on 1 March 1929,

Worthington #1 - 53

with orders to the Tutuila for duty.

Q: Was this something you sought?

Adm. W.: I sure as the devil didn't seek it. I wanted to come home. The ships got ordered home and they detached all of us young people.

Q: You were not married?

Adm. W.: No. They just took us all. It didn't make any difference whether you were married or not, they just took us all and scattered us among the fleet. This was from the ships that were ordered home. They were only out there on temporary duty.

So I proceeded via Chaumont, Captain W. D. Puleston in command, stopping at Hong Kong, then to Shanghai. Thence, by three river steamers from Shanghai to Chungking, reporting on the 22nd of March. [Diary of this trip up Yangtze, Appendix 2.]

Q: What was the purpose of the Tutuila? I mean what was her duty?

Adm. W.: The Tutuila was a new river gunboat designed for patrolling the upper river at low water. She had been in commission about two years and I was reporting to her first skipper at the end of his tour.

Q: Her patrol duty was exclusively for the protection of American citizens?

Adm. W.: Protecting American citizens, and the same order about property, not much about property -- not much was said about property. Of course, her presence being felt tied up, for instance, to a Standard Oil pontoon as protection to Standard Oil property there. The same way in Chungking or Wanshien, and the missions were always close by. So by our presence, we were protecting property, but we were not to take any risk to defend property at that time. I'll go into this a little more as we get along because some of the counter orders we had varied.

The day after my arrival in Chungking I was made recorder of a board of investigation into the sinking of a brand-new motor boat the previous day in the rapids near Chungking. This boat was the pride of the upper river at that time, the newest design but not appropriate for the Yangtze's rapids.

The second day we sailed downriver, stopping at Wanshien en route. On March 26th, sailing from Wanshien at mileage 102 in the river, we struck a submerged rock and had to be beached within three minutes to prevent loss of the ship.

Q: This was a kind of ordinary occurrence, wasn't it?

Adm. W.: I've got a list of the shipwrecks up there. There were 15 of them in the period 1919-29. [Appendix 3.] It was a very dangerous water.

Q: Did the same penal code pertain to the captain of a ship that hit a rock in the river as would prevail in the ocean?

Adm. W.: Well, the captain was being tried - we were proceeding downriver at the time at this low water, so they tried the captain and a special disbursing agent for the loss of some silver dollars. The silver dollars were stored in the magazine, there being no safe of sufficient size to hold them. The keys to the magazine, by naval regulation, belonged in the captain's cabin, and, although never proved, it was presumed that persons unknown carried the silver out of the magazine in buckets to the extent of about $800. By the time the ship had reached downriver, the special disbursing agent was tried by general court-martial. The captain was tried for two previous actions on the rocks plus this one. The sum total was that the special disbursing agent was acquitted and the captain lost some numbers. But there's no real possible relationship between what a captain has to do in an upper river, dependent on native pilots and native quartermasters and waters for which there are no charts, just local knowledge, to have the same code that we have in other places. That happened to be the case in this event -

Q: But they still go through the form. I mean, he was tried.

Adm. W.: Yes, they tried the special disbursing agent and they tried the captain. When we got to Shanghai I was one of the two line officers not under arrest in the ship.

Q: Dangerous service!

Adm. W.: I could elaborate. However, the less we say about that the better. But I did want to cover the reason for this hurried trip downriver. The river was at low water, dangerously low, and we knew it. But going into these groundings, I've always been convinced in my own mind that they were caused by the fact that the Chinese quartermaster had shown some communistic tendencies and was not following his pilot's precise hand movements. This was the method by which they conned the ship, never by spoken words. The pilot stood in front of the pilothouse and by motion of the hand, right or left, slow or fast. We were using triple rudders, but even that isn't enough. We sometimes used the engine and the rudders to make the turns. I would think it's the trickiest navigation in the world, probably.

What was I doing when we ran aground? Down below decks taking inventory of the first lieutenant's department. I soon found myself with the massive job of being responsible for getting the ship plugged up and afloat. Remember, this particular area, just below the Wuchang Gorge, the water can rise rapidly as much as 170 feet. We were beached. With our forward gun removed, everything we could take off was put on the beach to try to get her afloat. Then we placed canvas mats under the ship. We had to drag through the sand because she was beached, to try to cover the hole. We stuffed mattresses in the hole from inside, we put wooden plugs in the hole from inside. We built cement blocks on top of that hole, we had two merchant ships, one on each side of us, with their emergency pumps, also our own pumps going. We had cables from the merchant ships stretched under our ship to try to bring lifting pressure, and in several days, inch by inch, we were able to get off the beach. Once we had the ship afloat, then we were able to get enough cement in there to plug the hole — nine tons of cement. By that time, we pulled things back aboard. Fortunately, the river had not risen and so we were afloat. And on the 1st of April we were under way again downriver.

At the next port, Ichang, our new captain had arrived but in view of the situation in the ship it was decided not to relieve until we arrived at Shanghai. We went into the dockyard at Shanghai and not only repairs made for this work but some very important improvements. One was putting double bottoms in the ship. None of us could understand why the ship wasn't built with double bottoms - every other ship in the Navy had them. Another thing we did was put an 11-inch connection to the main injection to the two big compartments. As a result, with our own pumps we could pump the displacement of the ship within an hour.

After this long stretch in Shanghai getting through the courts of inquiry and the general courts-martial and with a new skipper and new officers, except I was left alone to go back upriver, we got out again in July, a much improved ship, and took a leisurely cruise upriver, visiting various ports, trying to test out the engines. It was quite an undertaking.

Q: You force me to ask you a question. Do you know anything about the background of the design for these gunboats? Who designed them? Where? Were they designed in the United States by someone who was not familiar with the problems of the Yangtze?

Adm. W.: There's quite a story about that. I think Tolley covers that pretty well in his book, but basically they were designed, yes, by American constructors. We had a superintendent of construction in Shanghai. These gunboats went through quite an evolution and they were supposed to have been designed by our people with advice from the people out in China, but I'm not at all convinced that they knew as much about the upper river as they should have. For example, this motor sampan. The only recommendation we had in the loss of this motor sampan was that the next would be one using the hull of the Chinese sampans that had been successful up the Yangtze for a thousand years. That's what they did. The new sampan we had was fine. It had a proper hull and decent engines. No problem.

The _Tutuila_ engines were built in Shanghai. The hull had to be built out there. But the first two boats were built with a British engine, Thorneycroft boilers, and this engine had a Lockwood and Carlisle piston ring that was vintage of about 1880. I'll give you some data on the construction of the ship.

The _Tutuila_-class gunboat was designed to answer the long-felt need for a type of vessel capable of steaming in any section of the Yangtze River, from its mouth to Chungking, at any water level. This type of ship was particularly designed to operate in the upper river between Ichang and Chungking during the dangerous low-water season. Her construction was begun by the Kiangnan Dock and Engineering Works in Shanghai, China, in 1926 under the direct supervision of United States naval officers. In her trials, held off Woosung, 17-20 February 1928, she made 15.6 knots, turning 360 revolutions per minute. Her maximum design speed was $14\frac{1}{2}$ knots with 322 revolutions per minute.

Now about the engines. The Tutuila had two vertical triple-expansion reciprocating engines built by the Kiangnan Dock and Engineering Works, Shanghai. The Tutuila and Guam were built by this one. The others were built in the States. Similar to those engines installed in upper river merchantmen of the I'ping type and a combined horsepower of 1,950. Steam is supplied by two Thornycroft boilers for the water tube express type located in a single fireroom. Two large reciprocating blowers supply forced air. Electricity is generated by two 25-kilowatt turbo generators, Westinghouse, and a 10-kilowatt auxiliary kerosene generator. Refrigeration is supplied by York one-ton carbon dioxide ice machines. There is installed a rugged steam steering engine to operate the three rudders simultaneously and an ingenious device for rapidly shifting to hand steering in an emergency. The ground tackle is very heavy and designed especially for upper river duty. The anchor engine drives the capstans either for

Worthington #1 - 60

handling chains or wire cables used to heave the rapids, should that be necessary. Radio equipment consists of a low- and high-frequency transmitter, one each, low, intermediate, and high-frequency receiver.

This history of the ship is the one I was ordered to write just before my detachment. I finished it on my way down-river. Maybe it would be better to put this in an annex. Wouldn't you think so?

Q: Yes, I would. [See Appendix 4.]

Adm. W.: So, we're at Shanghai, right?

Q: Yes.

Adm. W.: We started back upriver, visited Fukien, Hankow, Changsha, Ichang, Wanshien, Chungking. My duties also included chief engineer, gunnery, and special disbursing and supply. Then I go on to the new policy which I think is rather important and might best be quoted from this long letter of Admiral Craven's. It's dated 7 November 1929.

Q: Who was Admiral Craven?

Adm. W.: Commander, Yangtze Patrol, from May of 1929 - he was there two years - to 1931.

> With a view to being prepared for unsettled conditions
> up the Yangtze River, it has been decided to organize

two units of armed guards for the protection of merchant ships flying the American flag. One unit will be provided by the vessel stationed at Chungking and the other by the ships stationed at Ichang -

Q: These were sailors?

Adm. W.: Sailors, yes. One officer and six men.
- each unit to consist of one officer and six men. Personnel selected for this duty will be the most dependable type. Armed guards are to be supplied with rifles, riot guns and Browning automatic machine guns.
When put into effect and until further orders, an armed guard will be put on board merchant ships shortly before they sail from Chungking and Ichang. In those cases where it seems desirable to senior officer present the armed guards will take passage on merchant ships.

Actually we had an armed guard station ship at Chungking, one at Wanshien, and the Palos at Ichang, so we had them stationed in three places.

Q: This became necessary because of bandits?

Adm. W.: Yes, this is a report about the bandits, a report from commanding officer, Palos, Ryland D. Tisdale, dated for the month of October 1930: [Appendix 5.]

An armed guard incident I believe of interest is one

which occurred on a trip from Wanshien to Chungking in February 1930. Remember we departed from Tutuila at Wanshien where we had the friendliest and most cordial relations with the general in command of that area, General Wang Fang-tso. Shortly after departing, the Chi Chuen, the ship in which the Tutuila's armed guard was embarked, was fired upon from the bank of the Yangtze across from Wanshien. This fire was silenced by some 23 rounds of armed-guard weaponry. Checking over the situation and trying to determine why we should be fired upon in an area where the commanding general had been very close to our commanding officer caused me considerable concern, when suddenly I was informed through the Chinese interpreter ". . . that general on board." Not daring to leave the bridge and my armed guard, I requested that the general report on the bridge at his earliest convenience. He appeared somewhat excited and said, "Don't shoot, those are just frivolous boys that like to shoot the guns. They don't mean any harm."

I said, "General, I happen to have some young Americans who are frivolous and young and they love to shoot their guns, especially when somebody's shooting at them." Then I realized who he was and said, "Are you General Dai Tien Min?"

He said, "Yes."

I said, "Well, I'll have to ask you to debark at the first convenient stop of the ship. Our regulations are very strict. We cannot permit American ships flying the American flag to transport troops."

We were fired upon once or twice more by a shot here and there, but there was no convenient place to debark the general until next day. When the time came, he appeared in full uniform with his full staff, some 15 Chinese officers and men, all armed to the teeth. And here I was standing there with our small armed guard. He debarked without further incident and we continued our journey.

Q: How did he happen to get on there in the first place?

Adm. W.: Smuggled on. He'd paid off the Chinese comprador who was responsible for the passengers, you see, and was smuggled on. But it turned out when I reported this incident he happened to be acquainted with our friend General Wang Fang-tso, and when our captain took the matter up -- by the way, his name was General Dai-Tien-Min -- with General Wang Fang-tso he said he was terribly sorry that this incident had happened but he had authorized these troops, who were not his troops, to pass through this area provided there would be no disturbance to anything in his area. Nothing further was heard of the incident. [For dispatch report, see Appendix 6.]

Two further incidents in the spring, which I will mention. One, the trip of Admiral Craven, commanding the Yangtze Patrol in the *Tutuila* from Ichang to Chungking and return. I'm thankful to say this trip went off very smoothly and nothing untoward happened, even my engines functioned perfectly. I was designated personal aide for the visit in Chungking which was rather an interesting experience with Admiral Craven.

The next occurrence, which I believe was shortly after this trip with Admiral Craven, we took General Wang Fang-two up from Wanshien to Chungking in the gunboat, and he could not have been nicer. He was really very much of a gentleman, beautiful discipline all the time except for this one incident of these troops that were supposed to be passing through.

The next happening in 1930 - there were a couple more interesting things. One was on 8 September in the Middle River, 81 miles above Chengling. One shot fired from the shore was silenced by a round of machine gun and four 3-inch. This one had fired on the gunboat at rather close range, and it was rather interesting for me because, as gunnery officer, I was given the after gun which got a direct hit and the captain - L. P. Bischoff was then the commanding officer - said he would control the forward gun from the bridge. At any rate, we silenced the fire.

The next day the Tutuila was fired on again. Range 75 yards on the port quarter, red flag hoisted. We silenced that fire with a few rounds. The dispatch reports on both these incidents will be appended, also the commanding officer's war diary of those dates [Appendix 7.]

On 9 September 1930 we began to be convinced that gunboats were now targets. When we approached Kwai yin tzo, nine miles below Shasi, a rifle shot rang overhead, a small puff of smoke was seen on the bank to the left of the city. A little later, another, but didn't see the puff. A red flag was perched on the bank when the first shot appeared. Soldiers appeared on the bank, waving red flags, and fired at us. Opened fire with starboard battery, range 200 yards. After 3-inch put one shot in bank near red flag. In midst of firing, soldier again appeared with red flag and disappeared. 3-inch shell high explosive made a beautiful hit, tearing a big hole in the dike and shot the red flag, and I believe destroyed those behind it.

Q: What was the purpose of these attacks and the red flag? Explain that to me.

Adm. W.: Communists, all bandits. We reported most of these incidents as bandits because for Chinese face - if you told the Chinese general that his troops were shooting at you, he'd be very much hurt. No, his troops couldn't do that. But if you reported to him that bandits were shooting at you, he'd say, "Fine, I hope you shot back at them." You see, they had stragglers in all their units. Some of them we never knew. In this particular case, since they were flying the red flag with the hammer and sickle, we felt they were Communists. And there were Communist bands all through that area. But, generally speaking, the military had control of them. They would just as soon us shoot the stragglers as we would.

Worthington #1 - 66

Q: But they didn't have any concept of the fact that they were shooting at a foreign vessel?

Adm. W.: Yes, I was convinced that it wasn't necessarily a foreign vessel, it was anything that moved. It may have been that they would shoot because the U. S. flag was flown-- a great big flag marked on the side of these gunboats. The gunboats were well marked, but I had the feeling that they liked to shoot at anything that was moving.

Here's one the next day, very similar.

Q: There was a whole series of these then?

Adm. W.: Yes.

Q: I think you've given the picture, really, of what could be expected by American gunboats on the river.

Adm. W.: Yes, and this one thing will show you, then I'll go on to maybe the last one of these armed guard incidents and I will try to abbreviate that.

The motor vessel I'Fung at Hankow, China with an armed guard. As we were moving along we sighted lots of soldiers, a group of reds mounted on the left bank, gun mounted on the right bank, small detachment showed over hill -- all the way along the river we were sighting and so forth. In another place Chinese mounted officers.

Mileage 166 - this would be above Hankow - fired on by mortar, range 1,800 yards. Returned fire with 40 rounds of machine gun. No casualties observed.

8 November, two mortar shots were heard from the direction of Kwai ying tzo, mileage 294, followed by another village fire visible from motor vessel I'Fung anchored off Shasi.

I think I can cover this armed guard business briefly in something I have here.

In 1930 I commanded seven armed guards in various ships, silenced fire on the American flag four times and, as previously mentioned in this, aboard Tutuila silenced enemy fire twice.

This about covers the armed guard activities and the gunboat of that period.

Q: You want to record an additional incident of a gunboat?

Adm. W.: Yes. An additional incident of the past year is believed worth recording here.

The Chinese steamship Shuhuo was wrecked in the Hsin Tan rapids and, in view of the low water, It was considered unsafe to steam by this wreck. In mid-January, the captain decided the Tutuila could do the job.

Q: She could do what?

Adm. W.: Steam this rapid, by the wreck, in spite of the dangerously low water. To do this job, first, we anchored below the wreck and inspected it and the position, then got underway, increased our steam and increased our speed from the maximum design speed of the ship of $14\frac{1}{2}$ knots at 322 revolutions. We attained somewhere in the neighborhood of nearly 400 revolutions per minute on the engines, bypassing the high-pressure steam to intermediate cylinders. This was an undesirable procedure but it gave us an extra lift to steam the rapid on that date, and we did so with no further trouble.

Q: Pretty hard on the engines, wasn't it?

Adm. W.: Well, you can only hold the steam a few minutes -- terrible on the engines. But we'd done it before. We'd always had to bypass the steam but it was a question of how long you could hold it. We had a special arrangement between the captain and the chief engineer, which I was, and he gave the emergency bells on the bridge. That's when the ship stopped. When you steamed these rapids, you watched the shore on $14\frac{1}{2}$ knots you're going like the devil and all of a sudden you observe the shore and you suddenly stop. When he rings the extra speed on the throttle you put the high pressure steam into the intermediate pressure cylinder and you get a little jump and get over it. We never, in my time, had to be pulled over those rapids, as was done at other times and other ships. I believe this is an engineering step that is quite interesting, but I do not recommend it.

Q: What was the life of a gunboat?

Adm. W.: Given over to Chiang-kai-shek.

Q: So, obviously, these stresses and strains didn't wear her out.

Adm. W.: In Tolley's book he gives a very vivid description of her and turning her over to Chiang-kai-shek for a communications ship. The crew was taken down over to Burma and flown out, came out through the south. I think there were only about 20 crew left by that time. I'm glad I wasn't there.

I believe that pretty well covers the *Tutuila*.

Worthington #2 - 70

Interview No. 2 with Rear Admiral Joseph M. Worthington, U. S. Navy (Retired)

Place: His home on Gibson Island, Maryland

Date: Thursday morning, 18 May 1972

Subject: Biography

By: John T. Mason, Jr.

Q: It's good to see you on this beautiful spring morning, Sir. Today I think we enter another educational phase of your career. Last time, you told me about your duty in the Far East and, when we concluded, we had arrived back in the States and you were about to report for duty at the Naval Academy.

Adm. W.: I reported for temporary duty in the Department of Seamanship and Flight Tactics in March of 1931. Then for temporary duty at the Army Chemical Warfare School at Edgewood Arsenal, and finally to the postgraduate school general line course on 30 June.

Q: Tell me what each one of those temporary assignments entailed. First, at the Naval Academy?

Adm. W.: In the Department of Seamanship and Flight Tactics I was assigned primarily to substitute teaching in various classes in seamanship, depending on what instructor happened to be on other duty on that particular day or days.

Q: This was your first effort at teaching?

Adm. W.: That was my first effort at teaching, and it was intensely interesting to me because when we were talking of practical seamanship we got into discussions of towing which I had considerable experience in surveying and salvaging a ship that had run on the rocks. The midshipmen really listened and seemed to be very much interested.

Q: Well, there's a certain amount of glamour attached to that, isn't there?

Adm. W.: It was practical experience. Outside of those hours I taught sailing.

Q: That must have been a pleasure!

Adm. W.: That was a real pleasure, and I'd had a lot of that surveying so it was not exactly Greek to me.

Going to the Chemical Warfare School at Edgewood Arsenal was intensely interesting to me in this respect. We were studying the use of chemicals with excellent instructors and the Army instructors had a little different idea of what would be done with these chemicals in naval ships. I took particular pains in making my final presentation, pointing out that I did not believe we would ever sacrifice the ability, or capability, of armor-piercing projectiles for gas warfare for the simple reason that the Army would use chemical warfare for anti-personnel effectiveness, while the Navy used armor-piercing projectiles to sink the ship.

And I believe that was a fair appraisal, and although we never used chemical warfare we were prepared with defense against it.

Q: Did the Army instructors have a knowledge of the Navy? Had they been indoctrinated in those areas?

Adm. W.: I would say not very much in those days, except we did have a naval officer assigned to the staff but more or less for administrative purposes. I do not believe he had any classes.

Reporting to the postgraduate school, Captain Frank H. Sadler was the head of the school, a very dynamic individual, and he had a splendid staff in my view. P. V. H. Weems instructed in navigation and piloting. He gave us a splendid course. T. N. Vinson, instructed in maneuvering and tactical graphics. The publication which he had personally developed and was used a great deal later on in maneuvering divisions of ships I found very useful.

Q: Weems himself had written some sort of a textbook, hadn't he?

Adm. W.: A number of textbooks. He not only taught the textbooks he had written, but he believed in teaching us all the different methods of navigation, whether it was Ageton or Weems or the old Hydrographic publications -- I think it was H.O. 204 in those days. He wanted us to know how to use a variety of publications on navigation. He was a very inspiring instructor.

The other part of the course, on piloting, groundings, and so forth, I thought was particularly useful because his textbooks were the records of the groundings of the various Navy ships in the last twenty or thirty years, and the findings of these courts of inquiry showed you the mistakes that were made and how easy it was to make them.

The head of the Electrical Engineering Department was Terwilliger, a splendid electrical engineer from MIT and instructor, and his assistant LaCausa. Then we had an instructor in history who lectured once a week, Dr. Charles E. Hill from George Washington University and his weekly discussions on --

Q: International law, wasn't it?

Adm. W.: He was a professor of international law but in relationship to our history and government and international law, and it was very valuable to us.

Q: Yes, he was a particularly knowledgeable man.

Adm. W.: He was fascinating. He'd really keep you spellbound. Next, I went on to the Army Industrial College.

Q: How long did you spend at the PG school?

Adm. W.: June 30th to June 10th the next year. It was nearly a full year -- an 11-month course.

Q: This was not for a degree, then?

Adm. W.: No, this was a general line course and had the practical subjects which we all needed for regular duties aboard ship.

Q: How many men were assigned to the PG school at one time?

Adm. W.: To my recollection, we had about sixty in the line course, but, of course, at the same time we had a group of maybe a dozen taking postgraduate communications –

Q: Specialists?

Adm. W.: Specialists. Another group in engineering, mechanical engineering, electrical engineering, for a second year. Then they went on for a master's degree to either Columbia or MIT, a couple of them did, and to the West Coast to the University of California at Berkeley.

Going on to Washington, since the Industrial College course did not open until the latter part of August, I reported to the Chief of Naval Operations, Materiel Division, for duty. The start of this was rather unusual. I had to drive through the Bonus Army encampments and also between lines of troops when MacArthur's group evicted the Bonus Army from the Capitol grounds.

In the Materiel Division of the Chief of Naval Operations I had one specific duty and that was to study our war plans day in and day out.

Worthington #2 - 75

Q: With what purpose in mind?

Adm. W.: Logistics, because I was to take the Army Industrial College course and my seniors in the Materiel Division felt that I should know of the war plans and in particular the logistic part of the war plans, or the materiel part maybe, which were not too extensive.

Q: These war plans were concerned with the Pacific, were they?

Adm. W.: They concerned the Orange Plan for the Japanese, and the Red Plan for Britain I believe. Blue plans were our own. White plans were internal. And Latin America, we had plans for Latin America. I can't remember the names of the different ones, but they were our basic plans.

Q: Were they updated all the time?

Adm. W.: Oh, yes. We had very good plans at that time but, of course, they were working on them all the time.

Q: Where were they formulated, in the Department or at the Naval War College?

Adm. W.: Oh, no, in the Department, in the office of the Chief of Naval Operations, which had a War Plans Division which did the primary planning. On the other hand, they coordinated them with the Intelligence Division and the Materiel Division. This division I was assigned to was working on the materiel sections of the plans. There were several officers in there at that time working on them, so it was an ever-growing product. My assignment to the Industrial College, I believe, was with the intent that I should some day come back there and be working on those plans.

Q: That was in the early 30s. How did the Navy in those days view the materiel aspect of naval conflict? What status did it have?

Adm. W.: We were ever-conscious of the need to build up the Navy and the combatant ships and some bases. Of course, our plan for the Pacific in those days was one rush across the Pacific and we did not have built-up bases to support it. We had a small place at Guam and in the Philippines and Hawaii, but even Hawaii, which I'll touch on more later, was not in any way prepared. This was a fleet dash across the Pacific and wind it up. We did not have the backup at that time to do it. We were trying to get ships built in Congress; we were trying to get tankers, supply ships. I would say we were just beginning to get into the real logistic backup of a Pacific Fleet.

Q: Was the emphasis largely on land-based depots and so forth, rather than supplying at sea?

Adm. W.: Yes. We had very little training in supply at sea

in those days, but I will touch on that later on when we did have these exercises in supplying at sea. But I would say in 1933 we were just beginning.

Q: Yes, I know, but did anybody conceive of what did develop in World War II, the supplying at sea and the great effort?

Adm. W.: Yes, there were plenty of people who knew, people who were advocating and trying to get into our Navy better ships and better logistics. There were studies at the War College and Admiral Ingersoll way back in those days was thinking very much ahead and what we required to go overseas. But the problem was in 1933 we had no funds -- 1932-1933.

Q: That was the nadir.

Adm. W.: We had no funds. We couldn't buy ships, we couldn't build ships, and we were cutting down our personnel. It was drastic. It was hard to get a ship to go to sea. It was another one of those dead periods of the Navy. After the stock exchange, after the cut in naval appropriations, the cut in personnel -

Q: The cut in salary.

Adm. W.: In salary, which I always thought was illegal for us. We'd get promoted and not get it! We did have plans but they were plans based on limited personnel, very limited -- both military and civilian.

Q: I suppose it's fair to say that at that point in time no conflict was really anticipated anyway?

Adm. W.: That is correct. But the United States never anticipates these conflicts until they happen. I mean World War I and right on back through our history -- the Spanish War -- you can keep on going back and find we weren't prepared and suddenly it hits us. And that's one of the things that worries me today more than anything else. We're cutting down our Navy and our ships and everything and suddenly we'll need everything. Take the Tonkin Gulf. We've never been able to have the influence over the State Department and the President until they get scared. The military has the same thing as the Navy.

Q: In that time you spoke also of the war plans that involved possible conflict in the Atlantic. What was the concept for supplying the fleet in the Atlantic?

Adm. W.: Well, in the Atlantic we were near enough to our Atlantic coast naval yards. We had naval yards and bases up and down the Atlantic coast and Guantanamo, and that's not so far, of course, in the Atlantic. But it's a whale of a way across the Pacific in distance. We just didn't have it. We were just beginning to build our 8-inch gun cruisers, for example. At these conferences we kept on losing.

Q: In terms of materiel and supplying the fleet, were we in any way circumscribed by these arms limitation treaties?

Adm. W.: Yes, we couldn't add to Guam; we couldn't add to the Philippines.

Q: You mean we couldn't fortify them?

Adm. W.: Fortify them or increase the units over there. We had an experience over there where we tried. Some planes got in difficulty in the Philippines based on aircraft tenders, which were perfectly legal. But the weather was bad and the plane couldn't get to the tender and went down in Subic Bay. The people there got hold of this thing and worked up to the dock and pulled it aboard, onto the shore. The Japanese immediately made a protest through our government that we were violating the treaty about naval bases -- a naval base, an air base ashore.

Q: They were ever-vigilant!

Adm. W.: They were ever-vigilant everywhere. This particular instance, I was there at the time but didn't know about it. I found it in Dyer's book on Turner. He describes the whole thing and exactly what they were doing. So we were kept back. We couldn't build; we could only build ships of certain types. Don't let me mislead you but we had the ablest man we could ask for as Chief of Naval Operations then -- W. V. Pratt. He was the top brains of our Navy for a good period there. He was followed by Admiral Standley. You can't find any two more able people. But when you're curtailed by the Congress and by the public all you could do was try.

Q: Well, all of this digging did prepare you for the Industrial War College?

Adm. W.: Yes, it was very useful to me for background. We reported to the Army Industrial College, as it was known then, and Lieutenant Colonel William A. McCain, Quartermaster Corps, was the commandant, a brother of John S. McCain, and a very dynamic individual.

For the opening class, for example, he immediately turned around and introduced Major Dwight D. Eisenhower and Commander W. S. Farber of the Navy. He said, "I'm doing this merely to show that the Army and the Navy are working together." It happened to be two people who later on were rather prominent in the Army and Navy. But, as he said, they helped educate in the joint work of the two services. And the staff we had -- John C. H. Lee was one member; Major Quinton another, later Chief of Ordnance. I was going to go into that and maybe I'll do it now -- some of those members of that staff.

I've mentioned Eisenhower, Lee, W. S. Farber, Morton C. Ring. In this class were Clifton B. Cates, Paul Hendren, James Kirk, John Dale Price, John A. Waters, Henry Williams, and Walter

Worthington #2 - 81

Weaver, who was the Billy Mitchell of that day. You can judge by those names who were present daily that we had some rather lively discussions of problems and diversities of view in the several services.

Q: Was that a year?

Adm. W.: From the 20th of August until the 20th of June. We worked on problems together and we heard some splendid lectures. One of them was Bernard Baruch, who was the top advisor to presidents through a great many years, from World War I on. In World War I he was head of the War Industries Board.

Those people all came and talked to the college at their own expense. They considered the invitation a chance to get military appreciation of the industrial backup and problems were worked there. I could mention many others, but I will not at this time.

The final problem that was assigned to my group, several different branches of the Army -- I was the only Navy man -- was world communications in World War II. We worked on that problem for several months, with quite a bit of digging and research, including visits to various places. And then as a junior member of the committee I was assigned the task of presenting it to the class. It went along, I thought, very well for a while, until I did mention the fact that in World War I the Army took entire units from AT&T and other civilian companies and put them in the

Signal Corps and they operated as units, put them in uniform and so forth. This brought quite a discussion. The Signal Corps said, "Oh, no, we had our own." One of the visitors was then a colonel in the Signal Corps, David Sarnoff. He was an Army Reserve, and he got into quite a discussion with the Army in which he backed up my statement. I was let out of the argument entirely.

Q: The Army people didn't want to -

Adm. W.: Well, it was quite a natural thing to do. They did the same thing in World War II. They'd bring in whole units and use them. When you expand -

Q: Why not accept this as a fact of life?

Adm. W.: The then chief of the Signal Corps was the one who took exception to it. The other questions were answered by the other members of my committee. I found it well worth the effort.

Q: Talking about the complexion of the student body, these came from the two services. Did they come from the State Department too?

Adm. W.: Not at that time. The Marine Corps, the Navy, and, of course, the Supply Corps of the Navy was represented rather heavily. Each branch of the technical services was represented.

What we're getting to, and I might point this up now, is that we were reaching the point where we had to get the Army and Navy and their various technical subdivisions working together on this mobilization, because on my checking through the various problems I would find that the Corps of Engineers had a complete plan of their own. The Signal Corps had a plan, and the others. But the coordination -- when they started working with the Navy, I think we learned quite a lot. One of the differences between the two services at that time was the Navy had mostly line working on these materiel problems; they also had Supply Corps and Engineering Duty Only officers, but they were mostly line, whereas the Army had mostly staff. For example, they had a Quartermaster who was commandant of the Industrial College. They rotated. The previous one was Signal Corps. They changed it around and later it was Ordnance Corps, then Field Artillery.

I believe the Industrial College accomplished quite a lot in those early days in getting the services working together and exchanging ideas.

Q: What relationship did it have at that time with the Naval War College and the Army War College?

Adm. W.: None whatever, except that we went down to one lecture at the Army War College, which was then at Fort McNair. The latter had another name then.

Q: In that area?

Adm. W.: It was in the same building. It was then the Army War College. They moved to Carlisle, I believe, to make room for the National War College. As I recall, there was only one lecture down there that we attended. The Naval War College had nothing in that respect. They worked independently. It's a fine college and I'm not running it down. I can tell you later some of the battles I had to get the Navy line completely backing up the Industrial College phase of it. That's a later story.

Q: Was there any evidence that the Army men who were assigned to the Industrial War College also had an opportunity to go to the Army War College at some time or other in their career?

Adm. W.: Yes.

Q: This in contrast to the Navy practice?

Adm. W.: This in contrast to the Navy for this reason. Here's the way the Army operated nearly always. The first thing they think about when they get out of West Point and get some field duty, if they could get any -- in those days there weren't many troops on that duty -- they'd go to Fort Benning, maybe, the Infantry School or the basic school and then to Fort Leavenworth to the Junior Staff College. Then, if they were successful there, to the Army War College or the Army Industrial College.

Worthington #2 - 85

The Army basically wanted their technical people to go to the Industrial College and their what you might call line people to go to the War College. That's basically the way they operated at that time.

It was much later I think before we had any Army at the Naval War College. You see, the Naval War College worked at that time of course on national policy, but basically on the naval phase of it, which was a big problem for them and they had a great deal of trouble meeting the requirements for that. Later on, the Army War College started getting naval officers on the staff and with the war coming on there were Army officers on the staff of the Naval War College.

Q: When did these colleges begin to accept State Department people? Not in this time?

Adm. W.: Not in this time. I could give you that later on because when I was deputy commandant at the Industrial College in 1946 to 1948 there were then State Department members of the National War College, and I believe the Industrial College started taking representatives shortly after that. But it was after my time of three years as deputy commandant. Then they brought in the other services. That's really another phase of this because the bringing together I will try to bring out in the three-year period as deputy commandant, because I had a lot of problems.

Worthington #2 - 86

Q: Yes, but it all was a broadening of the base?

Adm. W.: Yes, but at the beginning we had a very small staff. We had people wanting to work with us and the Navy backed us up and the Army, but you see at that time the Industrial College was under the Assistant Secretary of War and that was Secretary Woodring, and then Payne.

Q: I want to ask you one question about this. I do know that men who have gone to the National War College and so forth have benefitted by the association with men from other services and this has proved useful to them in their contacts in their careers. Did you notice this as a result of your — ?

Adm. W.: We felt this at this time. Not only with other services but with people of our own service. So many of this particular group got right up to the top.

Q: They were all promising men, yes. That's why they got there.

Adm. W.: Cates, general, USMC; Price Hendren, Farber and Hiltabidle got to be vice admirals. Ring, I don't think was a vice admiral but he should have been. He was tops. Waters and Buck, rear admirals. But these other services -- I'm just trying to spot some of them here right now -- oh, Colonel Scott, infantry, in this class was a brother of Norman Scott, an awfully nice person. J. C. H. Lee became a lieutenant general, Quinton and Kirk, major generals, and a number brigadier generals.

Q: I only meant to say that this did benefit you immediately, as your career unfolded?

Adm. W.: Oh, yes. Of course, I didn't get back to it again until I was deputy commandant of the Industrial College after the war, but I did find it a very useful intermingling of individuals and getting an understanding of the different service views, which I had no idea of before. How the Army, for example, was divided into these technical services. A very close-knit organization, each one of them, so that the Army themselves had to finally amalgamate them, as it were.

Q: This would cause me to speculate that it might be useful at the Naval Academy to have some sort of a course that taught the midshipmen about the detailed structural setup of the other services.

Adm. W.: Here's where you put me on the spot. I'll tell you why. I think it's very useful for them to know that at the Naval Academy. I think the superintendents over the last few years have done a great deal for this interchange of cadets and midshipmen and Air Force people between the academies to get to know each other and learn about each other's working. My hesitancy about recommending another course at the Naval Academy is looking at it from the director of education point of view, which I had for two years at the Industrial College, or maybe three, what course do you take out?

Q: Where do you find the time?

Adm. W.: That's a problem that I had literally hundreds of recommendations from people in the three years at the Industrial College, and I'd always bring up this one question, what do we take out. I felt we had a pretty good course. Of course, it improves every year, they've added to it every year, but it's the number of things, and that's why, without having been close to the Naval Academy in recent years, I would hesitate to say what to take out. For example, I think it's wonderful what you've done on this naval history business. I hate to say it, but our naval history was rather feeble in the Department of English, History and Government, and the appropriations committee in Congress tried to take this little history lecture course out of the postgraduate school. They said "Why does a naval officer need to get a course on history? He should be able to read." That was the attitude of people with budgets. So I think this symposium and business to me was a great inspiration, and these meetings with the midshipmen the last three years. We're beginning to get them to think of the lessons of history and think in terms of the future.

The Industrial College gets difficult because I was there so long.

Worthington #2 - 89

Q: Yes, but if you do it in the chronological sense, you were there for a year for this course.

Adm. W.: For this course, yes.

Q: Then I think we go on to something else.

Adm. W.: Well, graduating from the Industrial College I was extremely fortunate to be assigned to the 8-inch-gun heavy cruiser Pensacola. We had so many ships in mothballs and so few operating at sea that year that there seemed some doubt as to where I might end up. They were sending naval officers to the Civilian Conservation Corps, as well as a whole group of Army officers attending this Industrial College course. So I took particular pains in getting orders for a ship that was going to sea.

Q: Would you digress for a minute? That's a very interesting thing, which I did not know, that naval officers were assigned to the CCC. Whose idea was this and what did they do there?

Adm. W.: The little I know about it is from officers coming to ships with me afterwards. They ran camps or parts of camps just the same as any of the Army officers. Many Army officers did that, and they took the same type of a job. A line lieutenant, for example, would have a section of a camp. Their primary need was supply and medical officers from the Navy but they also got a great many line officers. How many I have no idea. I just know from talking to them afterwards what a harrowing time they had.

Q: Was there any thought that here were potential reservists that they were dealing with in these cases?

Adm. W.: Oh, yes, they realized and fortunately they did because they got a lot of them. They taught them how to live, and how to keep clean, and how to eat, and how to work. On the whole, it was a very, I think, good factor in our country.

Q: Then it was by design that the military men were involved in this?

Adm. W.: Yes, well frankly it was because they were the only people that could run it, I think, in a hurry. They were people used to doing things like that, and the Army did not have many troops, and the Navy was reducing their number of ships, so they accomplished a great deal, I think, in doing that conservation program. But I think maybe they need it now -- get some of the people off the streets.

Q: I didn't mean to digress because you were starting to tell me about the Pensacola, but it was an interesting facet.

Adm. W.: I reported to the Pensacola in New York, Captain H. H. Michael, commanding officer, and one whom I'd had the privilege of serving with in the Texas eight years previously.

Worthington #2 - 91

The executive officer, Commander W. H. Pashley, whom I'd met in China; the gunnery officer, Walter C. Calhoun, who is one of the finest officers I have ever had the privilege of working with. He assigned me to Number 3 turret and the Third Division, 8-inch gun turret, which I felt very fortunate to get, shooting again where I wanted to be.

We sailed immediately for Belfast, Maine, which was the town where Admiral Pratt, retiring Chief of Naval Operations, was retiring to live and he was very fond of that area. This was a gesture from the Secretary of the Navy, I believe. At any rate, our visit proved - the 4th of July - a political tour, in which some naval officers were taken around to these various towns, Rockland, Portland, Camden and Northport, for decoration while the politicians spoke.

After that, we sailed south, stopping at Norfolk to take on supplies and personnel for the West Coast, proceeded to Panama. A nice independent cruise which was mostly occupied in getting the ship cleaned up and painted up after a Navy yard period. We had a greeting party to Captain Michael in Panama, which we all liked. Steamed up the West Coast and at that time were able to get in some serious gunnery training.

Q: Did you then become a unit of the Pacific Fleet?

Adm. W.: Yes. Our home port was changed from New York to San Pedro. We stopped in San Diego to leave our planes and get a chance to check our directors in the still waters of San Diego Harbor, which was very useful to us.

Q: You had catapults, then, on board?

Adm. W.: Oh, yes, catapults and planes.

Q: What were the planes used for?

Adm. W.: Scouting and spotting gunnery practice. Later on I'll tell you about taking them off the ships, but at this time we had them.

Then we had to proceed to San Pedro. We fired short-range battle practice, and I was very fortunate in commanding an "E" turret, which, except for the economy time, would have given all the crew prize money. We fired on one principle, safety. In this I was supported by the gunnery officer and the captain. The cruiser staff gunnery officer, for example, observed my firing and told me I was entirely wrong, that with this excellent crew I could make a much higher score. I replied I was merely complying with the safety rules, which I insisted on doing.

To make a long story short, many "Es" were plastered on the cruisers in the harbor that month and when the word trickled to Washington that the safety precautions had been played with, those "Es" were taken off, but mine and our turret 2 in the Pensacola stayed. It was unbelievable to me that people would take those risks.

Q: What kind of risks were they taking?

Adm. W.: You're supposed to bring your gun down to level and hold it there until you can see the air pressure take the smoke from the preceding fire clear of the muzzles, so you can see daylight. Then you give the signal and the gun is to reload, and then the gun is hoisted up into position. They were jumping the gun on this particular operation.

Q: Not waiting for their clearance?

Adm. W.: And it was dangerous, in my opinion. At any rate, the Navy didn't go along with it and I was thankful that they didn't.

Q: Were you limited in the amount of ammunition you could use?

Adm. W.: Oh, yes.

Q: Admiral, if you would comment on the practice of working for an "E" in contrast with training for battle?

Adm. W.: Item 1, training for battle. You've got to have the greatest emphasis placed on safety, loading as fast as you can safely, closing the breech, and then elevating the gun to some position which might be, if it's long-range, quite a high elevation. In training for short-range, you actually depress the gun to get on the target, and in that way there is little danger of the load, powder bag and shell, dropping out because your depressing the gun will hold it in, but the point I want to make is that the short-range practice, the score practice, and for battle you elevate. The minute you get in the habit of starting to elevate before that breech is closed and locked, you take the danger of the powder dropping back into the turret and the shell dropping back. Or, the shell becoming unseated, in which case you get an entirely different range when you fire than the one you had calculated. I believe that's the main point.

Q: That's an interesting point and it leads me to ask how general was this practice of relaxing on the rules and regulations in order to achieve excellence in the contests?

Adm.W.: I have no exact figures on this, but I do know there was another cruiser that did the same as we did. I blame this in part on the emphasis placed on it by the particular individual gunnery officer who had influence on the gunnery officers of the ships. I know no one in that responsibility in all my time in the Navy that would do something like that, and I was utterly amazed that it was done.

Q: Of course, it's a feather in one's cap to earn an "E"?

Adm. W.: Sure. Look at these "Es" all over the turrets. I was riding past all these turrets one day with these "Es" on them with Walter Stratton Anderson, whom you must know, to play tennis ashore and he sort of blew up. He said, "What's going on with these cruisers? Where do they get all those "Es" from?" Well, at that time, I was so annoyed about the situation that I said, "Well, they don't comply with the rules, in my opinion."

I think he might have stirred them up in Washington. He was on his way back there. Because he knew gunnery and he was a dynamo for getting efficiency ratings. I don't know, I never served with him, I only played tennis with him. But I do not believe that he would violate any safety rules or permit anybody else to.

Anyway, it was straightened out and after that we went back to regular practice. You couldn't get away with this. You had to change your methods, you see. Once you had a practice that you don't depress any gun, you were in danger. Then you had it drop out on you and you were in real trouble. I felt very keenly about this at the time and still do.

The Pensacola thing might be quite long. It was quite a cruise.

Q: Well, is there anything of particular interest, or was it mainly routine?

Adm. W.: One thing I was going to mention was Jap discourtesy on the high seas when they broke through our division. This was the feeling of the time and I'm getting that from something I wrote at the time. It's dated October 1933:

Worthington #2 - 96

> We put to sea for U. S. Fleet tactical exercises
> and an impudent Jap merchantman caused the <u>Northampton</u>
> and <u>Pensacola</u> to scramble to avoid collision.

Q: Where was this?

Adm. W.: On the high seas, off the West Coast. On the high seas. The Jap clearly violated the rules of the road and the laws of civilized nations. It was typical of their attitude.

I will just touch briefly on the <u>Pensacola</u> being assigned the position of taking a congressional delegation to review the fleet off San Diego. To me, this was a fascinating opportunity to see the U. S. Fleet pass by and, from my position in the foretop with a high spotting glass, it was something entirely new.

To pass on from there, and this I must quote. The <u>Silver Palm</u> crashed into the <u>Chicago</u>.

Q: The <u>Silver Palm</u>?

Adm. W.: A british merchant ship. This is under date of 25 October 1933:

> We were steaming along yesterday morning in a heavy
> fog in close column (600 yards foremast to foremast)
> at 12 knots. Commander, Cruisers, in the <u>Chicago</u> led,
> followed by the <u>Pensacola</u>, Commander, Cruiser Divi-
> sion 4 in the <u>Chester</u>, and Commander, Scouting Force

in the Northampton bringing up the rear. About 0720 the Chicago signaled us to disregard her movements. Pensacola take formation guide, increase speed to 14 knots, and change course to starboard 25 degrees. The Chicago stood on and increased speed to 17 knots to test out some new boiler cement. At 0806 the Silver Palm (British) rammed the Chicago on port bow forward of Number 1 turret. At 0815 we received an SOS from the Chicago, turned toward her, and a few minutes later could make her out through the fog. The merchantman was just backing clear. We manned all boats but were shortly afterwards directed to proceed back to the scene of the collision to search for personnel believed to be overboard. The Northampton and Chester convoyed the Chicago to port while we, assisted by a division of destroyers, continued searching until dark.

I wanted to bring that out for two reasons. One is we had steamed the night before in that same formation in the same fog with zero visibility, and it was so bad that with the 36-inch searchlight from the ship ahead trained astern we could barely see their towing spar which they had astern for us to follow. But primarily no one seemed to realize, and here were three flag officers and their respective captains that we were doing anything out of the ordinary. I learned later that Captain

C. C. Gill from the Vestal cruising north at the same time had steamed out to sea ten miles in clear weather. Of course, this was war training and that was probably the reason for it, but here, in my description I just read of that time, although it's perfectly clear that our ship, the Chicago -- at that time the Chicago was independent -- had the right of way. The courts fought this back and forth, to the best of my knowledge, for some seven to nine years, and I cannot tell you at this time whether the final decision was in favor of the United States or in favor of the British.

But that was how this collision which, to my mind, should never have occurred, took the two nations into their respective courts to try to get a settlement.

Q: What happened to the captain of the Chicago?

Adm. W.: He was not promoted.

At this time, November 1933, I would like to point out the problems extreme shortage of personnel were giving those of us who were trying to conduct battle practices. In this case, for night battle practices, my turret had to use personnel from another turret to fill seven vacant stations, and likewise part of my crew filled vacant stations on the other turret at this night battle practice. So it had to be fired in two sections. At that time, a ship's complement was down to 73 percent of that required to man our stations.

Q: 73 percent of the minimum required?

Adm. W.: Well, your ship has a complement to man a station and if you have less for the station you're not ready for normal operations. In this case, just ordinary battle practice. Of course, in wartime you step up the complement. But here we were training personnel, powdermen in one turret to point - vice versa, the pointers were getting the training but the powdermen were getting it in the opposite turrets, which was a very poor arrangement.

Q: Would you comment on the caliber of the enlisted personnel during the period of the depression?

Adm. W.: Excellent. That will come in again a little later when we get into fire control in the Pensacola. We were getting at that period - in this next assignment I had, which was the fire-control division, I had the pick of the personnel assigned to the ship except those who were engineers. I looked for fellows who had had some college experience and frequently got them, or high-school graduates, but in many cases they'd had a year or two of college.

Q: The educational level was high then?

Adm. W.: The educational level was higher and we could train them quicker. Of course, we lost them quicker, too, after the

Worthington #2 - 100

depression was over, but at least we had some very high-grade personnel in those times, and it was really a pleasure to work with them.

Q: Since you mentioned the fact that you were engaged in night practice, let me ask how extensive was night practice, battle-order practice, gunnery practice, or what have you, in the fleet at that time?

Adm. W.: All ships - it was part of the regular gunnery exercise. We started out with the short-range battle practice. That's primarily for training the crews in handling their guns and their turrets and safety precautions, and then short-range pointer fire. Then you move into the night practice, where you use your searchlights and your star shells for illumination, and it is a more difficult practice. And then a more high-speed target practice at a greater range. Then you get into more extensive practices like the long-range practices. I mentioned that earlier about the Texas long-range practice, where you really test out your equipment, such as firing at almost maximum range, the skill in range-finding, spotting, and everything else.

Next, I want to mention something which to me was of extreme interest.

In the spring of 1934 we were having a fleet exercise off the West Coast - this was in February - and while cruising in a fleet disposition we sighted the Macon, the CRS-5 air ship, commanded by Lieutenant Commander H. V. Wiley, in smoke and going down. As soon as the Pensacola could clear the cruising disposition we proceeded, as did other ships that were much closer, to the rescue of the Macon personnel. This was about sunset and by the time we'd gotten close enough - and I was assigned the lifeboat, the officer of the deck at the time commanded the lifeboat - it was dark and the wreckage and gasoline on the water was burning and we had to be careful approaching this burning wreckage with a gasoline motor boat. We found no personnel. Fortunately, they had been rescued a little earlier by other ships that were closer, all except two, I believe. But we did find the navigator's log of the Macon, the ship's bulletin board, some of their ballast tanks, and some other articles. Probably the navigator's notebook was the only one of real value.

In regard to that accident, we learned later that she was returning from sea to Point Sur, California. She was returning in a storm from these fleet exercises to her base near Point Sur, California. During the storm, she was caught in a sudden updraft that caused a structural failure of her upper fin and resultant gas leakage and loss of control. Later on, this same commander, H. V. Wiley, reported to the Pensacola for duty.

It was terrible seeing the Macon go down. She was the last of our big ones, I believe. He was such a marvelous shiphandler that the entire crew got off and from the dense smoke and then later flames that we saw you wouldn't have thought anybody would be alive.

Following this exercise, the fleet made a cruise to the south, Fleet Problem XV, and during this cruise one of the most interesting actions was an emergency transit of the canal, which I believe was 17 hours and the first time this had ever been accomplished.

Q: This was a practice emergency?

Adm. W.: Yes. We suddenly arrived off the entrance and were going to pass through in the normal manner, then Reeves sent out this signal, "Emergency and we'll transit without delay." That's the way they did it, with the pilots back and forth, fascinating. It was a good drill.

Q: This was Admiral Reeves?

Adm. W.: Yes. He was assigned the responsibility. Admiral Sellers, I believe, was fleet commander, but Reeves was assigned the task. It was probably Reeves' suggestion that we do it.

Q: It sounds like him!

Adm. W.: Just like him. Then we steamed on to New York for the Fleet Review by the President, and on to Newport, where we had a fleet critique. To me, this was quite a memorable occasion, for Admiral Reeves took the podium of the Naval War College, disposed of the loudspeaker, and said, "I believe you can all hear me." He was a very forceful speaker with a booming voice, as you probably know.

Q: Was this the total officer personnel of the fleet assembled?

Adm. W.: Everybody that was not on watch was designated to attend this critique. They were his officers, and he really gave us a splendid pep talk and dissertation and so forth. I think everybody should have benefited by it.

We were en route to Provincetown when we received orders in the middle of the night to return to Newport immediately for special duty. The special duty seemed to be in no real hurry when we arrived there. It was to be target for some fancy torpedoes we had, electric magnetic things that they wanted to test out. So we had several delightful weeks in Newport, going out to sea every day and being targets for these torpedoes. The experts took all their readings and observations, then we were anchored for the evening to enjoy Newport.

Meanwhile the trials for the America Cup races were going on, so we had a chance to see those every day.

Q: A fortunate arrangement of time, wasn't it?

Adm. W.: It certainly was. We did very well!

The Pensacola was suddenly detached from this work and proceeded to Annapolis, where the remains of the late Belgian ambassador to the United States and his family were embarked for transportation to Antwerp. This was a quiet trip, with no untoward events until arrival in Antwerp when, with a regiment of Belgian infantry drawn up on the dock to present arms, everyone in full dress uniform, a minute gun salute being fired, the casket being hoisted over the side, when it became apparent to all that the casket was far too big for the Belgian hearse. Bluejackets, ever resourceful, proceeded to take off the outer layer and the next layer and, after some forty minutes, the procession proceeded to Brussels, where the funeral had to take place before sunset by Belgian custom.

We recovered from this in Gravesend, England, and had a chance to visit London, returned to the United States for some operations off the East Coast, routine drill and tactics, until proceeding to New York Navy Yard in October for the final chance to get the ship repairs before returning to the West Coast in January.

Captain Michael was detached in April, we engaged in fleet problem, 29 April to 16 June, to Hawaii and return to San Diego for another fleet review and critique. Upon return to the States, the gunnery officer was detached, many of the other gunnery personnel, and there were a great many changes in the ship.

I will not dwell much on the next gunnery year, although I could at some length. Unfortunately we had four or five acting gunnery officers in that time. I still had the responsibility of the main battery, and we did reasonably well in most of the practices, short-range, night battle, but the climax to the year came with a long-range battle practice which I had every reason to believe would be perfect. There was only one hitch in it. The captain would not let me use the procedure which we had found extremely successful in the previous two years -

Q: This was the new captain?

Adm. W.: The new captain - and directly ordered me to fire his method. Even so, we would have still been successful, but the best director firing pointer, in this case a trainer, I have ever seen happened to be off-target on the first salvo in deflection. No spots were possible. By the time the first fall of shot was observed, most of our ammunition was already in the air. It turned out that we had perfect range at 29,000 and would likely have made a killing by stopping five seconds to get a check on that first fall of shot.

At any rate, that's gunnery for you, and it was excellent war training because in war you have to get those first hits or else you're in trouble. But it made a very unpleasant ending to my three years of gunnery in that ship.

Q: It causes me to ask you to comment on this practice of reassignments and battle practice, the effectiveness of training of that sort when personnel is constantly changing.

Adm. W.: Well, we had so much of a change in personnel in this ship at the time that it was extremely difficult to do a decent job.

Q: Very little continuity.

Adm. W.: Yes. As I mentioned, by the time the next gunnery officer reported I was the senior officer in the gunnery department with any experience of the previous years' firing. My work was main battery which, of course, I thought most important and it was. But the point is we went to an excellent gunnery school by the time they got aboard ship to work with the new captain. The Pensacola went on a cruise and I was among those who attended gunnery school aboard the Minneapolis, based on Long Beach.

We had in that gunnery school the most experienced main-battery officers from all the ships, eighteen cruisers involved. The new gunnery officers from all these ships, except my own, many of whom were inexperienced in gunnery but were due for a head of department cruise before coming up for selection for commander. I felt that this gunnery school was the finest thing I'd ever seen. Among the people in that school were Joe Wright of Annapolis in my class, Laidlaw, Crowe and Adams, all of them experienced in main-battery firings, and all except myself were postgraduates in gunnery. So we lived all day between firing and shooting and discussing firings. We had some ammunition to fire these various practices, and they were the same practices that the cruisers were all supposed to fire during the gunnery year. And aboard with us was the new cruiser gunnery officer, a perfectly splendid individual, Alexander S. Wotherspoon. He was not only brilliant, but he had common sense and knew how to handle young people and captains and admirals and everything else. And he knew gunnery. He was, of course, the key behind this school.

The quarters aboard the Minneapolis were rather tight at the time. A great many of us lived in what had been Admiral Hart's cabin. He was in another ship at the time, so we could use this new ship for gunnery. We had good results from the gunnery school. My only problem, returning to my own ship was to sell these new ideas to the new captain. The assistant gunnery officer, who had the antiaircraft control, was on another ship, attending another gunnery school. I had two ensigns with me who were brilliant and they really worked. They got commended by the cruiser gunnery officer for what they did in this gunnery school, and they stayed with me for a while after we got back to the ship.

But the turnover in personnel was out of this world. We had a new captain, a new executive officer, a new gunnery officer, a new first lieutenant, and then going on along to the lower ranks - new turret officers. The Navy suffered from that. I don't know the answer. The Germans, you know, put a crew in these 6-inch-gun cruisers they built between the wars and they stayed there for six years, ten years, and the whole crew were lined up to be officers when they expanded the German Navy. But ours had to do different things. It's a very difficult problem and I don't know whether we've solved it yet or not. I sometimes wonder.

I wasn't going to touch much on the latter part of the Pensacola cruise because I didn't know what would be accomplished by it. I did want to mention that in the Pensacola among the people who were shipmates and that I thought very highly of in the earlier part were A. S. Merrill, who became a quite famous admiral -

Q: "Tip" Merrill?

Adm. W.: Tip Merrill. He's a gem. J. Hord Armstrong, one of my turret officers, who lost his life in the Jarvis. Otto Nimitz was one of our navigators. He knew gunnery, but he was a navigator, and he wasn't about to get in on it under the circumstances.

Q: What kind of a man was he?

Adm. W.: I liked him very much. This is Otto Nimitz, the brother.

Q: I know. Half-brother.

Adm. W.: He was a very technical man. Frankly, at the post-graduate school - he taught us gunnery there - and I thought it was a mistake for a plain line officer to be taking all this technical gunnery he was teaching us. He practically went into the wiring diagram of all the new ships. It's a good thing to know for an ordnance postgraduate, but on the other hand he was an excellent naval officer. He was a good shipmate, and I liked very much working with him. I think he worked on the captain, too, which was a help.

John Brown, my old friend, was assistant engineer. We had a chief engineer, Johnson, who I thought was an old man then. He was 58 years old. He'd been a fireman aboard the Illinois when my uncle was chief engineer and Sims was gunnery officer, back in the early part of the century. He used to give me some great tales about the Navy in those days and then I'd have to go to my uncle to get some ways to refute some of them!

I believe we've pretty well covered the Pensacola.

Q: You were in her for three years, you say?

Adm. W.: Three years, the longest I ever stayed in a ship. We did go to the Navy Yard in Mare Island in April. Then the captain became senior officer present and I had another job as his aide. The good thing about Mare Island as far as I was concerned was a Board of Inspection and Survey came aboard and

I was assigned the job to inspect the ship with them. They had a very fine person by the name of Bradley. A great many people were scared to death of him -- Willis W. Bradley, who had been captain of the Portland and he gave us a beautiful materiel inspection. It was a real inspection. That made things better for the ship. Also, the Navy Yard gave us all the repair work we'd asked for, which I thought was an accomplishment in itself.

Then the captain assigned me as aide to the senior officer present afloat, which he was, so I had all the details of the flag duty, the staff duty, and assigning the berths to the ships, and medical guards, court-martial reviews, and all kinds of things. But that didn't make any difference to me because I knew I was leaving shortly.

I did want to say, before leaving the Pensacola -- I mentioned H. V. Wiley before. He was the first acting gunnery officer, and we fired the short-range practice and he told me -- he was the damage-control officer of the ship -- "The captain says there's to be good results." I said, "That's fine."

"Well, go ahead and fire," he said. "I have not been in gunnery for many years. I've been in lighter-than-air." Which was perfectly fine and he knew the wind and the direction and things like that, which was very helpful, and we had a very fine practice. Then he resumed his duty as damage control.

I didn't mention the new executive officer of the Pensacola that year. He was Alfred Zimmerman, who was extremely able,

Worthington #2 - 111

extremely capable, and he worked sixteen hours a day. I thoroughly enjoyed working with him because he would make a decision, after getting the facts.

Q: You were next assigned shore duty at JAG in Washington. How did this come about? Had you asked for this?

Adm. W.: I was stupid enough to ask for it. Frankly, in the time of reducing naval personnel, which I just went through in the depression days, so many officers from the Navy were retiring, I felt that my naval postgraduate work was purely and simply of naval use later on, whereas if I could take a law course I would have something else to fall back on. That is the fundamental reason that I went to the JAG.

Q: This reflects the thinking in the Navy at that time.

Adm. W.: A lot of us were looking for jobs and a lot of us were not being promoted.

Q: It was a dead-end career?

Adm. W.: That's right and that's why a lot of people were getting out.

Then I reported to Admiral G. J. Rowcliff, the Judge Advocate General of the Navy, and then Commander T. L. Gatch, who was Assistant Judge Advocate General. I was directly under Commander C. J. Parrish, who had the court-martial section of

Worthington #2 - 112

JAG. My specific assignment was the general court-martial desk, which involved taking a law course in the forenoon at the George Washington University, reviewing general courts-martial in the afternoon and on Saturdays in the office of the Judge Advocate General, and, in particular, keeping track of every general court-martial that came into the JAG office, whether it was sent to the Marine Corps or the Chief of Naval Personnel or the Secretary of the Navy or the Chief of Naval Operations.

Q: Were these numerous?

Adm. W.: No, but there were enough to see the tragedies in the Navy -- a ship collision, a ship sinking, stealing of funds, mess funds or ship's service funds.

Q: How many in a given year?

Adm. W.: I wouldn't pretend to say because I have no recollection at this point. All I can remember now is that I was everlastingly busy with these coming across the desk, because each one might come across my desk several times.

For example, after it had been reviewed in the office and I'd prepared an endorsement for the next up the line. Now, if we found nothing wrong with it in the JAG office, then Naval Personnel might have it, if it was a naval case, or the Marine Corps might have comments. Then it came back for passing on up to the Secretary of the Navy. Most of the time I was in this job Admiral Standley was Chief of Naval Operations and Acting Secretary of the Navy. So in many cases endorsements were prepared for his signature. The then Secretary of the Navy was ill.

Q: Was that Claude Swanson?

Adm. W.: Claude Swanson, for a long time. Admiral Standley did a marvelous job.

Q: That must have been not too pleasant a duty because you were dealing with people in trouble all the time?

Adm. W.: That's one of the things I never forgot. I thought I was getting a warped attitude of the Navy because I'd read about battleships running aground, cruisers colliding, destroyers colliding, and each one of them was a tragedy for some individual, and in many cases it was someone I knew.

Q: It was a kind of inexorable thing, too wasn't it?

Adm. W.: That's right, but it taught me a great deal in later commands, what to watch for in the way of safety of ships. Previously the line course taught all these histories and navy groundings from the records in the Office of the Judge Advocate General. I would see these long cases and, of course, review what every witness had to say, and how little it takes to be between safety and disaster.

Q: What is the line of demarcation between a court-martial and a lower censureship?

Adm. W.: Usually determination can be made right within your own organization in the chain of command, the senior on a court of inquiry or a board of investigation, as the case may be, if it's not serious enough to warrant a court-martial, a letter of reprimand or a letter of admonition. But I never saw those because they were handled in the fleet itself, within their own organization. But generally it was serious damage to materiel, as it would be in the case of a ship. I think the feeling was that a court-martial was one way to either clear it or make the responsibility clearer than a court of inquiry, which ascertains facts in the case.

Q: What percentage of them were exonerated as a result of this?

Adm. W.: I would say not very many. Once the convening authority afloat who had all the facts closest to him, had decided that this individual should or should not be given a court-martial, he would not order a court-martial unless he was pretty well convinced that the evidence was there. I have known cases when a court-martial has been ordered and there was some doubt, and the convening officer just wanted to be sure that the individual involved was given a fair chance. To me it's a sad part of the Navy, but it's a necessary one.

Worthington #2 - 115

Q: When a man is court-martialed, then he leaves the service?

Adm. W.: Not necessarily. Many people lose maybe five numbers, twenty-five numbers, in seniority, or are fined. But once it's on the record, the chances are unlikely that he will go further. Some of our top people during the war had courts-martial or reprimands or something on their records.

Q: Was JAG involved during the time you were there with the preparation of testimony before congressional hearings?

Adm. W.: If they were, I just do not remember any of that. If it was a court of inquiry though that was going up they would have maybe had to make a special thing. Maybe that was handled by some of our civilian lawyers. For example, we had a case of a court-martial of one of our lieutenant commanders who had sold some of our plans to the Japs. That was one of the cases that came across my desk. Well, we wound up with a civilian lawyer in JAG handling it all the way through, and he kept it until the offender went to federal prison. It was a very unforunate thing. It happened in 1935 aboard a destroyer down in Charleston.

There was another, to me, tragic case that I handled entirely, the Marine legation at Peking. Three Marines, young kids, hoisted the red flag, hammer and sickle, over the legation. It was just a kid's prank, I think, in their view, but then they got scared when they heard about it, so they got a gun away from a guard and went absent without leave. They were caught, of course, and they were tried right there on the spot, and they got very heavy sentences. By the time it got back to Washington, to the commandant of the Marine Corps for endorsement, the sentences were finally reduced. It started out, we think, as a childish prank, but you can't grab a gun away from a guard, or you were in trouble.

All the letters from senators and everything else would come across my desk. They were the ones I always had to prepare a reply for the signature of the Judge Advocate General.

Q: How did you deal with that kind of political pressure?

Adm. W.: It so happened that we were able to tell them what the law was, which, with good conduct in prison, was that they'd get out in two-thirds of the time, or something like that.

Q: Yes, but in some cases that doesn't suffice, does it?

Adm. W.: It usually did. I don't remember any cases where -- once they'd write the letter, you see, they'd cleared themselves and had something to send back. I don't know of any case where the Navy weakened on a clear-cut case.

Q: Let me ask how much law you learned that year.

Adm. W.: An awful lot more law than you'd ever think from my law school record, because I've used it in the years since so many times. I've had to.

But, to make a long story short, at the end of the summer -- at the end of the first year, which was June, I requested assignment to sea duty. I was wasting the U. S. government's time going to law school. Admiral Tom Gatch wrote a beautiful endorsement to the effect that I didn't have an aptitude for law but that in no way reflected adversely on my abilities as a naval officer. That cleared the situation, but the detail officer would not send me to sea. That was Harold Train. You probably knew him in Annapolis. He said, "I can't give you as good a job at sea as you had when you left. You're coming up for selection this year. I'm going to send you to the Naval Academy. You will be useful to them. You'll get some rest and be prepared for next year." And so I got my assignment to the Naval Academy.

Q: What was that?

Adm. W.: I was assigned to the executive department to be Ninth Company officer, which was a very delightful assignment. Within a month after arrival, they had this serious Board of Investigation at the Academy, in which charges had been made against the Dental Department, totally false.

Q: What kind of charges?

Adm. W.: A Dr. Jones had been allowed to have a chair in the Dental Department and try out a special invention on midshipmen who volunteered.

Q: This was a woman doctor?

Adm. W.: A woman doctor. To show, if this worked, that they wouldn't have any more trouble with holes in their teeth. Mrs. Roosevelt's pressure got her into this job, and it got so bad that the Dental Department's time was all taken up with keeping her records and re-examining the midshipmen every two weeks until it was seriously impeding their care of the midshipmen. So she was asked to leave.

Q: Was her system working?

Adm. W.: Nobody ever found out to my knowledge. With all this investigation that was going on, I never found it any good at all. Had all these midshipmen testify and the dental officers testify. She went to the Secretary of the Navy.

Q: She was ahead of her time, wasn't she?

Adm. W.: Oh, yes. They're getting things now. But she made all this story to the Secretary of the Navy, and all he did was put it in a letter to the Superintendent and he ordered a Board of Investigation.

Worthington #2 - 119

Q: Who was the superintendent?

Adm. W.: I think the superintendent was in Europe when this thing happened and the commandant was acting when she was brought in. I think she was eased out as soon as he returned. The superintendent was Sellers. This was 1937, October 1937.

She brought these four pages of court-martial charges against the Dental Department at the Naval Academy, and I was assigned counsel for the Dental Department. The investigation took three months, plus the time of Captain Jack Shaffroth, who was head of the station ship Reina Mercedes; Captain Hayden, the head of the hospital; Commander T. deWitt Carr, of one of the departments plus two lawyers for the court, Lieutenant Cady, of the postgraduate school staff, and Marine Captain Ross, plus daily meetings in Bancroft Hall with this Board of Investigation. And every evening meeting with the defendants, chiefly the head of the Dental Department and his assistant. They were both splendid naval officers.

Q: What were they being charged with? Failure to permit her to — ?

Adm. W.: Oh, mistreatment, failure to permit her to do what she was assigned to do, not cooperating, throwing her out of the building -- this thing was three pages or four pages of absolute trumped-up charges, in her mind, which never should have been accepted at all. I tried for three days in court to get the whole thing thrown out. These charges were brought without any rhyme or reason, as nearly as we could tell. So far as I've ever been able to ascertain, when the investigation ended they were sent to the files in the JAG office.

Q: What was the position of the Secretary of the Navy? Was that Edison?

Adm. W.: I don't know whether he'd succeeded Swanson at that time or not. Standley retired in December 1936, so the new Secretary, I don't believe he took any position. It might have been Janhnke, the Acting Secretary. Edison was later -- 1939-40.

Q: This was indeed, then, a political thing?

Adm. W.: It was a political thing. Mrs. Roosevelt had persuaded the then Chief of the Dental Corps of the great value of this cereal and persuaded him to let her make this experiment with the midshipmen. There was an Acting Commandant at the time, that summer, and he let her use it. Todd was Acting Commandant. He let her in and it was soon after the regular superintendent came back --it was Sellers -- she went out.

It was just such an unfortunate thing, but the Navy's still confronted with that. When a politician gets onto something and puts pressure on senior officers, it can have a most adverse effect on the whole picture.

Q: Especially if the White House is involved.

Adm. W.: That's right. And, incidentally, one of the dental officers concerned -- I was very fortunate that he was the best one in the crowd -- was the one making the fight, and he'd been the dental officer to the President and Mrs. Roosevelt. So he still had close contact with the White House. So I didn't have any concern, except to clear this thing for the Dental Department.

Q: Did Mrs. Roosevelt see this through, or did she just step out of the picture?

Adm. W.: As far as I know, nothing ever came to her, unless Dr. Jones went back to her again and somebody there told them forget it. I don't know. I'd gone to sea by that time.

The year in the Ninth Company as company officer was delightful duty. I enjoyed working with the midshipmen, dining with them in Bancroft Hall about every ninth day when I had the duty, and many of those officers, then midshipmen, I was to serve with later on board ship and got to know them quite well. Many of them are doing a very fine job right now, although most have retired, I guess -- class of '38, '39, '40, and '41.

Q: You left the Naval Academy in May of 1938 and the very next month you reported for duty on the cruiser Minneapolis.

Adm. W.: Yes, the flagship of the Commander, Cruiser Division 6.

Q: Where was she? In the Pacific?

Adm. W.: In the Pacific. I was assigned aide and flag secretary to at that time Rear Admiral F. H. Sadler, who was relieved by Rear Admiral Ingersoll - R. E. Ingersoll - in July -- 16 July.

The staff consisted of Lieutenant Joseph A. Flynn, aide and flag lieutenant, who lost his life in the Indianapolis; Lieutenant Jack S. Dorsey, communications officer; and Lieutenant Commander T. T. Tucker, who was Commander, Cruiser Division 6, aircraft, and additional duty as aviation officer on the staff.

Shortly after reporting in San Francisco, which was the day following the presidential review, the cruisers proceeded back to the Long Beach area for various drills and exercises. I believe it's desirable to point out the captains of these cruisers: L. F. Kimball in the Minneapolis; Kelly Turner in the Astoria -- first, C. C. Gill in the Astoria but shortly after Richmond Kelly Turner; Austin T. Beauregard in the New Orleans; John F. Shaffroth in the Indianapolis. The Indianapolis was also flag of Commander, Scouting Force, Vice Admiral Adolphus Andrews.

The division was engaged in drills, gunnery exercises, tactics, and was kept exceedingly busy this entire fall off the West Coast. My particular assignment included writing operation orders for the division gunnery exercises and became quite involved before the year was out. In addition, during tactical exercises, my specific assignment was operating the maneuvering board for obtaining course and distance to the next position for the division, as the orders from the higher commanders were issued. The flag lieutenant saw that these courses and speed changes were hoisted. This was an exceedingly live cruiser tactical exercise. It may be pointed out that Rear Admiral Husband E. Kimmel was Commander Cruiser Division 7; Rear Admiral G. J. Rowcliff, Commander, Cruisers, and Commander, Cruiser Division 5; and Rear Admiral Walter Anderson, Commander, Cruiser Division 4.

I can assure you that all three were dynamic, driving, dashing individuals. Meanwhile, the junior admiral in the Minneapolis was so brilliant in tactics and so quiet in his manner that he was well able to more than hold his own in this cruiser squadron. Some of the exercises included recovery of the cruiser aircraft from the several squadrons simultaneously by the method then known as "cast method." They made a turn and picked up one aircraft on one side -- the cruiser seaplane landed in the slick, made a turn to land 2nd plane in the slick, then turned again, for third plane and another turn for 4th plane, which was a very intricate maneuver with 14 to 16 ships involved. But all of this was war training and the individuals were able to instill a great deal of seamanship in their respective commands.

Q: Admiral, tell me, was practice becoming more realistic, with the thought that the enemy was looming on the horizon?

Adm. W.: I would say it was much more realistic, with these people on the scene at this time, as you can judge by those four division commanders of cruisers, plus the type commander, and the Commander, Scouting Force. They were very realistic practices and the firing was quite realistic, and the antiaircraft problems were most realistic. We did those in formation, which was quite a trick to write the operation orders for a division of antiaircraft guns and getting the planes which, in those days, were towed by someone else in the planes to come in at the right time and the right direction so all ships' guns could bear at the same time and not endanger the pilots.

In 1939 the cruisers were part of the fleet problem in the Panama area en route, supposedly, to the East Coast for another fleet review. The exercises in Panama combined the Scouting Force cruisers, the new light cruisers, and destroyers with the West Coast ships and were very live exercises, including a long stay in the Culebra area, where Landing Force exercises were made quite realistic.

With matters worsening on the West Coast -- in the West -- the Minneapolis was ordered back, after a short stay in Pensacola, Florida, and proceeded to the Navy Yard at Bremerton, where Admiral Ingersoll became senior officer present afloat. The Astoria was also assigned to Bremerton, after returning from a cruise to Japan. The New Orleans was in the Mare Island Navy Yard during this period.

The summer was exceedingly busy, even though the ships were undergoing overhaul. Commander, Cruiser Division 6, was assigned the redrafting of the Navy general tactical instructions, which he and the flag lieutenant and the communications officer worked on daily in the Minneapolis. Meanwhile, the flag secretary was endeavoring to have a great many files of the ship since the ship was commissioned crated and declassified and sent to storage.

At that time we drafted a letter for the approval of Congress on the destruction of many of these papers.

Q: It was difficult to declassify, I suppose?

Adm. W.: Yes, and difficult to get them to let you destroy anything! It was horrible. But there was a war at the time and we were trying to get rid of useless files.

The summer stay in Bremerton otherwise was quite pleasant and the duties of senior officer present which, as legal officer, didn't bother too much, were not too strenuous, and we were able to work on plans as well as we could for future operations. When the Navy Yard period was ended, the individual ships were directed to proceed to Long Beach. Admiral Ingersoll proceeded separately and drove his family there. After his departure we received a fleet exercise, to work out and submit to Commander, Scouting Force, upon arrival in Long Beach. As was the case on many problems, they were sent to Commander, Cruiser Division 6, desiring to get Admiral Ingersoll's personal view on the situation or solutions or suggestions.

Q: Why? Did he have an original mind?

Adm. W.: He had an original mind. He'd been director of war plans. He got all these tough jobs, War College staff, and he was known in the Navy to know the answers. That's how it was. But this time it did not quite work. The staff present, the flag lieutenant and I, worked out the problem on the cruise to Long Beach, making up our own minds that we were going to have the reply ready at the time required by Commander, Scouting Force, and we were not going to deliver it until Admiral Ingersoll had seen it.

So, upon arrival in Long Beach, we told him we had this ready. "That's right," he said, "the chief of staff called me at home and asked me if I had worked on it, and I said no, I hadn't seen it. He was very much concerned. He said it was due today." And Admiral Ingersoll said, "Well, my staff, I'm sure, will have it ready for my signature," and that's what actually happened. He was amazed.

Things happened fast when we arrived at Long Beach. Orders

were issued to form the Hawaii Detachment. Vice Admiral Adolphus Andrews, Commander, Scouting Force, in the Indianapolis was now named as Commander, Hawaiian Detachment. Two divisions of cruisers were included, and Rear Admiral Ingersoll was given additional duty as Commander, Cruisers, Hawaiian Detachment, which made him type commander with two divisions of cruisers.

Q: What was the purpose of setting up this detachment in Hawaii?

Adm. W.: I'll give you the others, then I'll tell you. A flotilla of destroyers and the carrier Enterprise were also in the Hawaiian Detachment.

The purpose, I believe, was very clear: to test out the logistic facilities at Pearl Harbor, to see what they could handle and what was their great gap. I will come back to this a little later because this is what we got into upon arrival. We had to do such things as assign berths where the cruisers could dock or moor, and the carrier docked at the big dock next to Ford Island, the destroyers at Merry Point. The cruisers moored at what later became the battleship berths. The Indianapolis cruiser flagship and the cruiser of Division 6 flagship, Minneapolis, docked alongside the Ten Ten Dock. That was my job, assigning berthing space and seeing that the admirals got good berths. One of the reasons it was so important to be close to the Scouting Force flagship, close to the Navy Yard.

Now, with a small staff, various individuals suggested that

the admiral get a captain for chief of staff and a commander for operations, with the proper ranks and so forth on his staff. He said absolutely no, "any time my staff cannot handle this job, I'll let you know." We really started working then because additionally gunnery exercise operations were being planned for the eight cruisers now and we had a logistic problem. We had to have oil, for example, for the cruisers diesel ranges. There was no diesel oil available. We had to buy it commercially in Honolulu and truck it down. Gasoline for the cruiser planes, for a while we bought that at other places, although we had the Ford Island thing. But it was a question of getting it aboard the ships, at the docks. The oil barge in Pearl Harbor was nothing to handle these ships. The gasoline barge was nothing. The supplies were very meager. Of course, the Pearl Harbor people were delighted. Admiral Bloch was commandant -- C. C. Bloch, who was recently commander in chief of the fleet -- and the yard gave what I would say was 100 percent cooperation. But it took a lieutenant commander who was a fuel master mind and handled all these demands for fuel. But each time this thing came up, the letters would go up through the chain of command. They would go through Commander, Scouting Force, we need this, we need that, and go through the commandant, we need this, we need that. Well, the people back in Washington realized they had to send stuff out to Pearl Harbor. They'd asked for it before but they hadn't received it.

So, if nothing else, the Hawaiian Detachment did to start with prove the complete inadequacy of Pearl Harbor as a base to supply the fleet.

Q: It was kind of a catalyst, then?

Adm. W.: Yes, to know what they were doing. Of course, things started pouring out there in the spring when the fleet came out. It was a great education.

Q: Whose idea was this?

Adm. W.: War Plans. It came from Washington, I'm sure. It might have been from J. O. Richardson, the Fleet Commander. He came out in the spring. I wouldn't know at the moment. I was trying to get the requirements back to the Chief of Naval Operations at that time.

Q: Stark?

Adm. W.: Yes, Stark had recently relieved as CNO. Admiral Ingersoll didn't become Vice Chief until the summer of 1940, and Kelly Turner didn't become Director of War Plans until October 1940. He was still in the _Astoria_.

But, to go further, with the _Enterprise_, a destroyer flotilla, and a cruiser squadron, which I considered a forerunner of the carrier task force because we were able to get together for tactical exercises off the coast -- off Hawaii. We were able to fuel at sea, the first fueling I ever did was a little later but it was from the carrier Enterprise at sea. We did fueling-at-sea exercises, we did operate destroyers fueling from the larger ships. We had a great many tactical exercises, and when we got torpedo boats out there we let them make attacks on our ships. We did just as many realistic exercises as we could, and a lot of it was getting good antiaircraft practice.

In the early spring of 1940 the battle fleet joined for exercises and stayed longer than expected for political reasons.

Q: What do you mean by that?

Adm. W.: That's when the President of the United States felt that by putting the fleet out there it would be a warning to Japan that we were closer and more likely to do something if they took drastic action. It was to discourage them from their movement to the south where they were gradually taking over place after place. The Japanese were moving in those days, and the President hoped that this would discourage them. But it did not, and it was maybe a false hope because we did not have the logistics to support the fleet. We were pouring our feeble tankers out there. They were merchant tankers. The lack of fleet logistics was appalling. It's all written up in Dyer's book. They tried to get them out then but they couldn't get the ships.

In June Admiral Ingersoll was relieved by Admiral Frank Jack Fletcher and the former became Vice Chief of Naval Operations.

Interview No. 3 with Rear Admiral Joseph M. Worthington,

U. S. Navy (Retired)

Place: His residence on Gibson Island, Maryland

Date: Wednesday morning, 31 May 1972

Subject; Biography

By: John T. Mason, Jr.

Q: Good to see you this morning, Admiral. Last time, when we broke off, you were departing from the cruiser Minneapolis in June of 1940 and you were ordered to duty as gunnery officer of the USS Northampton. You just told me that Admiral Ingersoll gave you a word as you departed. Do you want to repeat that for me?

Adm. W.: That he would not have me again on a small staff but should he be fortunate enough to have a job for me on a big staff I would be selected again.

Q: What did he mean by a "small staff"?

Adm. W.: A cruiser division staff, which had just four officers, whereas a big staff had captains and –

Q: Well, he was going on up the ladder and so were you!

Adm. W.: Yes.

Worthington #3 - 132

Q: So it was logical. Tell me about the tour of duty on the Northampton, Sir.

Adm. W.: The day following my detachment from Admiral Ingersoll's staff I reported to Captain S. S. Payne of the Northampton for duty as gunnery officer. I was perfectly delighted with this assignment and found Captain Payne and the executive officer, Commander L. O. Alford, and many other officers of the Northampton wonderful shipmates.

Q: You say you were delighted with this assignment. Did you know in advance - ?

Adm. W.: Yes. I had requested as had all Admiral Ingersoll's staff a year previously, knowing of his prospective detachment, the duty that I wanted and my preference then was for commanding officer of a destroyer or gunnery officer of a cruiser, in that order. This gave me an opportunity which I had hoped some day to have.

The Northampton at the time was flagship of Rear Admiral John Henry Newton, who was Commander, Cruiser Division 4, and also became Commander, Cruisers, Hawaii Detachment. Captain Payne's first instructions to me - and only instructions really - were, "I want results." No one could have been more easy to work with or more cooperative than he was. So we immediately laid out a gunnery schedule and I took it up to him and said, "This is what you want." He said, "Yes, this is it," and he got

Worthington #3 - 133

it approved by the Cruiser Division command and he gave it to all the cruisers.

So we settled in in earnest but we did it the way we wanted to, and I felt very fine about it.

Q: And you remained in the Pacific?

Adm. W.: Oh, yes, we remained in the Pacific, we operated in Hawaiian waters until the latter part of the month, when we took a familiarization cruise to Midway, Palmyra, and Johnston islands, engaged in tactics and other exercises all the way, and firing some gunnery practices.

Q: Were there any fortifications on these islands at that point?

Adm. W.: We were just starting to build up Midway, dredging the channel at Midway, and the same way with Johnston and Palmyra islands. There was almost nothing at that time. We were frantically trying to build up those bases for the future.

Q: There were no native people on any of those islands, were there?

Adm. W.: I do not recall any on any of those three at that time. There may have been a few. On Midway all I remember seeing were gooney birds. At least, there were many albatross there. There was a PanAmerican station on Midway. It was one of their stops on the transpacific PanAmerican planes and they had a small residence there where the station-keeper lived.

Returning to Pearl Harbor, we intensified our gunnery training and fired our first practice of the year, another short-range gunnery practice, which turned out splendidly for us, and we were pleased to get a good start on the gunnery year.

Next, we were ordered into the Navy Yard unexpectedly to have installed this newly developed radar. It was supposed to be quite secret, but rather difficult to disguise because you had this enormous bedspring on top of the foremast of the Northampton.

Q: Was she the only cruiser having this installation?

Adm. W.: At that time I believe she was the only one in the Hawaiian area. They were starting to put them on the battleship New York, I believe, in the Atlantic and on some of the carriers. The Enterprise was to get one shortly, but at that time I believe the Northampton was the first. It was originally assigned to the ship for navigation purposes and placed under the navigator. But as soon as I found out that it could take accurate ranges, I asked the captain to place it in the Gunnery Department, which he did. The navigator was quite happy for the gunnery to work with it, and we did a great deal of drilling with it, and testing it. We found out how good it was.

Q: Did you have somebody from BuOrd on board to - ?

Adm. W.: We had a chief radioman who came across from the Research Laboratory. He was a technician and had nursed this equipment along. Then we had a couple of others assigned to us who'd had some training back in Washington. But he was the only one who really knew much about this equipment. It was relatively simple if you knew what to do and had enough spare parts.

So every exercise at sea we worked with that radar, using it for navigational purposes as well as for gunnery purposes and were finding what great value it could be to us. I wanted to use it for the first night battle practice, but the powers that be ruled that out because it would give the Northampton an unfair advantage in the gunnery competition, which was quite true.

Q: Did the other ships in the squadron know about it?

Adm. W.: Oh, yes, certainly. Word like that spreads right fast when they could observe us firing and could see this equipment because whether it was allowed to use it in the practice or not didn't stop us from drilling with it all the time, because we knew we had an excellent war capability and we were going to get the most out of it.

Things started happening rather fast probably in late September. The Northampton was ordered to the East Coast, to depart the latter part of September. She was the flagship and the order appeared in the organization of the Atlantic Fleet.

We had farewell parties given by the other ships around to those aboard the Northampton, and suddenly in the latter part of September the orders were canceled.

Then the ship was placed on stand-by for distant duty on forty-eight hours' notice. We had no idea where we were going. Some of us guessed it might be Singapore. We didn't know.

Q: She was really a marked ship because she had this new installation?

Adm. W.: Yes, and I think that had something to do with our not going to Singapore, too, because I think they sent the Pensacola or one of the other ships. But, strange as it may seem, instead of going into Pearl Harbor every night behind nets, we anchored off Honolulu every night. We did our gunnery training in the daytime or in the evening and we anchored by midnight off Honolulu in the open sea.

Q: Why was this? Because of security?

Adm. W.: I never knew just why it was, because I think at the time they were not worried too much about the Japanese submarines in that area. They hadn't made themselves conspicuous by that time. It was about a year later before they did. But we did get a great deal of very fine training by not losing any time getting to the operating area, just up anchor, and we were there, instead of having this long threading through from the docks in Pearl Harbor, through Pearl Harbor, out though the channel, and out to the operating area. So it was, I thought, a very useful fall. We didn't lose any time in the training. We did damage control, gunnery and tactics, antiaircraft -- there were plenty of targets, and the whole thing worked out, I thought, very well for training the ship.

One of the interesting things that happened at that time and rather puzzed us. Naval families were passing through Hawaii, the dependents being sent back from the Asiatic Fleet by Admiral Hart, quite properly. He wanted to get them back in a safer place. Things were pretty tense out there. I remember I saw his family as they passed through Honolulu, Mrs. Hart and Isabella, and the picture they had of the situation out there was about the way it was but not the casual way. I think they were very much shocked by the casual way the people in Honolulu seemed to think.

At the same time, Army transports were taking families out to Manila, because I visited General Edward P. King, Jr., who was a cousin of mine and a long-time friend, who was on this transport with his family proceeding to Manila. Later, King commanded the gallant defense of Bataan.

Here you had the policy by the Navy Department of sending families home and the War Department of sending them out at the same time.

Worthington #3 - 138

Q: That probably reflected the attitude of the commanders out in the islands, didn't it?

Adm. W.: I think so. I'm not sure whether General MacArthur had taken over U. S. command yet out there but in the Philippines he wanted to give the impression that everything was fine. I believe that might have had something to do with it. But to me it was a serious mistake. We were getting ready for war and if the family was far in the rear, remote from the likely area of hositilities, we could be in a higher state of war readiness.

The Northampton was scheduled for Mare Island for regular overhaul and some modernization. Then they changed those orders, which were to take place in February -- changed those orders to modernization in Pearl Harbor Navy Yard. Well, I started the protest. I was strongly, and was supported by the chain of command afloat, of the opinion that the Navy Yard did not have the talent at that time to do the job that they were trying to do on the Northampton. This was a shock to them in the yard because they wanted to use the Northampton to build up these people, which was desirable but personally I was looking after the Northampton at that time.

Q: In what sense were they inadequate?

Adm. W.: They didn't have the skilled technicians to modernize the gunnery. The Northampton was going to have quite a modernization

Worthington #3 - 139

of her antiaircraft batteries to increase the arc of fire, and it took experienced technicians to do it. Later on Pearl Harbor got those people, but at this date we did not have them.

Q: How did you know this?

Adm. W.: I'd been dealing with them with this Hawaiian Detachment for the previous year as gunnery officer on the staff, and materiel, and everything, so I'd been getting reports as to what they could do and could not do from each one of these ships that had work done on them -- that is, among the cruisers -- as well as the people in the yard who were perfectly honest about what their capabilities were.

So our orders were changed to Mare Island, back again, but I was still anxious to fire this radar-control practice and we were able to persuade the Commander Hawaiian Detachment, and Commander Scouting Force, to give us an allowance of 8-inch ammunition to fire an experimental practice. They also allowed us to draw up our own procedure for the practice, which pleased me very much because what we did was draw up a practice where we would open fire at the maximum range of 8-inch guns on a closing bearing where all three turrets would bear on the target. So we were opening fire at maximum range, closing at maximum rate of speed to still have all these guns bearing. We were looking forward to conducting this practice with a tremendous amount of interest, until the morning of the practice when the Commander

Scouting Force and Commander Cruisers, of the Scouting Force informed us that their flagships would be in such and such a position where they could observe the target very closely. This was at 5,000 yards or something like that, which was pretty close. We were shooting at 30,000. But it turned out that Captain Payne, and it shows what kind of person he was, said, "We'd better hit this target. If we don't, I'm jumping over the starboard side of the bridge and you're jumping over the port side."

Anyway, the practice went off beautifully, better than I had expected. We opened up at about 30,000 yards range and closed at maximum rate. Of course, as we closed, the amount of elevation of the guns required less, so we were firing faster and faster as we moved in. And the practice was just about as perfect as you could ask for. Then we started getting these congratulatory messages from Commander Scouting Force and Commander Cruisers, even from the tug that was towing the target. After that, everybody was well pleased and we concluded our gunnery year with a bang-up job.

People knew what radar could do then. They were convinced after that.

Q: I guess Washington was pretty anxious about that?

Adm. W.: They were anxious, too, and they got their reports from everybody pretty fast.

We proceeded to Mare Island, arriving the 1st of February, for this two-month overhaul. It was supposed to be February, March, and part of April. I had an unfortunate happening by shattering my ankle the first day we were there. Leaving ship in a heavy rain I slipped in the fork of the Navy Yard crane track. Anyway, I was in the hospital but was able, as soon as the doctor would let me, to go out on liberty. I was able to still keep my job on the ship, worked from the gunnery officer's stateroom. We had a perfectly splendid group of officers in the Gunnery Department. They were not too experienced, except for this one year we had been shooting, but they were so enthusiastic and they would work very hard.

So we were able to effect this modernization and carry out the plans and get out of the yard pretty much on schedule, which was about April.

The new captain, W. D. Chandler, arrived. He was another splendid captain and arrived before our departure. When we had all this modernization business, I was rather perplexed by receiving a set of pressure gauges from the Bureau of Ordnance and another set from the Bureau of Ships, with their own specific instructions as to how these were to be placed when we fired the guns.

Q: These were identical?

Adm. W.: Well, they had the same purpose but the thing that

concerned me was why can't the Bureau of Ships take what the Bureau of Ordnance gave me to read, or why can't the Bureau of Ordnance take the Bureau of Ships'? Why both?

At any rate, we had them installed in the Navy Yard before we left.

Q: You had two sets then?

Adm. W.: Two sets of gauges doing identical things. They were trying to find the pressures the after turret would exert on the area around the after director, which controlled the main battery guns. These gauges were all around and so I decided if they were no more certain than that about this -- it was the borderline case whether it was just right to do this or not. Having been involved in the thing since the beginning of the installation, I thought, well, here's a good chance for me to fire the director. The captain permitted me to do it and it was quite an experience. I'd never actually fired an 8-inch gun director. They usually had good gun pointer and trainer crews do it, but I did this trial and it was just about all the human body could take in the way of gun blast. Of course, you had heavy earphones on which protected your ears to an extent, but it was quite a jolt from that after turret firing for maximum range, which we did, wanting to get to the point where they would affect the after director the most. The idea being we wanted to be able to fire all guns in battle at the maximum forward bearing. But it was successful and we concluded the tests. The curve showed it was just about on the pressure line it was supposed to be. Then we finished up in the yard and went to sea.

Q: Did you have to make separate reports to BuShips and BuOrd?

Adm. W.: Oh, yes, separate reports to BuShips on their gauges and BuOrd on their gauges. As far as I was concerned, the thing worked and I knew it worked because I was there on the director and so forth. Everybody was happy as far as the ship was concerned. We were perfectly happy. We knew it could be done. Ordinarily you wouldn't be firing that far forward, but if you had to in war you could.

The next problem was putting to sea, and we took on all the armor-piercing ammunition we could carry, lashing it around the barbettes of the turrets, even in the wardroom passageways and in the crew's quarters. We carried all the extra powder we could stow in the magazines. We carried several extra planes, lashing them to the catapults and strapped them down so they couldn't get adrift. We had a lot of extra personnel aboard. We were actually a big, loaded-down cargo ship from Mare Island to Long Beach, San Diego, and then out to Pearl Harbor. The ship was naturally a mess after that assignment.

The day after arrival we got unloaded and Admiral S. A. Taffinder hoisted his flag in the Northampton. He immediately gave us a personnel inspection of the officers' staterooms, the only one I've ever had in the Navy. This was really quite annoying to me because I felt we were getting ready for war and had other problems in addition to cleaning up the ship just as fast as was humanly possible.

Q: He insisted on inspection of quarters?

Adm. W.: Inspection of quarters. He came into my stateroom and I'd never had that happen before in my time in the Navy. Generally speaking, officers' staterooms are supposed to be spotless and generally they are in pretty fine shape, but I'd never had a flag officer do that before.

Q: You just trust the officers to do it?

Adm. W.: That's right. It's his responsibility and his captain's. Oh, they might walk by the door.

Q: Does this say something about Admiral Taffinder?

Adm. W.: It did as far as I was concerned! I won't make any more remarks.

Fortunately for me, we were to sail again on another trip to the islands and I received dispatch orders to command the Benham. They did not want to detach me on such quick notice, just before this cruise. This was getting orders at night and the ship was sailing in the morning. But Captain Chandler very kindly said, "I know you want your command. I'm not going to stop you. How are you going to get detached that fast?"

I said, "Well, the assistant gunnery officer can take over. He's been assistant here for a year. I'll get my baggage across the deck to the Indianapolis -- we were tied alongside the Indianapolis -- we're not sailing till six the next morning and I'll get my baggage over there and I'll be on my way." So, through the kindness and considerateness of Captain Chandler, I was able to clear.

I went over to the yard and they arranged transportation for me on the Lurline to San Francisco.

Before leaving Hawaii, I'd like to make some comment -- maybe it's a little out of position here -- that in all my cruise of that area I was able to work with some very fine officers, through Wednesday afternoon tennis with Captain Wilkinson, who was chief of staff to Vice Admiral Andrews, Captain Gill, who had command of the Astoria but I believe was the district intelligence officer at the time, Captain J. W. Lewis, who was chief of staff of the 14th Naval District. Almost every Wednesday the flagship was in port. Then, on Sundays, we had another tennis group on Captain Wilkinson's private court with Arthur Cayley Davis, Worral Carter, J. H. Hoover. And then a third place was over at Wailupe Radio Station with Captain Ray Thompson who had some of the same group and others.

The interesting thing to me was that playing this tennis with this group and discussing informally things that were going on in the Navy and what we were trying to do and so forth, with that group who pretty soon were mostly flag officers and all held responsible positions in the early days of the war -- Norman Scott was another in that group -- here I was just a junior lieutenant commander, and was seeing a couple of times a week this wonderful group of officers -

Q: Yes, but you were a Leech Cup man, too, weren't you?

Adm. W.: That's what got me started in it, maybe, because I had played with Captain Wilkinson before and with Captain Gill, of course, and Captain Lewis -- I played with that group in Washington, the Navy Department tennis team. But I learned a lot from it and they were wonderful people to work with.

Going on from that, I arrived in San Francisco in the Lurline. I was supposed to get off in Long Beach, but I received dispatch orders to fly to San Diego to take command of the Benham. I dug my baggage out and got it delivered to the plane. I never thought I'd make San Diego. The last meal on the Lurline poisoned me, but I went anyway, got to San Diego, got a destroyer boat out to the Benham, assumed command because the officer I was relieving was flying back the same day, Tommy Darden was to take command of one of the big transports. I think it was the Mount Vernon, in San Francisco. So there was no time for waiting and delaying.

Fortunately, the doctor took care of me immediately after the relief ceremony and that evening I received dispatch orders from the squadron commander, Captain R. L. Conolly, that he would be aboard with his staff at six in the morning and proceed to sea on ten days' special exercises.

Q: And here you were green and -

Adm. W.: Sick as a dog, but nobody could have been finer. It was a privilege to have the Commodore aboard and he immediately put me at ease. He said, "Don't pay any attention to me on the bridge. I'm going to be up there but I'm only your guest as the squadron commander. It's your ship and you run it, and I will try not to interfere."

Everything he did was such a comfort, any suggestions he made. Here I was on my first destroyer duty, first day in command, and the squadron commander aboard.

Q: And sick as well!

Adm. W.: Right. A lot of people could have made it quite unpleasant for me, but not Admiral Conolly.

Quoting from a letter I wrote at that time: "I admired him greatly for his friendship, friendly advice, modesty, and understanding." In my judgment, he was an ideal leader and a great naval commander. His war record bears out outstanding fighting qualities. Some of his helpful and frank advice which put me at ease at once: "I will tell you if you can improve things," "In destroyers we do not have time to think about past mistakes, we must always be thinking of the next move," and his parting remark was one I appreciated most, "You will do well in destroyers, you do not get excited on the bridge." And upon returning to his regular flagship, although not necessary for the short period of time involved, he made out a fine fitness report and sent it to me with the following note:

> "If you find this satisfactory, mail it to the Bureau of Navigation by clipper. Otherwise, return it to me for revision."

You know, there was no good reason to make a fitness report for ten days, but it was the biggest help that I ever had, and it was particularly helpful later on because by the time I joined up with my division commander he was just the opposite type.

Q: Conolly had an outgoing kind of personality, didn't he?

Adm. W.: Oh, yes, and he wanted to get action. He wanted his ships ready for action, and he demanded instant action. One of the things that I think helped me was the fact -- it did not help me with my division commander -- was the fact that he would give an order, he would just say "_Benham_," and he didn't designate _Benham_ according to his signal, he said, "Tell 'Dead Ready' to do it," whatever it was.

Q: Get ready?

Adm. W.: "Dead Ready." That was what he called without even

Worthington #3 - 149

speaking by name or by number. His signal force knew he meant Benham DD 397.

I had a habit of putting the rudder over and putting speed on as soon as I saw the message coming. I relayed it to my division commander as soon as I could, but I knew that Conolly wanted to see that ship move when he gave an order. The division commander got the message as soon as possible, but lots of things happened operating with carriers, with other destroyers, and you have to move fast.

But, to go on with the narrative of these ten days at sea, he said, "My staff will tell you exactly what kind of practice to fire, you don't have to worry about it. We're going in close at San Clemente and fire over the heads of the Marines who are camped there. They're going to be as if a landing force was going in." In this case the landing force was already there and we had to show what close-in gunnery can do.

Q: This was an amphibious operation?

Adm. W.: Yes, but the only difference from going in in boats was that the Marines were there. They had it all laid out on the range. They had a target range, and we closed in and that's where the first time, I think, Admiral Conolly got the name of "Close-in Conolly," because he did close and we found out that it could be done. It was very successful. He used that to great advantage later on. He used it in Sicily when he commanded the attack force going to Sicily. He used his cruisers' 6-inch guns to annihilate a German Panzer division and, later on, in Kwajalein he used his attack gunnery close in again. You see from time to time in histories mention of Close-in Conolly. Well, he studied it in this exercise aboard the Benham. As far as I know that was the first time it had been done. That was our ship firing over live troops.

That was the end of ten days' exercise which, to me, was most successful and evidently the Commodore thought so too. We arrived back in San Diego -- I'd been up to call on Major General Marston, whose wife was a first cousin of mine and who commanded the Second Marine Division. He said, "We're going to have to get some troops off San Clemente in a hurry." He said, "We're going to ask the commandant here for his help."

So I said, "Well, I'll give you odds you're asking me." I got back to the ship that night and the orders were "Benham and Ellet proceed to San Diego at dawn -- I mean to San Clemente -- embark the Marines and return them the same day." All speed restrictions were off.

Q: The other destroyer was what?

Adm. W.: The Ellet, Lieutenant Commander Frank Gardner, who was a classmate of mine and a very close friend.

So we proceeded and had our first chance at Marine transport. We were very heavily loaded, too, because they had just two destroyers to get their defense battalion. The thing about those Marines, they were trained in the tropics, embarked on transports in San Diego, taken to the East Coast with the idea of going, I think, to Parris Island first, with the idea that they would be available for the Azores' occupation, should that become necessary. When it was found not necessary, they wound up in Iceland, with Major General Marston still in command, and by the time the Benham had learned through a picture in Life that this Marine outfit was in Iceland, they were back down in New Zealand training for the Guadalcanal operation. So they got around right fast in a year's time.

The Benham during that summer off Hawaii operated with the other ships of Destroyer Squadron 6. The Balch was the flagship. The Dunlop was the flagship of the division. The Fanning and Ellet were the other two ships in this division. The other division, Gridley, flagship, Craven, Gwin and McCall.

We conducted very extensive training exercises in the Hawaiian area, battle torpedo practices were held repeatedly and the results were excellent, both in the scores and in the reliability of the torpedoes.

Q: This was rather unusual at that stage of the game, was it not?

Adm. W.: Having good results from torpedoes?

Q: Having reliable torpedoes.

Adm. W.: Well, these, of course, were target torpedoes. They did have trouble. I know we got a special message to the effect that they were unreliable, but I think the unreliability of torpedoes was in the warheads that came out later on, and I will mention that later on because we changed our settings accordingly. But the firings were excellent and the training was excellent, as far as I was concerned. This business of high speed chasing the torpedoes down the range, then stopping and picking them up was quite a good seamanship exercise, and we were fortunate in having them all surface perfectly. We didn't lose any torpedoes.

We also had to run a full-power run and this delighted me because it was the first time I'd ever had the chance to feel the ship opened up. We had to run this at over 32 knots, 34 knots I think. The Benham had made 41.8 knots on the trial. This run went beautifully. The only problem I ran into was the seas were such that I didn't dare turn around at that speed, so I had to continue going and decelerating and gradually coming around to come home.

We had numerous exercises that summer with the carriers out there, plane guard, the Saratoga, the Lexington, and Enterprise. Most of the Benham's plane-guard duties were with the Enterprise, and this was extremely fortunate for us in view of later events.

Q: You speak of "plane-guard duty," and this entails?

Adm. W.: Plane-guard duty entails steaming astern of the carrier, in those days they frequently had one at 500 yards and another at 1,000. The one at 1,000 directly astern and the one at 500, if they had two ships, just ten degrees off the starboard quarter.

In order to be able to pick up planes that were launched, if there were any crashes and that sort of thing, and when they were recovering, if they had any accident -- pick up the personnel, not the plane. We had considerable experience in that during that year, and I thought it was very fortunate as a preparation for war. Also, we got used to the carriers' maneuvering quickly, particularly the Enterprise with her small turning radius. The Saratoga and Lexington had a much larger turning radius and that was a little bit different proposition.

But all that summer the squadron drilled hard, and the commodore, Admiral Conolly, insisted that we do that, and we also had upkeep and damage-control drills. We were trying to get the ship in every possible way ready for war.

In the fall, we worked with the battleships. We had night torpedo attacks. These were, of course, drill attacks but the battleships -- we came in at high speed and the battleships turned their searchlights on us and that, to me, was one of the most tricky prewar exercises we had. The battleships zigzag and the destroyer is coming in at 32 knots and we had a searchlight suddenly thrown on the bridge. It's not supposed to be on the bridge but that's what they do, putting us on the spot for a while so they could see what was going on.

Worthington #3 - 154

We had very good success with the squadron divided into three attack units and going in on these high-speed attacks. The Benham was directly astern of the squadron flagship, the Balch, and the McCall was directly astern of the Benham. We made attacks two different nights during that fall and we were so close in getting in that the third ship in our section had to turn away. They couldn't go with us on the attack. They had to turn away and they joined us up at daylight. They couldn't make it at high speed, going through the whole battle formation.

That's the way the Commodore wanted to train, and it was excellent training.

Q: Would you say that there was a similar state of alertness at Pearl itself at this time?

Adm. W.: I think they were beginning to get that way. Yes, I do, I think the whole fleet was on an operating schedule that was pretty rigid now that the battle fleet had been sent out there, and except for the division of battleships and, I believe, a division of cruisers and two destroyer divisions that had been sent East, the fleet was still there. That's why they were caught there. They were operating in and out, but they operated as three units. One of them mostly battleships and some destroyers. One of them mostly cruisers and destroyers. Well, actually the Enterprise operated with three battleships, the Arizona, Oklahoma, and Nevada, and their destroyers, but they slowed down the high-speed maneuvers, of course. They couldn't make the slow battleships go over about 22 knots.

So I would say that we couldn't have been better trained than we were. Our commodore, for example, entering and leaving Pearl on every exercise, he had every man in the ship at his battle station. This started six months before December the 7th. So we were pretty well set.

Q: That seems somewhat in contrast with December the 7th itself?

Adm. W.: That's right. I'm getting close to that right now!

All this task force was ordered out on what we thought was a normal maneuver with the third group of the fleet, different units. Halsey had his cruisers and destroyers and three battleships, the Arizona and the Nevada and the Oklahoma, and we started out heading somewhat to the southeast. When we were well out of sight of land, he turned the battleships over to, I believe, Admiral Milo F. Draemel, Commander Destroyers Pacific Fleet in Detroit. Admiral Kidd was the admiral aboard the battleship division, but Admiral Draemel had other forces -- the cruisers and destroyers -- and was senior in the whole training area.

Then we turned to the west, after being out of sight of the islands, to the east, we turned south and west. At that time, the 28th of November, Halsey, just like Admiral Hart, perceived this as a war warning message. We received the same immediately from Halsey. He told us to prime our torpedoes and depth charges, put on our warheads and get our depth charges ready for offensive action against any contact we believed to be hostile -- words to that effect. At any rate, he interpreted the war-warning message for just what it was intended to mean, be ready for action against the enemy. There wasn't any question to anybody in this squadron, the Enterprise, the cruisers, the Northampton, and Salt Lake City were with us at that time, and the destroyers as to just where we stood. And then we headed west, for Wake Island.

We did not know it at the time, but the Enterprise had on board twelve fighter planes with Marine pilots who were to be flown off to Wake Island. They were flown off, I believe, on the 4th of December in sight of Wake Island. Most of those planes were lost in the defense of Wake Island. The Enterprise headed back to Pearl at their best speed with the task force. She was due in at 8 a.m. on December the 7th, according to our schedule, but head seas were pretty bad part of the way and some of the destroyers were low on fuel, so Halsey asked what destroyers required additional fuel and if anybody needed fuel to reach Pearl Harbor he would top them off at sea, which we did. That slowed us up a few hours maybe. Unfortunately, I knew we had enough fuel to get to Pearl Harbor but I didn't know what was coming. We'll get to that decision later on. But we made the best speed we could and were off Pearl Harbor on the morning of December 7th, when the Enterprise launched their squadrons, as

Worthington #3 - 157

they always did, 200 miles out to land at the Ford Island air station. Some of those planes were shot down by our own forces because they got in there about the time of the Japanese attack, but the Enterprise stayed at sea then. By that time we'd received the Pearl Harbor message. But we received all these various reports as to where the enemy was and we started once on a dash to the southeast and another time to the southwest, and late in the day westward.

Q: But you were minus your planes, from the Enterprise?

Adm. W.: Some of them came back, but I'm not sure how many came back because that night, I know, we were sent -- a surface contact was reported west of the force -- and our squadron got into a night search and attack position at high speed. We got up to 30 knots, but we didn't locate anything where they were reported, and we were recalled to rejoin the Enterprise.

Meanwhile, the ships that had gotten out of Pearl Harbor had all formed up I believe under Admiral Draemel. I think he was in the Detroit and had a number of ships that were able to get out of Pearl Harbor, mostly destroyers. By that time, the Lexington, which had been cruising to the westward of Hawaii, had gotten pretty close to us. We were able to assemble some of the ships and then we entered on the 8th, and that was a horrible sight, steaming through the channel with the Nevada beached to keep her from sinking right beside the channel, and then steaming past the battleships. The destroyer Shaw was still burning at the destroyer dock. The battleship Arizona still had a tremendous column of smoke pouring out. It was just a horrible sight, the whole harbor. But we went on in to the fuel docks and one of the worst mistakes the Japanese ever made -- the fuel docks were intact. We fueled all the destroyers and went out to buoys in the harbor until the Enterprise was ready to sail. By dawn the next morning we were on our way out again. We went out before dawn because we were screening the area and searching before the Enterprise came out.

Q: She'd gotten a new complement of planes?

Adm. W.: She had full planes on then, yes. She had all the replacements she could get. She operated as a carrier and operating northwest of Hawaii she sank one sub, I know. It was pretty rough weather out there, too. I mean for destroyer operations. But we stayed out for about ten days. We still were suffering from logistic support. We could not stay out long enough -- we might top off once from the carrier or the cruisers, otherwise we had to go back to Pearl and get some fuel. The slow tankers available at that time couldn't keep up with the task force.

We went in on I think the 18th and went out again on the 20th. Each time, we loaded up with depth charges and supplies and fuel, mostly fuel was the key thing. Leaving on the 20th, we headed west, passing the 180th meridian on Christmas Day and the crew was puzzled by a signal. They couldn't find it in the signal book. Halsey had spelled out "Merry Christmas" to us on the signal flags.

Q: You were looking for units of the Japanese fleet?

Adm. W.: We were headed for Wake. Halsey was headed for Wake, the relief of Wake, and as soon as they found out in Pearl Harbor, he was recalled. I'm not positive whether the new command in Pearl Harbor had recalled him or not, but I know he was quite upset about it. We had Halsey's force and we also had Fletcher's Lexington force not too far away.

We crossed the meridian for the second time, the date line, on Christmas Day and returned to Pearl Harbor, much to Halsey's quite obvious concern because we all thought we could be of some help.

Q: Why this recall?

Adm. W.: I think the powers that be feared the loss of our only carrier at that time. The other was on the coast, I believe. The Lexington was there, but the Saratoga was back on the coast. I think the situation was too bad to risk it at that time. That's discussed by some of the experts, so I won't try to get into it at this particular time. I believe there were so many people involved in that recall. You see, Admiral Nimitz took

Worthington #3 - 160

over on New Year's Day. He took over command of the Pacific Fleet from a submarine, I believe, that was in port.

We went out again right after New Year's and I believe we met a convoy that was standing in from the States, and then operated again for more firing. We did a lot of firing and training, waiting for the task force to go out again because Halsey and Fletcher both were preparing for the Marshall and Gilbert raids. After we got through all this training and everything ready to go out on these raids, they realized that the Benham had not been in dock for two years, over two years, and thought she should have her bottom scraped because it would help her speed somewhat, so we were ordered back to the West Coast to escort a convoy.

I was briefed for this convoy in all the various ramifications of convoy duty, departing the next day, I believe it was. That night, about midnight, a member of the destroyer staff came aboard and said, "How soon can the Benham get under way?" I said, "How urgent is it?" He said, "Well, the Saratoga's been torpedoed and they need some help."

So the Benham went off in half an hour, which was the required time to get up steam for high speed, and it was the only time in my life that I ever had to leave Pearl Harbor without a single light of any kind. It was a pitch-black night and we had to sneak from our berth and go around by eye and by ear to get out. As soon as we got past the buoys, we put on - Frank Gardner, my classmate, was two numbers senior to me so he commanded our unit -- we put on 32 knots and steamed for the Saratoga, 500 miles to the southwest.

About noon next day, we sighted columns of smoke and were horrified to find the Saratoga dead in the water with a destroyer escort still around her and the cruisers she had. But fortunately the Saratoga was able to get steam going and get underway at moderate speed. We just reinforced her screenoof destroyers. I don't know how good our contacts were, but there were Japanese submarines in the area besides the one that torpedoed the Saratoga, and we dropped a great many depth charges -

Q: She wasn't sunk at that time?

Adm. W.: Oh, no, she steamed back into port. There were a lot of depth charges dropped which at least kept other submarines from doing further damage to the Saratoga, and she was able to get back into port.

Then the Benham immediately was assigned another convoy to the Coast, and this was a 22-ship, 7-knot convoy. It was very annoying to me because the Benham in nasty seas did not ride too well at 7 knots or steam too well. That's about the lowest speed she could steam and keep a decent course and that way for fourteen days from Honolulu to San Francisco.

Q: What kind of convoy was it?

Worthington #3 - 162

Adm. W.: Miscellaneous. We had one cruiser with us, the Portland, and they were empty ships mostly coming back from having dropped their loads at Pearl Harbor or Honolulu, going back to the States. One of them was so slow that we had to send a destroyer back every morning to find her and tell her to steam up and catch up with us. She'd drop behind during the night and catch up in the morning. But we got safely to San Francisco, and the Benham entered the yard right away for cleaning and we proceeded right away to get all the help we could get in the way of modernization. We had installed in that time a high-speed dome which enabled us on one of our sound gear to get submarine contacts at much higher speed, nearer 22 knots rather than 15 which the installation we had had would do. A new type dome.

We also had part of the installation of two types of radar, one for our guns and one for our search. These were not completed in Mare Island but we got them completed after getting back to Pearl Harbor.

Q: They were not usable at that point, then?

Adm. W.: At that point, no, not until we got the tender work, but we had the essential work that the Navy yard had to do, or could do easier than a tender. I tried very hard to get permission to convert two of our store rooms to oil tanks. Seeing the plans, I knew that the ship made such wonderful economy records on her trials that they decided to make two of her oil tanks into store rooms, and all it needed to convert the store rooms back to oil tanks was to put two valves in. But I could get nobody in authority to let me do it because that change had been ordered by the General Board. I wrote the letter through official channels and we actually received approval for the modification in the last mail before the ship was sunk, signed by King. It went through all the channels it had to go through. Since the original decision was made by the General Board it had to go for Admiral King's signature. The change didn't help us any.

We had a very successful period in San Francisco. We went down alongside the tender <u>Dixie</u>, which gave the crew some good liberty in San Francisco. The <u>Dixie</u> was a splendid destroyer tender and did everything possible to help the ship and get things we needed done without too much paper work.

So we proceeded with the next convoy and to my amazement there were 22 ships, including 5 transports, with Navy captains, all four senior, but as lieutenant commander of a destroyer I was the task group commander. That was quite a sudden shock to me, but at any rate that's the way the rules were. We had one other destroyer, the <u>Flusser</u>, with Lieutenant Commander W. G. Beecher as captain.

We had an interesting trip. We were clearing the coast and had the old destroyer <u>Sands</u> to augment our escort and also the TC 14, a lighter-than-air craft, the first one I had ever had reporting to me for duty. At any rate, they helped us and I felt better with her screening overhead. That was just to clear the coast, and they returned to port at sunset. On the second day out, the Kanawha had breakdown trouble and I was really on the spot. I couldn't send the Flusser back to escort this tanker. I had five troop ships in the group, I knew there was a Japanese sub operating off the San Diego-Santa Rosa area, but the captain said he would have to return to port. You probably knew him in Annapolis, Walton R. Read. Anyway, I said, "Proceed to port at discretion," and he got safely in, thank goodness.

The next thing that happened on the way was that one of our large ships had to be told to proceed independently for Christmas Island. She was loaded mostly with cargo and base supplies for building up Christmas Island, so that wasn't as bad as it might have been. Then, getting closer to the range of our PBY from Pearl Harbor we reported in. They reported our position and gave a rendezvous for the official escort that was coming out from Pearl Harbor to escort the ships in. By that time, we'd been reduced by two. As we were approaching the entrance - we were trying to split the convoy between the ships that went to Honolulu and the ships that went to Pearl Harbor -- we heard over commercial radio air raid warnings, and this was quite disturbing because there was not supposed to be anything like that around. At any rate, we had only two ships that had any antiaircraft defense to amount to anything, and they were the two destroyers. We went to battle stations and everybody else was warned, that was

Worthington #3 - 165

all you could do. There wasn't anything else you could do about it. Fortunately, the air raid did not get any closer, but the Japs did have one of their long range patrol planes up there. It had dropped a bomb I think the night before somewhere over the islands.

Q: This was in the month of what?

Adm. W.: First of March 1942, and after that episode we split up the convoy and got safely into port.

We had a little time in port to do this work on the radars, finish up the job started at Mare Island, and also improve some of our guns. I neglected to say we were able to acquire four 20-mm. antiaircraft guns at Mare Island and they were a great addition to our armament because before that we had to depend mostly on the 5-inch 38 and 50 caliber machine guns, the latter of which are not too effective. Also, one of our changes, we had some K guns, which threw depth charges, which helped in our antisubmarine battery, and ever since December we had been adding depth charges in racks until the squadron commander told us to take some of them off, they were too many for the ship. But initially we were very, very short on depth charges. If we could carry a lot more, I thought that was worthwhile.

Next, we were assigned to the offshore patrol, much to my disgust, because I wanted the Benham to get back with her squadron, which was making raids on the Gilbert and Marshall islands.

But the offshore patrol duty was somewhat interesting. We operated in a certain area with various destroyers and smaller ships. George Hussey was a captain then and commander of the patrol at that particular time, a squadron commander from another squadron. He would send us off to escort a ship down to these various islands, Maui maybe, if there was a ship going there with supplies, or to meet some ships coming in -- I think the *Aquitania*, the *St. Louis*, and other big transports, we met some distance off. Then a sudden dash to Hilo to escort the *Lurline* back to Hawaii, loaded with troops.

About that time I decided that maybe the *Benham* ought to have more fuel. I knew that we had already covered the return of the *Enterprise* task group from these raids, and I didn't want the *Benham* to be forgotten. So I hoisted the signal that we had so much fuel on board, which indicated 30 percent, which was all we had. We'd been out ten days on these special runs, so we did not have too much. We were immediately ordered to proceed to port, fuel, and return immediately. That was a pretty specific order and I wondered how I was going to get around it.

Well, we got into port and, of course, the destroyer people got aboard to see what we needed, as they always did, and I said, "How about putting us back in DesRon 6 where we belong?" "Whose orders keep you from doing that?" And I said, "Right out here." And they said, "Make no plans to go out. We'll get your orders canceled by the time you're ready to go out," which was about two hours, but they had to go to CinCPac to do it. We rejoined DesRon 6 then and got ready for going out on the next expedition.

This was getting late in March and also the drilling was getting more intense because we never knew what Admiral Halsey was going to do, but we knew he was going to do something. Sure enough, we kept on fueling and exercising, antiaircraft shooting, long-range shooting, drilling with tame submarines for antisubmarine work. Finally, we set out in early April with just the Balch, Benham, Ellet, and Fanning and headed west, and then northwest. I believe this was the 8th of April.

Four days later we received orders from Halsey to proceed on a certain course and speed, deliver these orders to the senior officer in the group we meet. And, sure enough, not far over the horizon was the aircraft carrier Hornet with four destroyers and a tanker, and two cruisers, the Nashville and the Vincennes. We delivered the orders to the task force, effected a rendezvous between the two, and then formed one cruising disposition with Halsey in command, Mitscher, a captain then in command of the Hornet, and cruisers, destroyers, and two tankers -- the Cimarron and the Platte were the two tankers -- and we headed west at a pretty good speed.

Q: You didn't know where you were going?

Adm. W.: We had a pretty good idea by that time because we went alongside the Hornet to deliver these messages by breeches buoy over to the Hornet and all these P-40s were on deck! And we said, well, we're not going out of here for fun anyway. There were no Navy planes in sight. Of course, they'd all been broken down and were below decks.

At any rate, we made pretty good speed, not slowing for fueling or anything, and the day before the scheduled launch on Tokyo, it was very heavy weather. But we fueled the carriers, cruisers, and, by afternoon, they got around to the destroyers. It was really getting nasty by then. One destroyer was alongside the Platte, I think it was, and I was alongside the Cimarron. when I was taking fuel from two hoses and very happy about it, except that it was a rough job, when I get a sudden message, "Cease present exercise." I earnestly requested that we continue because we were taking fuel satisfactorily from both hoses.

Meanwhile, the other destroyer got in difficulty alongside the other tanker and Halsey couldn't dally any longer on that, so he immediately proceeded for the launching point with his cruisers, leaving Captain Conolly with his eight destroyers and two tankers. We did no more fueling that day. We hoped the weather would be better at dawn, which it was. We were able to fuel to capacity all the destroyers. Then the tankers, with an escort of two destroyers, were told to head home.

The Enterprise and Hornet cruisers rejoined us and immediately built up speed to 20-some knots. Still feeling we were in the range of Japanese carriers, we knew they had eight but we didn't know where they were. We also knew they had plenty of submarines somewhere in the area, but very fortunately we did not encounter anything on the way back. We did lose one of our search planes on the way back, and were able to get into Pearl Harbor I believe it was the 25th of April.

Q: The launching was sooner than they had planned, wasn't it?

Adm. W.: Yes, and this is my own personal opinion and it may be quite different from what the real reasons were, but my feeling is that, had Admiral Halsey had his full destroyer escort with him, they might have been able to dispose of the patrol boats that spotted the carriers sooner, and thereby make the early launch unnecessary. Also, he would have had better protection to go in farther with his antiaircraft screen and antisubmarine screen.

But this was not the first time that Halsey had left his destroyers behind. I believe the Makin raid was conducted previous to this and he went in with just his cruisers and carriers.

My own belief is that had he had his full outfit, he could have gotten in closer and would have, because realizing that he had lost part of his protection he thought he had to make the launch sooner. And the weather was bad, too, real bad when he made the launch, as you can see from the pictures of those planes. It was pretty rough. But that is only my opinion and may not be the true facts.

On returning to Pearl Harbor, we headed south with the Hornet and the two task groups combined under Admiral Halsey, and all the cruisers and destroyers we could get together to reinforce Admiral Fletcher's force in the Coral Sea, as action was expected there soon. We crossed the equator and prior to that Admiral Halsey issued orders that there would be no customary exercises for crossing the equator, "This force is preparing for battle expected soon in the Coral Sea."

Q: No levity!

Adm. W.: No levity, no foolishness. I believe the Coral Sea action had taken place when Nimitz told Halsey to rendezvous with Admiral Kinkaid's cruisers and some destroyers who were coming back, heading for Pearl. The carrier Lexington had been sunk and the Yorktown had taken a more circuitous route, I believe, by Tonga and back at a safer distance with her escorts.

To effect this rendezvous, Benham received orders from Admiral Halsey to deliver orders to Admiral Kinkaid at a certain point the next day or the day after -- it was two days away.

Q: Tell me why orders couldn't be delivered by dispatch?

Adm. W.: We never opened up our radio on those expeditions, except short-range radio, the TBS, the bridge communications.

Q: Communications from Halsey to the Benham?

Adm. W.: Yes, we used TBS for that all the time because that was very short range. Halsey never believed in opening up longer range radios and I don't believe the others did either.

Q: Was it fear that the code might be read?

Adm. W.: He didn't want them to know the ship was in the area. A submarine might be listening or something. It was possible. At any rate, we did maintain, I think, very effectively radio silence. It was all right for Admiral Nimitz, for example, because he was shore-based. He could broadcast his messages. You could broadcast them from the bases. They knew a lot of traffic was going from Pearl Harbor or the West Coast.

Q: That wasn't revealing.

Adm. W.: No, they knew that station was there and it was so arranged in quantity that even if it would show a difference that could be stepped up, we kept the activity up on the right circuits. To the best of my knowledge, communications used to do that.

When I received these orders from Halsey in the Enterprise I resumed screening station on the Vincennes. I was told to depart at a certain time from the task force, which was after dark. Of course, just about the time of departure I had a submarine contact, so the task force turned off and I stayed with the contact, was told to remain with the contact if desirable for a while, and then carry out my original orders. I stayed around there as long as desirable and I didn't have any better results but dropped a lot of depth charges to worry him if I didn't get him, I don't know, and started for the appointed rendezvous.

At noon the next day I received orders direct from Pearl Harbor from Nimitz, "<u>Benham</u> head east at maximum speed." These orders really shook me for a moment. I'd never received orders direct from the commander in chief before in the Pacific and I questioned the communication officer twice or three times that he was positive he had the right call.

Q: It was signed "Nimitz"?

Adm. W.: Well, from his call number. They were directed to <u>Benham</u> because I knew I had these direct orders from Halsey to proceed to this rendezvous. We knew his orders were important to the rendezvous with Kinkaid's group.

I developed speed and shortly after that sighted over the horizon an island that stuck up and looked just like it might have been the pagoda of a Jap carrier. Cocopia, I think, was the name of the island. I started to veer off a little bit from that until I could get a better look and was convinced it was the island. We identified it on the chart. Another little while later, we had just settled down to our speed —

Q: This speed being what?

Adm. W.: 32 knots, which was all I dared go with the situation as it was. I had to have some fuel in reserve.

The doctor reported he had an emergency appendectomy case, so I said, "Well, doctor, how about it?" We have these orders from Admiral Nimitz to proceed at maximum speed and this is no place for us to tarry. I know you can't operate at this speed. Can you make out until dark?"

"Well," he said, "I think we can."

"We'll have to take our chance and I'll slow at dark. I'll slow long enough for that."

"It's just a quick operation," he said, "it only takes half an hour."

They used the wardroom table for the operating table. The appendectomy was round the back, and they cut him open all the way around, and the operation took four hours. But, fortunately, it was successful, and we picked up full speed again.

Q: This was during daylight?

Adm. W.: Oh, no, dark. I would not slow down during daylight. I didn't dare after those orders. But I took a chance on saving the man and figured we had made a good advance toward the area we were supposed to get to.

When I made the rendezvous at dawn a day later, I had

Kinkaid's force almost dead ahead and I had Admiral Halsey's force not too far away in the other direction, so all the forces joined up at the same time properly, and I was able to deliver the orders to Admiral Kinkaid and actually to all his ships because they were orders for all the ships in the task force.

We turned immediately and headed back for Pearl Harbor with the combined forces. That was the time Admiral Nimitz decided the Japs were going for Midway, and we picked up other ships on the way, the Pensacola and another tanker, and went into Pearl Harbor, I believe it was the 26th of May, fueled and provisioned, and left again on the 28th. By that time, Admiral Spruance had relieved Admiral Halsey in the Enterprise. He'd shifted over from his cruiser flagship to the Enterprise, and with the Hornet Task Force 16 proceeded to the area northwest of Midway.

And on the 3rd of June Admiral Fletcher rejoined with the patched-up Yorktown and his cruisers. So we had Admiral Fletcher, then, in tactical command of Task Forces 16 and 17 for the Battle of Midway.

Worthington #4 - 175

Interview No. 4 with Rear Admiral Joseph M. Worthington,

U. S. Navy (Retired)

Place: His residence on Gibson Island, Maryland

Date: Wednesday morning, 7 June 1972

Subject: Biography

By: John T. Mason, Jr.

Q: Well, Admiral, I'm looking forward to a most exciting chapter today. You're planning to talk about the exploits of the Benham at the Battle of Midway.

Adm. W.: The Benham's task force, Task Force 16 commanded by Rear Admiral Spruance, rendezvoused with Task Force 17, Rear Admiral Frank Jack Fletcher, on the late afternoon of 3 June, northeast of Midway. At that time Rear Admiral Fletcher became officer in tactical command and he directed Admiral Spruance with Task Force 16, which included the Hornet, to remain within visual distance for easy communication.

The idea was to cruise out of range of Japanese land-based planes, hope to avoid being sighted by their submarines, and, when the Japanese started their attack on Midway, to search and destroy their carriers. [For Japanese plan see Appendix 8.]

Q: The element of surprise?

Adm. W.: The element of surprise was paramount because it was believed that the Japanese did not know of the presence of our carriers.

The first report came in at daylight, 4 June, by one of our patrol planes from Midway that they had sighted at least two Japanese carriers and a destroyer. Shortly thereafter a report that there were many planes approaching Midway. A little earlier Admiral Fletcher had launched his long-range scout planes to cover a sector not believed to be covered by our other search planes.

As the battle developed -- then Admiral Fletcher ordered Spruance to attack as soon as the position of the enemy carriers was definitely known and he with his force was in appropriate range, saying that he would do likewise as soon as he had recovered his search planes. So about nine o'clock on June 4, Spruance launched all aircraft that could be launched from the Enterprise and Hornet, the Hornet at that time having separated a short distance, which was the custom for battle operations in those days. At the time, the Benham's position was first screening the two task forces, but plane-guarding the Enterprise, and with the separation she continued with the Enterprise task force.

With all the planes launched, the Enterprise task force was keeping in position for recovery of any damaged planes or early recoveries. That operation, I believe, was largely completed by noon when the Yorktown who, at that time, was somewhat separated, reported their first dive-bombing attack from the Japanese carrier Hiryu, one of those not damaged in the battle itself.

I'm trying to follow this through. I think you intended me to do the Benham's part in it, and then describe the whole thing in the talk following?

Q: Yes.

Adm. W.: About noon the Vincennes, Pensacola, Balch, and Benham proceeded at about 32 knots in the direction of the Yorktown, at that time showing great columns of smoke and evidently she had suffered serious damage from that first attack. Upon reaching the Yorktown, these four ships reinforced the screen of the Yorktown -

Q: Were there any left to guard the Enterprise and Hornet?

Adm. W.: That leaves an interesting question. I was checking that this morning in Morison, and the Enterprise had the Northampton cruiser left and three destroyers of Destroyer Squadron 1. The Hornet had the Minneapolis, the New Orleans, and Atlanta, and three destroyers. I believe that was about all. I was unaware that the Enterprise was so stripped until this morning, on re-checking the figures. But I presume when they joined together again they rearranged the distribution of ships.

Meanwhile, in joining up with the Yorktown, the screen

formed up as well as they could on the ship making 5 knots and was just about getting into position, although a little wide for an antiaircraft disposition, when a report of another attack was coming in. The Yorktown launched what remaining planes she had as soon as she could get up any speed. She got up to about 15 knots and then 17 before this torpedo attack came in.

Q: That was a rather remarkable recovery, wasn't it?

Adm. W.: I thought it was remarkable and I think anybody who has studied the valiant efforts of the engineering force of the Yorktown in getting that ship moving at that speed and that time, considering the terrific damage they received, feels the same way.

The Yorktown planes were not lost to the battle, as those returning from the attack landed on the Enterprise, so they were able to take off again as soon as gassed.

But what planes the Enterprise could get into the air, their combat air patrol, and the Hornet, and the Yorktown all tried to fend off the oncoming Japanese attack, and they did extremely well on that attack except for about a dozen torpedo planes flying very low. The CAP was up high trying to break up the formation coming in and they did not get the torpedo planes, at least not all of them. This attack was directly opposite from the earlier one, which was a dive-bombing attack from high level, and this was a low-level torpedo attack. The planes flew as close to the water as they could. Most of them were shot down by either our fighters or our guns, as the task force by that time had closed in its defensive antiaircraft screen. Two torpedoes struck the Yorktown from planes that had gotten through the screen.

The Benham, meanwhile, was shooting with everything she had. She was on the side apparently bearing the brunt of the attack, so were the cruisers. The Portland was near her, and other ships in the screen were very tight and firing low. During this attack one 5-inch shell went through the stack of the Benham from the Yorktown, which mortally wounded one of our officers, Ensign Walter E. Pierce, and wounded four others.

But the Yorktown in desperation, to try to keep those planes who were still trying to strafe her from getting between the screen and the ship, so there was no choice, trying to save the ship by knocking down the plane and if anybody else got in the way we couldn't help it. There's no way to dodge that kind of thing. I think it's one of those acts of battle you can't help.

The attack lasted roughly ten minutes and with its two torpedo hits the Yorktown took a very strong list. I thought at the time that it was approaching maybe 25 degrees, but when a carrier deck lists over it looks maybe a lot worse than it is. At any rate, the Yorktown's captain, in my opinion, was very wise in ordering "abandon ship," and officers and men slid over the side, climbed down nets, and went over into the water. The normal thing to do is to go alongside and take off as many as you can, but this time it was not deemed expedient for the ships to go alongside. They were already in the water and, if we'd gone alongside, we would have either hit somebody in the water or it seemed to me there was great danger of the ship capsizing. Construction experts say no, but to those present –

Q: To the visual eye.

Adm. W.: To the visual eye it looked like the thing to do. In that operation we had, I believe, originally three destroyers going in to try to pick up those in the water, with the others still screening as antiaircraft screens and as antisubmarine screens. There was still that danger, and a ship dead in the water is a lovely target.

In that operation we were making considerable progress with the recovery but the commodore had directed ships to pull out, those loaded, to pull out into the screen and send in new ships to pick up more of the survivors. The Benham was not in a position to do that. We had too many survivors around our propellers. It happened to be that we were close to the stern of the ship and so when people went over the side and the ship had still some momentum, drifting, the survivors tend to crowd at the stern. I started to move and did not.

At that time we had another air attack reported.

Q: A third attack?

Adm. W.: Yes. And so the screen was getting into antiaircraft position, but there again I tried, as soon as we could get clear of the people in the water, to get moving to a position where we could do something on the antiaircraft defense. By that time, fortunately, the attack was beaten off by our fighters from the other carriers, and none of them got into this mass of humanity.

Though I'm told we had 725 aboard from the Yorktown, the other ships had as many as 500, 400, 300 -

Q: That must have been capacity for a destroyer, wasn't it?

Adm. W.: Far more than capacity, really. We had more than the flagship, which rather surprised the boss. He couldn't understand it at first, but eventually did understand it. If there are people in the water you have to pick them up. You don't question where you'll put them. You just pick them up. Having carried those Marines the year before from San Clemente over to San Diego, I figured we could carry a lot more than people expected.

After the completion of these operations, and the Yorktown was ordered abandoned, we withdrew to the eastward under orders from Spruance. He's been so much criticized for that. I thought he did the right thing. We did not know what the Japanese were doing at that time, we did not know the Hiryu was sunk or was out of action, and he withdrew to an area to protect these damaged ships and save as many personnel as he could. We had a very weak force to oppose against them.

We steamed to the eastward during the night and the following day, that is the Astoria group. Admiral Fletcher had his flag in the Astoria at that time as he had no communications from the Yorktown he had shifted to a ship that had some and he very properly shifted the fighter director command over to Spruance. He was turning it over to somebody who could handle the operation, and I thought it was one of the wisest things a person could do and it was done instantly. He didn't want to lose any time on it.

We were steaming that night, the Astoria, the Portland, and a few destroyers -- at that time we had five or six in the screen. Later in the evening the Hughes was directed to return to the Yorktown to observe, but I think primarily to get some confidential publications they thought were still loose. Also they had fear that there might have been somebody trapped below decks who could be rescued.

Q: But you'd rescued all those visible on the sea?

Adm. W.: Everybody visible on the sea and on board and known to be alive, I mean as far as we were concerned. But we didn't know what was in the ship. We just picked up everybody in sight, including a fighter pilot we picked up steaming away from the Yorktown. He was some distance away and just by the grace of God we spotted him in the water and picked him up.

During the night, the Hughes was detached to help the Yorktown, and the next day we were ordered, first, to transfer certain personnel, damage-control people, to the Astoria, and they were to be taken back by a destroyer to get aboard the Hammann, eventually transferred to the Hammann, and they were going back to attempt a salvage operation. This was a group of about 30 the Benham had but I don't know how many the total was.

Q: How did you transfer them?

Adm. W.: By breeches buoy. On completion of that, the Benham was ordered to transfer all remaining Yorktown survivors to the cruiser Portland, so by rigging four breeches buoys and the use of airplane crane in a period of about four hours we transferred what was left of the 725. Some of those were badly wounded.

Q: You transferred them anyway?

Adm. W.: We transferred the badly wounded by stretcher, swinging the ship in close each time, then the airplane crane in the Portland took the stretcher aboard. That was a slow and tedious procedure. Meanwhile, we kept the four buoys going continuously. One funny incident with that as far as I was concerned was the executive officer of the Portland, Commander T. R. Wirth at the time, said, "How many are you transferring?" I said, "Oh, about 400." He said, "We already have 400 by actual count."

So, I said, "Well, that's about half the number that are

coming, so we'll take your count."

Then he said, "What do you think this is? The Grand Hotel?"

Wirth was a great officer. He always had a sense of humor, no matter how bad the situation was.

Lawrence du Bose was the captain of the Portland at the time and F. J. Mee was the damage-control officer, friends of mine and shipmates from times gone by, Mee in destroyers, Wirth in the Texas.

Another thing the Portland did which, to me, just showed what a ship could do when they were trained. They were handling these breeches buoys, handling the stretchers, the ambulatory cases, and they launched and recovered planes for antisubmarine patrol. Fortunately the sea was calm and they were able to get them in the air, and pick them up by what they called the dog method on a sled. All this going on simultaneously, including fueling Benham.

Q: Was there any danger from Japanese submarines in that area?

Adm. W.: A submarine was evidently in the area because he caught the Yorktown the next day. There was one known to be in the area but how close we didn't know. That particular one I think moved up from Midway and got the message on the Yorktown, and I believe that night they had a plane out from somewhere, a long-range search plane that might have spotted the Yorktown. I don't know.

At any rate, when the transfer was completed we were sent

back to try to help with the Yorktown. By the time we arrived there the next morning, this would be the 6th of June, a little before daylight, the Yorktown was in tow of the ancient fleet tug, converted minesweeper, Vireo, which was making 1 or 2 knots maybe, not very much. The Hammann was alongside delivering power to the salvage pumps and light, and they'd put the Yorktown salvage crew back aboard.

Q: Was the list any greater than it had been?

Adm. W.: Not too much. No, they had corrected the list considerably by that time and things were looking in much better shape, but they only had Balch, Benham, Gwin, and Mugford -- I believe those were the destroyers in the screen at that time. Of course, the Hughes was still there. So with the ship dead in the water we started a circular screen and, incidentally, the bathermography of the Hammann, the only one on any ship present, was taking her readings and giving us a sound condition of very nearly zero. In other words, we were steaming this tight circle with our sound gear which, at best, wouldn't be good for more than 1,000 or 2,000 yards. The thermal layer showed the sound conditions were near zero and were not too helpful. But we thought we were making real progress on the recovery of the Yorktown and about 2.30 that afternoon we heard a report over the voice circuit that torpedoes were approaching the Yorktown. I am convinced that they were fired from over

6,000 yards, maybe more. It was a glassy sea, perfect visibility, still target, dead in the water. Nothing easier than for a submarine to stay way beyond any destroyer screen and fire the shots.

At any rate, at the time the report came "torpedoes approaching Yorktown" we were still steaming in a circle, the Benham as near as I can figure was on the port beam of the Yorktown and in its circle clockwise we had reached the bow of the Yorktown at that time. All that we saw as we got around was the bow of the Hammann sinking fast by the stern. The commodore, the senior officer of the screen, E. P. Sauer in the Balch, directed Benham to proceed into the area and attempt rescue operations, all other destroyers to continue their screen against this submarine.

Q: The Hammann had gotten in the way of the torpedo intended for the Yorktown?

Adm. W.: Actually, there were several torpedoes but they got under the Hammann and got the Yorktown, but when they went off they set off the Hammann's depth charges and torpedoes and there was a horrible mess. I'm not positive but maybe one of their torpedoes did get the Hammann, but I think most of the damage was due to the setting off of the depth charges by the explosion right next to it. At least three torpedoes hit the Yorktown, there might have been more. I know one full salvo got her.

I had to proceed into this scene of humanity very cautiously. At the time, we had no life rafts left, no boats left, and the

5-inch shell that hit the Benham two days before had cut the falls and when we were directed to get out of the area after the rescue operations, we had to cut loose the boat. The boat had been holed by shrapnel also. We couldn't stay for it. But we did go in and the only thing to do was to put men in life jackets, volunteer swimmers in life jackets, with life lines and we got in as close and carefully as we could with the ship to rescue these people in the water, many of them horribly wounded, and gradually pull them back to the ship with the swimmers and lines and put them in stretchers down on the water level and hoist them aboard. This time we recovered nearly 200.

Q: What had been the complement of the Hammann?

Adm. W.: The Hammann was about 235, I believe, and she had heavy loss of life. The number we delivered to the Pearl Harbor hospital was about 100 stretcher cases and about 75 ambulatory cases, and we buried 27 of them at sea. So she suffered fearful losses.

The next thing that happened, in this rescue operation, going in among this debris from the explosion, some of it fouled one of our condensers, so we had no backing power on one engine. Fortunately it was backing power and not go-ahead power. When we were satisfied that we had picked up everybody, the Balch meanwhile had signaled us they picked up the captain of the Hammann unconscious with two bluejackets also unconscious, clutching one on each arm. He was a good swimmer and had swum way off from the scene apparently, and that's how the Balch and the screen happened to spot him. He's still alive, I think, Admiral Arnold True.

Well, with this operation completed, Benham was directed to proceed to a certain area in the rear where a submarine tender had come out, acting really as a hospital ship to take all these people back and as soon as I talked to our doctor he said "We can't transfer these people again. Some of them will die. They won't stand another transfer; they're in that bad shape." So I reported to the commodore, "Urgently recommend taking these survivors to Pearl where they can get medical attention and I believe we can save some lives." He didn't hesitate. He said, proceed. Meanwhile we'd borrowed a doctor from the Balch, an extra doctor, and we transferred him back to the Balch and we picked up the doctor from the Hammann, although he wasn't in good enough shape to be of much help at the time, after the rescue. But we proceeded back to Pearl and I checked with the doctor on what speed we could make without affecting these patients' comfort. So we got about 27 knots, I think, in the calm waters on the two-day run back to Pearl Harbor. Of course, every bunk in the ship was taken up as a hospital bed.

Q: That must have been a trying run.

Adm. W.: It was a very trying trip. Of course, there were still

Japs around. We didn't know where the submarines were. We'd just experienced one of them.

Q: But it was pretty obvious the battle was over?

Adm. W.: The battle was over, yes. We knew the battle was over and we knew Spruance was chasing them with what was left of his force, and this was a question of getting them back in time to get some medical attention. Our doctor, Lieutenant junior grade Seymour Brown, did a fantastic job of looking after them. His pharmacist's mate, first class by the name of Dykes, did a splendid job and some of the others. Everybody pitched in on helping with first aid and looking after them. When we got back to Pearl Harbor we went in to the harbor much faster than I had any business going, but I had neglected to take off steam early enough -- I was trying to get them in there. We got in to Merry Point and made what I do not like to do in a destroyer, one of these fast landings because by that time I'd forgotten I only had one backing engine! But we made it all right. The crew came to the rescue.

At Pearl Harbor Admiral Nimitz was on the dock, members of his staff were on the dock, and the ambulances were lined up to take care of all the wounded. They took the men off and got them to the hospital through the various facilities at Pearl Harbor. [See article "A Destroyer at Midway, appendix 9.]

Then Captain Arthur Cayley Davis, later of the Enterprise --

at that time he was a captain, he was Aviation Plans for Admiral Nimitz -- asked me to come up to debrief him on what I saw and he was going to debrief me on what had happened at the battle, what he had heard about the results. You see, this was the first combatant ship returning to Pearl Harbor after the battle.

I believe that covers the return to Pearl Harbor. After transferring the wounded, we were sent over to the Navy Yard for limited availability for repairs and it turned out to be the longest time the Benham was in a Navy yard during the entire war existence, because the Enterprise was brought in several days later and placed at the same pier the Benham was. The captain of the yard did not want to move the Benham for the Enterprise so he had to squeeze her by the Benham at the other side of the dock. So we stayed there for about twelve days and got a lot of work done.

The commander, destroyers, sent over a working party of about 100 men to clean up the Benham. She was spattered with oil halfway up her stack, in all the staterooms, everywhere from rescuing all these people from oily water. We had some repairs made in the yard; the stack job was rather minor.

Q: Did they add anything new in the way of ordnance?

Adm. W.: I always picked up some machine guns and 20-mms. and depth charges, extra depth-charge racks, Y-guns, whatever we could handle. There was not too much time for that. We were damaged in the yard by a crane one night, which was very disconcerting to me, but I asked for repairs the next day and I was told that our availability was over, we could not make any more repairs. We got the repairs. I went up to see the admiral, who was very cooperative. He said, "And look, you don't need any paper work to do it." I think it was Admiral Paine, who was engineer officer of the yard, around Admiral Hill's class.

Q: 1911?

Adm. W.: 1911, I think. He was an engineer and I'd known him at Hill's. I'd met him before and seen him in the yard. He was very cooperative and did everything he could for us. The captain of the yard was wonderful. Harry Hayes had been a shipmate of mine in the Pensacola. He told me, "Every service your ship needs you'll get it right now." They were really out to help.

Q: What was the state of morale among the crew?

Adm. W.: I would say the morale of the crew was excellent. We did what we could for them. The only thing we could give them for recreation was beer and steak parties. We had certain picnic areas that they had in Hawaii for that, and we were able to send them out several times, so all the crew got some picnic. That was about all you could give them. Pearl Harbor at that time and Honolulu was so jammed up with everything it was hard to give them any kind of recreation. Then, there were blackouts at night, of course. There was still concern about what the Japanese would do next. Then that curfew. I think they did get some liberty in town in the daytime, but not very much.

All we were doing was getting fixed up and cleaned up and ready to go to sea again. Let's see, we got in there the 9th of June and we went out on training exercises around the 20th, and did a lot of antisubmarine training with live submarines, a lot of antiaircraft firing of various types.

Q: Were you still considered a part of the task group of the Enterprise?

Adm. W.: Oh, yes. We were still considered a part of Destroyer Squadron 6, but Destroyer Squadron had changed considerably by ships being separated from us. We still had the Balch, Benham, and Ellet together. I believe the Gwin joined us as another ship when we went south. The rest of that period before proceeding to the Solomons was entirely doing all the training we possibly could because we knew things were going to be tough down there.

Q: And you had a much better idea of the way the Japs operated?

Adm. W.: We certainly did. And another thing we did. Some way or another you hear things. One of the ensigns came aboard one day, the day before we were sailing, and said that "I get the rumor that we're going on distant duty." I said, "That's very interesting, but don't tell me that. Get the supply officer or at least the commissary people to go ashore and get all the canned goods and storage materials they could get on emergency requisition." They asked, "Where are we going to put these?" So I said, "Well, it's against Naval Regulations but stick them in the bilge. We'll need them."

So we had some extra weeks' rations and they were a god-send at the end of that mess in the Solomons. The other destroyers were just out, and they couldn't get anything. Some of them had almost gone hungry, the supply system was so poor. We were still eating on Spam and canned goods and this kind of artificial potato you have.

Q: You mean dried potato?

Adm. W.: Dried potato. We learned to use that.

But when the task force went out, I think on about the 15th of July, it sailed south.

Q: This was with the Enterprise and the - ?

Adm. W.: Oh, yes, the Enterprise and the Hornet.

Q: As you left Pearl, you say, the task force had changed in complexion somewhat?

Adm. W.: Task Force 16, Enterprise, flagship, North Carolina -

Q: She had come up from?

Adm. W.: She had just joined up. This was her first time in the Pacific, to the best of my knowledge. She was the first fast and powerful battleship in the task force. Portland, Atlanta, an antiaircraft cruiser, Balch, flagship of DesRon 6, Ellet, Gwin, Maury, Momsen, Grayson. The latter three ships had joined the task force at the time of the Tokyo expedition.

We proceeded south to Nukualofa Harbor, off Tongatabu, in the Tonga Islands. Since the dateline had not been taken into account, it was July 26th and the task force had to depart immediately to make the scheduled rendezvous with the other task forces.

Q: We hadn't yet gotten used to operating on both sides of the dateline, had we?

Adm. W.: I don't know how that happened! We had been operating on both sides. At any rate, Benham, North Carolina, and Atlanta were allowed to delay departure to top off provisions and fuel. The fuel Benham obtained slowly from the Aldeberan, an auxiliary poorly fitted for fueling, was consumed in catching up with the task force after midnight. At that time Task Force 16 screened Transport Division 2, composed of Crescent City, President Adams, President Jackson, President Hayes, and Alhena. Next joined the New Zealand division of the amphibious forces and Task

Force 11, that was Rear Admiral Fletcher's carrier force in the Saratoga, and Task Force 18, Rear Admiral Noyes in the Wasp.

Q: Before we get involved in this next operation, Admiral Worthington is about to give us an account of the Battle of Midway, a considered account as he prepared it for delivery to a group in Baltimore.

Adm. W.: The Battle of Midway, fought in the Pacific in June of 1942, is vastly important, in that in this battle the rapidly advancing tide of the Japanese forces was stopped and they were turned back, after suffering heavy damage. To start the story of this battle, I think it's desirable to go back to information available to the opposing forces prior to their meeting.

The United States Navy started a collection of certain codes and cryptographic studies as long ago as 1915. This was supplemented in the early 1920s by being able to capture the Japanese commercial code in one of their offices in New York, by some very careful sleuthing at night, copying this commercial code, and returning it to its Japanese safe without the knowledge of their representatives. It so happened that, at that time, this commercial code was also their naval code. This is a long story and I will not take that time here. But as a result of that long-ago thinking ahead and constant work by a very few individuals and observing the utmost secrecy, it resulted in the U. S. having a vast amount of knowledge of the Japanese plans prior to the Battle of Midway, and enabled Admiral Nimitz to position his task forces accordingly.

As for the Japanese advance information, they too had been collecting a vast amount of material over many years from every source they could find, but apparently they had no information about our forces prior to Midway and were completely fooled by the position of our carriers. When Halsey was in the vicinity of the Coral Sea battle, before turning north, he was sighted by a Japanese plane, patrol plane, and evidently reported. Apparently this convinced the Japanese that we had no carriers -- or would have no carriers -- in the Battle of Midway.

To go to disposition of forces, I'd like to trace it back to, first, the Enterprise task force, which we've already been through in the story of the Benham, but she went out to Wake Island to deliver the Marine fighters prior to December 7 and participated in the raids in the Marshalls and Gilberts, back for the raid on the Tokyo area, back again to Pearl Harbor, down to the vicinity of the Coral Sea, and in position northeast of Midway on the 3rd of June ready to strike.

The Hornet task force has been mentioned previously, with their proceeding from the East Coast to San Francisco Bay to pick up the Army planes for the Tokyo raid, down to Pearl Harbor, the Coral Sea, back to Midway in position for this action.

The Yorktown started from the East Coast about December the 7th and brought her squadrons, a cruiser-destroyer task force, proceeded through the Canal to the West Coast, San Diego, embarked Admiral Fletcher and his staff, proceeded directly to the Southwest Pacific, was able, with the Lexington, to stay the advance of the Japanese toward Port Moresby, stopped the Japanese in the Battle of the Coral Sea, inflicting severe damage on the Japanese carriers in that battle, badly damaged herself, trailed oil all the way from Tonga to Pearl Harbor, patched up in a matter of hours, replaced some of her lost planes with those training for the Saratoga, and reached her position in the Battle of Midway.

I'd like to point this out to show the tremendous distances our naval task forces traveled with very little upkeep beyond anything that the forces afloat or the tenders or a quick stop in a Navy yard somewhere. In other words, they were operating at sea, overseas, for six months of the war when they started this battle.

The defense of Midway is an interesting operation because Admiral Nimitz had sent everything he could find out to defend Midway. He had Marine planes, some new, some old, and their pilots, a Marine defense battalion -- a reinforced defense battalion. He had anything that could be of use to defend that island sent there. Army planes, B-17s, based I believe at Kauai, went to Midway and then went on from there to attack the enemy forces.

One of the interesting facets of this Midway business was the uncertainty, at first, of the decoders as to actually where the main Japanese attack was going to be. They did know that it was a base known as AF, so the decoders sent a message out to Midway to send in plain language that they were out of water. That message was picked up by the Japanese and came through in their code, which convinced our people that Midway was the point of attack.

Q: That was a clever ruse!

Adm. W.: Everybody was on their toes.

As for the Japanese plans, the Japanese had their landing force -- about 5,000 landing force in transports were to sail from the Guam-Saipan area. Their minesweepers from Saipan and their landing force from Guam. Their main body and their carriers from the big Japanese bases in the Inland sea. They proceeded north to their last outlying base there before they started across the Pacific. The Japanese forces -- an interesting comparison with ours [see appendix 10].

Japanese preliminary movements. The Aleutian occupation force and second mobile force from Ominato. First Carrier Striking Force, main force, and Second Fleet from Harashima Jima. Midway occupation force from Guam. Minesweeping group from Saipan. Submarines from Inland sea bases. Type-2 flying boats from the Marshall Islands.

As to the strength of these forces: The Japanese had five large carriers, three CVS type -- seaplane type, eleven battleships, twenty-three cruisers, sixty-five destroyers, twenty-one submarines.

I have a correction on the battleships closer to the Midway operation -- five; combined heavy and light cruisers, fourteen; destroyers, fifty-eight; submarines, seventeen. In comparison to these forces in this area of the operation, the United States had three carriers, one partly damaged; eight heavy and light cruisers; seventeen destroyers; twenty-five submarines.

Q: And no battleships?

Adm. W.: And no battleships. I believe this covers the forces, except air, which I will go into later, in the vicinity of the Midway attack.

Now then, to go into the narrative of the battle.

About 2:40 light carriers of the Jap second mobile force attacked Dutch Harbor and inflicted moderate damage -- Dutch Harbor in the Aleutians. This was June 3rd. About 8:40 our Midway patrol planes sighted Jap occupation forces about 700 miles southwest of Midway. Midway's defenders and Fletcher's carrier task forces were significantly alert. As I recall this particular dispatch was received in the task force instantly and right after that moment Admiral Nimitz' headquarters sent another dispatch confirming that this was the occupation force, that the main body had not been located as yet.

About 4:30 the B-17s from Midway attacked the occupation

force with negative results -- 4:30 p.m.

June 4th. Patrol planes made night torpedo attacks on Jap occupation force and damaged a tanker. About 5:34 patrol plane made contact report on enemy carriers. 5:45 contact report many planes heading Midway. Shortly after 6:00 Midway Marine fighters engaged attacking planes. About 6:30 antiaircraft batteries opened up on attackers. Shortly after 7:00 our surviving fighters were able to land and refuel. Damage had been done, but the all-important airfield was operational.

Starting shortly thereafter and continuing until about 10:00 there were eight separate successive attacks made on the enemy carriers. TBFs, B-26s, and B-26s carrying torpedoes, scout bombers, B-17s, Vindicators, the obsolete planes, all from Midway. Then the 15 Hornet torpedo planes, 14 Enterprise, and the 12 Yorktown struck. They were shot down almost in their entirety, but during these operations they had tremendous effect upon the Japanese maneuvering. Their carriers were fighting off repeated attacks and, though undamaged by ten o'clock, they had not been able to properly launch their planes or recover their planes, gas their planes, change their ammunition. As a result, they were open to our dive-bombers when McClusky from the Enterprise with 37 dive-bombers drove home his attack at about 10:26. Within four minutes his forces had three of the Japanese large carriers out of action. Having caught their carriers with planes on deck in the process of gasing planes, with some of their fighters in the air but not their maximum number, and in the process of reloading, his attacks were far more effective than they might have been.

I would like to point out that this flight of Lieutenant Commander McClusky had reached almost the limit of its endurance in order to return to its carrier, yet he chose to start a box search and, in making that box search, found a Jap destroyer and sensed that it was returning to the Japanese carrier, and in that way he was able to locate Japs.

This attack decided the Battle of Midway.

One other interruption which I have not mentioned, the Jap carriers had during the course of these various attacks was a submarine that appeared in their midst, and in their attempts to dodge the submarine and sink the submarine, which they did not do, their air operations were further impeded.

Q: Pretty disconcerting!

Adm. W.: Yes. The next part of this affair was the attack by the remaining carrier Hiryu on the Yorktown, with a dive-bombing attack. I described this earlier in this talk at some length, but not the reply from our planes to the Hiryu.

By about five o'clock in the afternoon the Hiryu was located. We started out planes from the Enterprise, from the Hornet, some still-remaining Yorktown planes that were flying off the other carriers. We diverted B-17s who had flown from Hawaii toward the Hiryu, and some other long-range planes from Midway. So, all in all, the Hiryu was pretty well covered. But, once again, it was the carrier dive-bombers that finished the Hiryu or, rather, put her in fatal condition.

Now, to go back to the previously mentioned withdrawal Admiral Spruance ordered. Remembering that he had recovered many of his planes after dark, and I believe this was one of the first of our operations in the carriers at sea in recovering planes after dark —

Q: Had he lighted the deck for the recovery?

Adm. W.: I think he had some lighting on the deck. He had to. But he recovered his planes and headed eastward. At this time there were several things pretty important to him which he did not know. One was the exact location of the Japanese main body -- and I have it down as seven battleships, one light carrier, cruisers and destroyers. When he withdrew, he did not know the location of these strong forces. He knew toward midnight that they were behind the carriers, not too far. How far he did not know.

Now, what was happening at Midway Island. The Japanese heavy-cruiser division was supposed to attack Midway -- first, the submarines started to shell Midway, but the Marine gunners there drove the submarines underwater, and that was the end of that attack. The Japanese four heavy cruisers coming up to the bombardment group were to shell Midway at 1:00 a.m. Ninety miles from their target, they were recalled. On their return, our submarine Tambor got within firing range and, in the resulting confusion, dodging the Tambor's torpedoes, the Mogami rammed the Mikuma, costing that ship a bow.

Then they tried a night attack. Our planes did not have any success from Midway, on these damaged cruisers, being unable to locate them at night; the two Japanese crippled ships, the Mogami and the Mikuma, were retiring. Their other cruisers, I believe, had been recalled by that time to join Yamamoto's force. On their retirement, at dawn on June 5th, the Marine dive-bombers from Midway, Vindicators, still were in the fight and in the attack Captain Fleming's plane was in flames, yet he was able to maneuver his flaming plane into the turret of the Mikuma and did a tremendous amount of damage.

After that, Spruance sent off a search first for the Hiryu because he had received no report that the Hiryu had been sunk, and also for the retiring Japs. Of course, they were fortunate in retiring under a weather front.

Q: They came out from the weather front and went back.

Adm. W.: Yes, and they went back into it, so it was very difficult for us to find them. Our planes did find a destroyer and did some damage. I believe that was the only ship of the retiring force that we were able to find.

On the 6th Spruance -- the Mikuma was damaged, later the carrier planes finished off the Mikuma. The Mogami was damaged so badly that she was not able to get into the war again for two years. So that evening, late on the 6th, Admiral Spruance evaluated the situation, with his carrier screen reduced to six cruisers and four destroyers -- I might explain this somewhat. When the destroyers ran out of fuel he sent them back, but he kept on going ahead with his carriers and cruisers.

Q: Sent them back where?

Adm. W.: To the fueling rendezvous, and, as I say, at midnight on the 6th he realized that with his light forces and also he was due not only to the fueling rendezvous but to rendezvous with the carrier Saratoga that had some additional planes and was coming out from the Coast. So that, I think, explains some of the main points of this action, but I would like to sum it up in two or three items here.

First, even though I've already mentioned them, I want to tabulate what I consider critical decisions. The first was on June 3rd when Admiral Nimitz sent out to all his forces "Ships sighted by PBY are occupation force, not enemy main body." I think that instant recognition of what the force was was vital.

On the 4th -- I mentioned this earlier -- Fletcher to Spruance -- this is, mind you, when he still had his planes in the air, "Assume command and attack. I will recover search aircraft, then attack."

Spruance to Mitscher -- this was shortly after the battle began, on the 4th, "Operate independently generally conforming to my movements," this was when the two carrier forces split.

McClusky to his dive-bombers, "Am reversing course and following enemy destroyer to carriers." This, to me, was one of the big decisions of the day.

Q: What induced him to do that?

Adm. W.: He'd sighted this destroyer and he figured it was going back to join the carriers.

Q: He'd already gone the limit? I mean fuel-wise?

Adm. W.: Yes, he was taking a chance. He didn't fly again that day. He was wounded also in this thing.

On the 5th now, Spruance to search for carrier to limit of plane radius. He was looking for the Hiryu, which he did not know had been sunk. And on the 6th to his forces, "Keep outside of 700-mile radius from Wake." That's where the shore-based planes were able to attack. That order to retire to fueling rendezvous.

Certainly the most important fact that contributed to our decisive victory against overwhelming enemy forces was the courage and determination displayed by fellow Americans who participated therein. Here again, it was clearly shown as in past history that battles are won by men. Other important factors contributing to our victory were our very simple and flexible command structure: Admiral Nimitz at Pearl Harbor; Rear Admirals Fletcher and Spruance embarked in carriers; Rear Admirals Kinkaid and Smith in our heavy cruisers; Captain Simard and Colonel Shannon at Midway. I don't know how you could have a more simple command structure for such enormous forces. Timely arrival and most effective disposition in the battle area of ships, planes, pilots, Marines, and guns. Instant decisions and aggressive actions in launching our planes and attacking enemy carriers as soon as located and within range. Incredible intelligence information of enemy plans and splendid scouting and prompt reporting of enemy contacts. And, finally, Divine Providence certainly must have been on our side at the Battle of Midway.

That's the end of this description, but I've got an insert I think I should make.

I believe I have not touched on the disposition of the submarines on both sides. Admiral Nimitz' disposition of our submarines was, one might say, as perfect as humanly possible. They covered all areas of the Japanese approaches to Midway. The Japanese submarine disposition had a similar initial plan, which might have been far more effective. However, the three submarines that failed to reach their station on the approach which our carriers passed through from Pearl Harbor to Midway left a hole in the defense information service which was of tremendous value to our forces.

Q: Was that explained afterwards? Why did they fail?

Adm. W.: They broke down. They were a day or two late. Everything was gone by that time. I mean our carrier people had passed through.

There's so much more to this, but I think I should make it brief.

Q: Our destroyers had torpedo capability.

Adm. W.: Yes.

Q: Were the warheads as effective as they proved to be with our submarines?

Adm. W.: I would say not by that date. My own belief is, I know for a fact that shortly after our first submarines came back from patrol and told our people in Pearl Harbor -- and I would say this was probably February of 1942 about these torpedoes, without any authority from the Bureau or anyone else, I directed that the Benham torpedoes be set to take care of this error, at the proper depth. Much later on, instructions came out and I would say by the time of the Battle of Midway the instructions must have been out. So our destroyers should have been all right, but we never were too successful in our destroyer attacks. I can't explain it but we weren't.

Q: Were our destroyers designed for this type of action?

Adm. W.: Night fighting? Yes. Once the torpedoes were properly adjusted and crews trained we had wonderful results in runs and torpedo practices. We trained regularly for it. We had every morning general quarters at sunrise. We exercised at torpedo-director control. Of course, we didn't fire torpedoes but we had everything ready and target-tracking and so forth. We did the same thing with the evening general quarters.

We were just overwhelmed in that. Look at it this way. Had the Japanese battleships, which should have caught up by midnight, we would have run smack into them, had they kept going, but they turned around and had we met head-on that enormous force with the cruisers we had and destroyers. That's a question that's been asked me every so often. In fact, Admiral McClusky asked me at the last talk I gave what would Halsey have done if he'd been there. So I said, "I probably would not be here because he may have dashed in." You have to answer in two ways. Had the Japanese battleships come head-on and had Admiral Halsey dashed in, we would have been in a bad way. On the other hand, had they retired we might have been in a position to do more damage to their surface forces in the morning. They didn't have any carriers left to attack, so we had to keep looking for the Hiryu until we knew she was down.

Q: It seems to me one of the key elements in the explanation of

Japanese tactics is missing in the person of Yamamoto. I mean he was not around long enough to explain why he did things and why he failed to do things.

Adm. W.: Even reading the Japanese accounts, I've never seen any good explanation why he turned around, except that his carriers were all sunk. He knew that. He knew he'd lost his carriers, so he had nothing left but battleships, and by that time he knew we had two carriers. I'm convinced in my own mind that had Spruance kept going any farther west -- Yamamoto by that time had decided to turn around and come back and with his planes from his seaplane tenders -- he still had four smaller carriers and the ones from the Aleutians who were supposed to join up and reinforce him and more battleships coming down to reinforce him. He had a massive force to come in there. Had we gotten in range, had we gone a little bit farther, and that's when Spruance turned around.

Q: Yamamoto also continued to have a capability of making a landing, did he not?

Adm. W.: No.

Q: On Midway.

Adm. W.: Of course, his landing force hadn't been hurt, really, that's true, and he had plenty of cruisers. Yes, he had the capability of pushing ahead, but he'd had enough of our aircraft for that day, I think. I would have thought he could have because his landing force on the transports was intact. I didn't mention this in the account, but in the first night attack on the landing force a torpedo plane from Midway damaged his tanker, so his fuel supply for that force might have been knocked out. But I think the Marines on shore at Midway could have handled that 5,000-man landing force. They had very few casualties.

Q: Has any suggestion ever been made of the possibility that Yamamoto's own physical condition had something to do with —

Adm. W.: I think some of the books indicated that he -- no, I think he trained on rice gruel or something like that. That's all he could eat after he heard about the carriers, according to one of these books I picked up.

Q: Now I think we're about to go back to Tongatabu and the Guadalcanal operation.

Adm. W.: Proceeding from Tongatabu, Task Force 16 screened Transport Division 2, Crescent City, President Adams, President Jackson, President Hayes, and Alhena. Next joined the New Zealand division of the amphibious force and Task Forces 11 and 18. Task Force 11 commanded by Admiral Fletcher, and Task Force 18 by Admiral Leigh Noyes. The combined amphibious force proceeded north on July 27th, fueled July 28th -- the first night fueling for the Benham.

Q: Did you run into any difficulties with that?

Adm. W.: Actually, no. Surprisingly it went very smoothly, but it was a good big tanker, very competent to fuel in daytime and the only problem was having to put flashlights on the hoses because you couldn't use any other light.

Q: And it wasn't done under duress? I mean there wasn't any danger from the enemy?

Adm. W.: Well, submarines were known to be not too far away.

Q: Did you know what operation you were going to be involved in?

Adm. W.: Really, I do not think we had very much information in individual ships, other than that we were going on a big landing at Guadalcanal. We didn't have detailed operation orders. We operated a task force, Enterprise flagship with Rear Admiral Kinkaid as Task Force Commander, and had very little detailed information as far as individual ships were concerned. Later on we had these enormous operation plans, but not then.

Presumably the carrier with the Task Force Commander had information.

We joined up Task Force 18 and Task Force 11. On July 31st Enterprise aircraft launched a drill attack on Koro Island and the task force, in company with Task Forces 11 and 18, conducted a rehearsal landing operation in preparation for the planned attack on Guadalcanal. I believe that's the first information we had of what we were up to, when we had this rehearsal on Koro Island.

Then screening Enterprise and combined task forces. On August 1st joined Task Force 62, Task Groups 611-612-613, amphibious forces.

On August 3rd Benham had to search for the pilot of a burning plane with negative results. The plane crashed and sank immediately. Fueled from Cimarron. Now, this is important. It's the last fueling of the Benham until the 10th of August, and it's a question that's been argued about so much by various writers.

Q: What was her capacity?

Adm. W.: Her capacity as nearly as I can tell you at the moment was about 160,000 gallons, and in a day's steaming in aircraft operations we would use 24,000 gallons or maybe more -- 24,000 to 30,000.

Q: Six days was pretty -

Adm. W.: I think I'll go into that a little later to show why we couldn't have had very much left.

August 5th and 6th, task forces steaming in echelon - that means all the carrier task forces and all the amphibious task forces for the initial landings on Guadalcanal. Benham screened

Enterprise. Several unidentified aircraft reported, all, fortunately, friendly, for the operation was not disclosed to the enemy. This was on 5 and 6 August. Remember, we were landing on the 7th.

Q: And the enemy was not aware of it.

Adm. W.: Had not located us, no.

Q: How was that accomplished?

Adm. W.: We'd moved up from the southward. I think by good fortune as well as other things.

Q: Did they have reconnaissance planes?

Adm. W.: Not that far south. I think they mis-guessed, mis-estimated, what we were doing or how soon we were doing it, maybe. At least, they missed us. But they could have had plenty of submarines down there. They didn't show up till later.

On August 7th 1942 U. S. landing forces, consisting mainly of the 1st and 2nd Marine Divisions, took the enemy by surprise and landed on Guadalcanal and Tulagi. Benham was in the screen of Task Force 16 supporting this invasion. In this operation the Enterprise was launching and recovering aircraft almost continuously from first light until dark on August 7th and 8th and for combat air patrol and standby support operations on August 9th. The only unidentified planes reported on this date turned out to be U. S. Army B-17s.

Q: There was really no opposition to this landing?

Adm. W.: That's right. They moved ashore. They had the pre-bombardment from the air, the pre-bombardment from the ships that went in, the cruisers with the amphibious forces. At Guadalcanal there was practically no opposition. They just moved right ashore in their boats and started inland. They captured a lot of Japanese food. Japs went for the woods in the initial attack on Guadalcanal. The problem was unloading the ships. They got piled up very fast on the beaches. They were not cleared and were not as well prepared when the counterattacks came later.

On Tulagi we encountered quite fierce opposition from the small forces there. They were well dug in and they had good shore defenses, and our people had to shell them out, and the Marines had to fight them out. They really had a tough landing and they suffered severe casualties on the Tulagi side of the operation.

Meanwhile, we were trying to unload transports, and the carriers, as I previously described here, had combat air patrol over the carriers and they had search over Guadalcanal, giving all the support they could to the operations that went on.

But to dwell a little bit on this fueling situation in this task force, Kinkaid was probably more concerned than other task forces over the amount of fuel being consumed. But in the operations of that day we had the Benham steaming at probably over 30 knots from dawn till dark. She went up ahead of the carrier as antisubmarine screen, dashing back astern when she went into aircraft launching or recovery. And while combat aircraft operations were going on the planes returned unexpectedly, either damaged by being hit or they had other trouble, so there were frequent launchings and recoveries.

The carrier naturally had to turn into the wind for these -- which was fairly low that day, requiring high speed -- and between launchings and recoveries had to try to move back to what is known as Point Option where the carriers leave for their planes to come back to. So there were high-speed operations on both those days.

Q: Would you give me a footnote on Point Option? Was this a workable experience?

Adm. W.: Oh, yes, it had to be. The aircraft prior to take-off from their carrier of the task force for their operations instructions to the squadron tell them where to rendezvous when they return. So when the aircraft carrier conducting air operations in one direction would get that far away from this Point Option, frequently a moving point on the map, they would have to steam back to that position. It was workable, but they were steaming high speed all day in order to maintain it with the direction of the wind and the low force of the wind.

Q: But the exigencies of the situation sometimes demanded a

change in speed, and then what?

Adm. W.: That's right, they changed speed, but then in the time between they went in the direction necessary to launch or recover planes, at whatever speed was necessary to launch and recover. As soon as they'd completed that then they made effort to get back to geographical position where they told their pilots they would be. And the pilots keep that plot very carefully because they've got to know when they've finished their offensive operation how to get back to their carrier. In good visibility it's not too difficult a problem, but in low visibility it's a very difficult problem. They sometimes get lost and get to different carriers. But it was used as far as I know all during the war. In every operation I was in they had established a Point Option. They may change it by voice radio. If, for instance, they had to steam a much longer time in one direction than they anticipated and they couldn't get back by the time the planes were due, then they'd give them a new Point Option. But the pilot has the job of working that maneuver to get him back to his carrier. That's his most important task of navigation beside the target, is how to get back to the carrier.

I believe I've covered this enough about the speeds and about the fact that the carriers were in that area on the 7th of August for this attack, the next day on the 8th and most of the 9th when they decided they had to go back to their rendezvous with the tanker which was about 100 miles to the east or the southeast. And that was the move that was criticized because it made them not available the next day to chase the Japanese cruisers that sank our cruisers. But, as Admiral Fletcher has stated since, had he received information a little sooner he could have gone on the chase anyway, but since they were already out of his range he continued with his fueling rendezvous.

That night, the 10th, the Benham fueled from the Kaskaskia and it took two hours and twenty minutes, which indicates to me that our fuel tanks must have been almost empty, as from previous experience with those big tankers we fueled at over 1,000 gallons in a minute, and that's 140 minutes, that's 140,000 gallons. So it would appear to me that we were almost empty and, as I recollect, at the time I was very much concerned about our fuel capacity, I mean what was left. And so was Admiral Kinkaid, and he so stated in his message to Admiral Fletcher at the time. There were other destroyers that had a lot more, but they were not doing this high-speed plane-guarding that the Benham was doing. Probably another one doing the same thing was with each of the other two carriers.

Q: Was this type of operation in which the Benham was involved, was this envisioned when destroyers of that type were designed?

Adm. W.: Not at all. We developed that task force high-speed carrier operation in the pre-Pearl Harbor days. When the Benham was designed she had ample fuel capacity, to such an extent on her trials -- her economy was so good on her trials -- that the General Board had two of her tanks made into store rooms. I think I mentioned this earlier. None of our destroyers were designed for that long range.

I think it's well to bring out the difference between early in the war, when we had the individual carriers working with two or three cruisers, four or five destroyers, and that was all they had. Later, when we put three carriers in a task force with a screen all the way around them and you fueled every morning, basically from the larger ships until you could slip back every fourth day and join a tanker, maybe. But by that time they'd changed the tactics.

Q: How did our destroyers compare with the Japanese destroyers at that point in time in terms of long-leggedness and so on?

Adm. W.: As far as I know, our destroyers were just as good, if not better, than the Japanese destroyers of that day, except for one or two things. The Japanese seemingly had better control of their destroyers in night actions until we obtained radar. They had better star shells and they cooperated in using flares from their night planes. They had much better pyrotechnics than we had.

Q: Was this due to the fact that they had exercised

more frequently with night fighting?

Adm. W.: It may have been, but I think it was more the fact that they had used a more rapid burning explosive. We were interested in trying to have safe explosives. For instance, they used in their cruisers, I know, and I think the destroyers the same -- they used cordite, which is a very deadly explosive and much more rapid than what we were using. I believe we were vindicated later on when we finally were getting into action with Japanese cruisers at night and they suffered pretty heavily from the fact that they had cordite and planes on deck. We had taken our planes off cruisers because of the danger of increased gasoline fires. But they used their planes effectively with their cruisers and with their destroyers round the cruisers.

And in their defense of carriers, to go back a minute to Midway, the Japanese had a tight screen around their carriers with fast battleships, heavy cruisers, and destroyers, and they were good, but we were able to get through their defenses at Midway, as we've been talking about earlier, with the dive-bombers. They had, later on in their actions, defense of their carriers which was very good, but I think we were getting much better defense by the time the next battle came along. I'll show you when we get to that in the Eastern Solomons, our defense was improving with experience. They were still the same ships and there were still far too few for the job they had to do.

Now, to go on from the operations -- we still were in that area south of Guadalcanal some days after the initial landing at Guadalcanal and, to show you what was going on, we at night put on after the Savo affair, we formed a screen of cruisers and destroyers in a straight line 21 miles ahead of the carriers and other cruisers, so there would not be any further danger of a night attack by the Japanese on these carriers. And we were successful in those days remaining in the area in spite of the fact that the Japanese moved submarines in there and in spite of the fact that they knew where we were. They did not try to get down there until preliminary to the Battle of the Eastern Solomons, which took place the 24th and 25th of August.

We had some warning of this. Well, let's go back to the 20th when we had an air alarm and a search for a Jap plane that was shot down by one of our fighters. So we knew we had been discovered, assuming that the plane had gotten the information through.

On August 22nd torpedo wakes were sighted by our cruisers. The Benham ran a search for one of those submarines but I finally convinced the officer in tactical command that the torpedoes were black fish, but it took four hours of antisubmarine searching to convince them. I didn't have a visual sighting but I was positive that that was a fact.

That was an interesting evening for the Benham. Returning to the task force after this four-hour search, we were reported as an unidentified ship. I kept on the approach, determined I wouldn't get within gun range until somebody accepted our identity, and finally they sent out an order for the heavy cruisers to go to their guns. That was quite an eerie feeling that your own people were about ready to fire at you. Finally, Kinkaid over his circuit said the incoming returning ship is the Benham, do not fire. And then he sent a destroyer out to escort us in and exchange visuals. So the destroyer came out and, first, it was having difficulty getting recognition signals, but finally I convinced him that we were the Benham over the voice circuit. It was quite close. And we got in safely that night, but it was not a pleasant feeling.

Next, we get into the Battle of the Eastern Solomons.

At the start the Benham was at normal station in the screen of the carrier Enterprise. The first warning of the presence of enemy carriers was received from ever-reliable PBYs on patrol who radioed the message of contact and also closed to visual signal to be sure the message got through.

Extracts of notes made at that time follow.

1427 our fighters engaged enemy planes. Task force forming antiaircraft cruising disposition.

1501 enemy forces, one carrier, two heavy cruisers, one light cruiser, three destroyers bearing 50° true, distance 150 miles, on course 180°, speed 20 knots.

1655 enemy planes, distance 40 miles.

1700 Enterprise launched aircraft.

1704 enemy planes attempting simultaneous dive-bombing and torpedo attacks on Enterprise. Benham opened fire with all batteries, maneuvering rudder up to full speed up to full power conforming to movements of Enterprise.

1714 - notice this is a ten-minute battle like at Midway practically -- Enterprise hit in flight deck near stern causing jammed rudder and making maintaining station exceedingly difficult for formation.

1720 cease firing. More than 20 attacking planes shot down by antiaircraft fire, many more by our fighters. Four planes which attacked North Carolina shot down at once.

Fascinating to observe was the terrific concentration of fire this fine fast new battleship could now pour forth with accuracy, volume, and deadly effect. In this very brief action, the Benham expended 109 rounds of 5-inch, 510 rounds of 20-mm. ammunition, and sustained no casualties to personnel or materiel.

I might add that having the North Carolina in the formation was a tremendous boost to morale and to our antiaircraft defense, because I believe she had 22 of the 5-inch antiaircraft plus 40-mms. in quadruple mounts, something like 40 of them, and 20-mms. She had a tremendous antiaircraft battery. Her only limitation was that in this particular action her maximum speed I believe was 27 knots, and the Enterprise must have been up to 33 or something like that.

But the next thing that happened, and the battle wasn't over by any means -- meanwhile the Enterprise task force was retiring to the southeast, which was in the direction of the wind -- the Saratoga recovered some of her planes and I believe some of them went to Guadalcanal, but she had another explosion and this disabled her steering gear. The rudder jammed all the way over and they could not, for thirty minutes maybe, clear that rudder and get steering control, but they handled the ship with her engines and the screen did their best to keep approximate station. While this was going on there was a large group of planes -- I think something like forty or fifty heading toward the Enterprise. They knew she was damaged and they had failed to locate the Saratoga who was to start within sight of us practically, but they were out to get the damaged ship. Fortunately, a rain squall interceded and they passed us by at some distance. We had them on the radar all the time and they headed straight south and we were heading to the southeast and missed us. They lost quite a few of their planes because they couldn't get back to their own carrier -- they'd gone too far.

The question has been raised about the Eastern Solomons in some books. I think Morison called it indecisive, and other historians I've read say the same thing. I claim that it was a decided victory for us for the simple reason that the Japanese, to the best of my knowledge, made no further attempt by their carriers to intercept our amphibious line of supply that was going daily from Noumea running up to supply Guadalcanal and Tulagi. If they had felt they could meet us, I feel very sure that they would have gotten into that supply line, which was the sensible thing to do. So I believe they were hurt in planes much worse than the figures at the time seemed to indicate.

The *Enterprise* was escorted back to Tongatabu. Her bombers and torpedo planes were sent to Guadalcanal and based there for the time being. The aircraft carriers *Saratoga* and *Wasp* were still in the area, but they were damaged later on. Submarines were thick in that particular area within another week. I remember having reported contacts, at one time having eleven Jap submarines on the chart in the area in which we were operating, and we suffered from them. The *Wasp* was sunk, the *Saratoga* was damaged, the *North Carolina* was damaged, the *Chester* was damaged. It was a rough area to operate in, but we did get the *Enterprise* safely back to Tonga, then she was sent north for repairs at Pearl Harbor.

The *Benham* was detached from Admiral Kinkaid's task force and sent to report to Commander, South Pacific, Admiral Ghormley. We departed Tonga on the 31st of August, escorting auxiliary ships *Antares* and *Arctic*. This is going to be a little detailed but I just want to get somewhere in the record what a terrific moving around an individual ship did and the number of different people that we had to work under in a period of thirty days.

Worthington #4 - 225

Q: At that stage in the war?

Adm. W.: Yes. It could have come to sixty days, but thirty of that was under Willis Lee, which was no problem, but the other thing shows.

Benham was escort and task group commander. Shortly after midnight we departed on the 31st Commander, South Pacific, who was then Admiral Ghormley, ordered Arctic detached from this group to return alone to port of departure. That's the refrigerator ship we had and was supposedly urgently needed in Noumea. On September 5th sighted Amedee Island light. Shortly after arrived Noumea, New Caledonia, and reported to Commander, South Pacific.

September 6th reported Commander, Amphibious Force, South Pacific. This was Turner now. Commander, Task Force 62.

September 7th fueled from Kanawha, then underway and screening transport Zeilin, Captain Buchanan, went to Wellington, New Zealand.

September 10th sighted land-based aircraft New Zealand. And 11th approached Port Nicholson. Moored at Aotea Quay, Lampton Harbor, Wellington, New Zealand. In response to signal, reported immediately to commanding officer of His Majesty's New Zealand Ship Monowai loaded with survivors from Guadalcanal destroyer Blue and other ships. Received orders to escort his ship to Sydney, Australia.

1622 underway screening Monowai. Had a rough but uneventful

voyage to Sydney, arriving on September 15, entered that beautiful harbor, Port Jackson, Sydney, Australia, was assigned to Buoy No. 1 in Man of War Anchorage, called on Rear Admiral Muirhead-Gould, naval officer in command, Sydney, commanding officers of the Dobbin and His Majesty's New Zealand Ship Monowai.

September 17th departed Sydney, again escorting Monowai.

September 19th, pursuant to the following orders -- this is when I received a poem from the New Zealand captain. I won't quote it here, but it's quite unique -- orders in poetry.

Q: Dealing with what subject?

Adm. W.: What I was supposed to do next. Shall I read it to you?

Q: Yes. You should put that poem on tape because I don't think that any of our -- I don't think our Navy was capable of that kind of thing.

Adm. W.: No, they never did it.

Q: This was the New Zealand Navy.

Adm. W.: On 17th September departed Sydney, again escorting Monowai and at 0001 September 19 proceeded pursuant to the following orders. From HMNZS Monowai to USS Benham:

"When the hour of midnight strikes

Let's set our separate hikes.

With silent foot and cheerful heart

Without a word our ships will part.

When next you meet the wily Jap

I hope you will wipe him off the map,

And as you sock him, one, two, three,

Slip him an extra one for me.

We thank you for your kind escort

And wish you safe return to port.

May many bags of mail from home

Be coming towards you o'er the foam."

Proceeding, we shortly encountered a contact.

Q: A submarine contact?

Adm. W.: A surface contact. Prior to departure, I checked all the intelligence information available and was told there were no friendly ships that might be expected between Sydney and Noumea but there was a Japanese raider on the loose, and be on the alert for trouble. As we gingerly approached this ship with all guns trained, all torpedo tubes trained, and all directors pointed, and repeatedly endeavored to exchange recognition signals without any response, things looked rather grim, and at least my gunnery officer requested permission three times to open fire. But, by the grace of God, I held off. Finally we got a recognition signal.

The ship identified itself as the U. S.-flag tanker <u>Charles</u>

Worthington #4 - 228

S. Jones, course 100° true, speed 9 knots.

Proceeding on to Noumea –

Q: Why would she fail to answer?

Adm. W.: Somebody not alert, I would suppose. She couldn't help but see us. It was a dark night but she must have known we were there, and recognition signals you can see at a pretty good distance. She just didn't do it. Either didn't get out the book or didn't try and look up the answer. I don't know. You're supposed to have those recognition signals right at hand on the bridge always, but a lot of ships did and some did not.

Remained off Noumea for several hours and attacked submarine sound contacts with no positive results. Finally entered port and reported to Commander, South Pacific Forces.

On September 21st fueled from Kanawha, and the ship received a visit from Hanson W. Baldwin, military and naval editor of The New York Times.

On the 24th reported to ComDesDiv 24 in Lansdowne. That was Captain Ryan, Tommy Ryan. Thence underway in Task Group 66.4. Helena, flagship, Salt Lake City, Atlanta, Lansdowne, Walke, and Benham, to join Task Force 70. At this time, Benham was beginning to feel like an orphan, reporting successively as follows:

September 23rd Commander, Destroyer Squadron 2, in Morris.

Then to Commander, Squadron 12, in Farenholt.

Finally, on September 24th, to Commander, Battleship Division

6, in Washington. That was Rear Admiral Willis A. Lee.

The task group in which the Benham had sailed from Noumea had joined another group at sea. Seemingly, it was a fairly formidable force but no carriers were in, since the Enterprise had steamed off for repairs a month earlier. While this was a fast-moving mobile surface force, the Japs still had aircraft carriers in the area and were bent on doing all the damage possible to the all-too-meager forces striving to their utmost to supply and hold Guadalcanal.

The Benham received a signal to join this unit and the large fast battleship on the outside of this most formidable formation. She was not aware that the Washington, flying the flag of Rear Admiral Willis A. Lee, had left European waters. The unit consisted of Washington, Atlanta, Benham, and Walke and immediately departed from the formation. It was a real pleasure for Benham to escort this big and fast battleship with plenty of guns of all sizes and descriptions, modern radar, in fact an armored tanker and fully capable of maneuvering in the manner of a destroyer. Next day, Benham fueled from Washington. All hands had been cautioned to make every effort to show how smart a destroyer could be in this operation. Upon completion of fueling, cast off all hoses and all lines simultaneously and made a fast seamanlike departure from alongside the battleship.

The admiral told the commanding officer later that the operation was well done but not to try it again unless under air attack because his new crew were not used to such speed.

Q: By a destroyer?

Adm. W.: Well, the Washington, you see, had been operating in the Atlantic and was a brand-new ship just commissioned.

Q: But she was not used to the speed of a destroyer?

Adm. W.: Of handling lines and getting off. We'd been trained to clear expeditiously for safety and other reasons.

September 25th -- you see, these things are just a day or two apart -- Benham took station on Atlanta to act as reference vessel for the Washington's long-range off-set battle practice. It was a real treat to have such a grandstand seat for such a shoot and to realize that now, for the first time, we had the big and accurate-shooting 16-inch guns on our side.

Benham proceeded to Tongatabu to replenish supplies. The Washington had departed for the Pacific so fast that they were short even such staples as flour. As the ship approached Tonga on the 26th September and on course to one of our own minefields, the commanding officer became considerably concerned and signaled the flagship, "Is it your intention to enter port using the other channel?" The course was changed promptly. Afterwards, at the commanding officers' conference, the Admiral said, "Questioning the navigation of the flagship was quite proper when in doubt," and that he had been somewhat disturbed by the message from the base commander, Captain Olson, inquiring what salvage operation was required. In successive weeks the base had to make emergency repairs to Enterprise, Saratoga, North Carolina, several heavy cruisers and destroyers and expected the latest arrival also to have received war damage.

This logistic visit was very short but some vital upkeep was received from the Vestal before departure.

October 7th underway from Nukualofa Harbor in company with Washington, Atlanta, and Walke. Commander, Task Group 17.8, in the Washington steamed generally west.

October 10th fueled from Washington.

October 11th and 12th operating some 50 miles east from Malaita as a distant covering force to transport group McCawley and Zeilin carrying the American Division en route to Guadalcanal.

October 12th sighted Ulawa Island.

Generally, this little task group endeavored to keep out of sight of enemy long-range air, but remained in supporting distance of the supply line to Guadalcanal. On at least one occasion it steamed well west and acted as a decoy to divert the Japs from the vital supply lines at work.

October 15th, entered Espiritu Santo and commenced fueling from Washington. At 1935 this operation was interrupted by an air raid alarm, and the task group was ordered to sea immediately, then was underway at 1938. This emergency sortie after dark on the air raid alert in a narrow winding channel between minefields, the key navigational turning point, a rock on shore painted white, was a unique experience.

Benham was directed to lead the column out and, despite orders to the contrary, had to turn on a small signal searchlight on the white rock to make the treacherous turn in the channel. Ships following did likewise. The destroyer Tucker had already been lost in one of these minefields, and the President Coolidge was later to be lost in the other one in broad daylight.

October 16th Benham sighted two enemy observation planes with no friendly air.

October 19th fueled from Washington.

October 20th assisted by Laffey detected submarine contact including six 600-pound depth charges, indeterminate results.

2130 same day, three explosions were observed beyond horizon, and soon thereafter Chester reported having been torpedoed.

October 21st unidentified aircraft sighted.

At 1700, October 22nd, Chester was sighted escorted by four destroyers.

On October 23rd entered Segundo Channel, Espiritu Santo. Then fueled and provisioned from Lackawanna and Delphinius respectively. Sailed in the afternoon in company with Task Force 64, Commander, Task Force, in Washington, ComDesRon 12 in Aaron Ward, ComDesDiv 24 in Lansdowne, Atlanta.

We got into so many different commands and so forth and I want that to show in this thing, if possible, because a lot of people don't believe it. Other destroyers were in the same situation, I'm sure.

October 24th Benham was assigned to Destroyer Squadron 12, Captain R. G. Tobin, flying his broad command pennant in Aaron Ward. Then followed two weeks of intensive activity in the Guadalcanal area. Benham took part in night sweeps through Lunga Channel, in the San Francisco group under Rear Admiral Dan Callaghan, the Atlanta group under Rear Admiral Norman Scott, and in escorting convoys to Guadalcanal.

On these particular sweeps it was not the Benham's fate to meet her destiny. Although the enemy did not appear on these occasions, all the elements of battle imminent were present. With the enemy's preponderance of air, particularly carrier air, it was not deemed expedient to tarry long in this area.

October 25th Benham left Washington and proceeded to join Task Force 64.2 and take screening station on San Francisco. Sighted enemy patrol plane Rennel Island and Guadalcanal.

1750 Task Group 64.1 joined up, formed battle disposition-column of ships proceeding to locate and engage enemy forces off Savo and Guadalcanal islands. Admiral Lee in Washington was in command for the sizeable force of cruisers and destroyers. On this occasion, in approaching Savo Island from the west, Benham was in the van, but the Tokyo Express did not show up that night.

At 1:30 October 26th enemy not contacted, commenced retirement from Guadalcanal area.

9:08 sighted enemy float plane. At 0323, October 27 Lansdowne reported torpedoes fired at Washington. At 5:10 Atlanta reported torpedo had broached between her and the Washington.

October 28th, fueled from Washington, then formed up in Task Group 64.2, Atlanta flagship, Rear Admiral Norman Scott, ComDesDiv 12, in Aaron Ward, Lardner, Fletcher, and Benham. Proceeded to Guadalcanal Island to bombard Jap positions just west of Tenaru River while troops were unloaded from transports. These troops were General Pedro del Valle's much-needed Marine artillery.

On October 30th Atlanta embarked a Marine officer from the troops ashore who pointed out the Jap positions. Atlanta opened up on steaming close in and destroyers followed the motions of the flagship, successively firing on targets initially fired on by the flagship. The only signal given in two and a half hours of bombardment was "turn one-eight" repeated at intervals. In this operation the Benham expended 696 rounds of 5-inch 38 caliber ammunition.

9:06 commenced retirement.

That is my idea of a perfect bombardment support situation. One signal.

On returning to Espiritu Santo on October 31st, considerable debris close to the unmined channel was observed and ship proceeded with great caution. No information had been received that the President Coolidge had been sunk in our own minefields several days previously. This fine transport carried an Army regiment and heavy weapons sorely needed at Guadalcanal. This was one more inexcusable tragedy of war. Fortunately, due to fine rescue work by harbor personnel, the loss of life was small.

A most exasperating incident occurred on this logistic visit to Espiritu Santo. Benham was directed to obtain fuel from a commercial tanker anchored in the harbor. On making her approach, none of the crew was observed on deck to handle lines, no information received from the master except that the crew was having tea and were not inclined to work on Sunday afternoon anyway. Consequently, the crew of the Benham broke out grapnels, went alongside the tanker as in the days of boarding parties. This merchant crew was supposedly of Americans who received very high wages and double pay for being in a war zone. The master was advised that the Benham was going to receive fuel and, if it was not properly forthcoming, her crew would man his pumps. Most reluctantly she pumped fuel amidst unpleasant remarks from tanker personnel.

Q: Admiral, may I interrupt? This sort of thing occurred so frequently in the accounts of the war in the Pacific. Did it improve any as the war went on?

Adm. W.: Oh, yes, I think it improved. Of course, I left shortly after this, but I never ran into anything like this in the latter part of the war.

Q: There was an incident at Midway, just before the Japanese attack.

Adm. W.: I didn't know about that.

Q: Where they refused to do it because they were haggling over overtime pay --

Adm. W.: On the island itself. Were they workers on the island?

Q: No, no. This was some sort of a ship, and consequently the Marines had to take over or something.

Adm. W.: Yes, well, right here all I could do was report the incident because we were standing out to sea again right away and I don't know whether anything happened about it or not.

Q: Wasn't some attempt made to do something with the labor unions, to make them realize the situation?

Adm. W.: Yes, I think they got at them. When some of these reports got back I think they did do something about it, but I know publicly this was denied later on, that this ever happened -- I mean this type of thing. But that was for the newspapers. There's no question about it, it was just inexcusable. I think they got over it pretty soon, but, believe me, the crew were really mad at that situation because they were going back into the war and this was as far as the tanker got, about 600 miles away.

I want to get this across, if I can.

It was on this occasion, pursuant to war instructions, that the commanding officer had to report to Admiral Scott that the Benham had developed turbine trouble and could not make full power, but if he would permit this ship to sail all hands were competent and repairs would be effected before making the Guadalcanal area. Admiral Scott's immediate reply was, "I shall not worry about the power of your ship as long as your heart is in the right place. You sail with me."

The next day Benham reported "Task completed and able to make full power." Rear Admiral Scott was a gem.

November 6th Benham was ordered to report to Commander, Destroyer Division 10, Commander T. M. Stokes in Cushing, to escort a group returning to Noumea and there obtain ten days' urgently needed upkeep.

On 10 November Benham reported to Commander, Destroyer Squadron 2, Commander H. R. Holcomb in Clark, and arrived at Noumea, New Caledonia.

11 November Commander Worthington was relieved by Lieutenant Commander John B. Taylor as commanding officer, and Benham sailed on her last cruise, again screening Enterprise.

This is a short last account of the Benham. Do you think it ought to go in here? It's not from my personal experience but gotten from everybody connected with it.

On this day, November 11th, the Japanese made heavy air attacks on Henderson Field preparatory to their main landing and assault. Every available American ship was steaming north towards Guadalcanal to oppose what our intelligence had indicated was to be a grand-scale attack by the enemy. On the evening of November 13th, Walke, Benham, Preston, and Gwin became the escort screen for the battleships Washington, flagship of Rear Admiral Willis A. Lee, and South Dakota, designated Task Force 64. These warships departed from the Enterprise carrier force and steamed north to the east of Savo Island to intercept enemy transport force reported approaching the Solomons. They found their quarry the night of November 14, when they intercepted the bombardment group which included the Japanese battleship Kirishima, four cruisers, nine destroyers, and four transports. Two other destroyers later joined the enemy bombardment group, which was under the command of Admiral Kodo in his flagship, the cruiser Atago. This enemy force was split into three groups between Savo and Guadalcanal islands, presenting a confusion of targets to Admiral Lee's forces, which were steaming in one column with his destroyers in the van about 4,000 to 5,000 yards ahead of the battleship column.

At 2317 Lee's ships opened fire on the cruiser Sendai, destroyer Shikinami, which immediately made smoke and retired out of range. Meanwhile at 2322 Walke, Benham, Preston took under fire the destroyers Ayanami and Uranami. At 2326 Gwin detected the cruiser Nagara and four destroyers and engaged them in a private duel. At 2330 these Japanese fired torpedoes and by the time they arrived at targets only the Benham had escaped serious damage by gunfire. The Walke had her fo'c'sle blown off as far aft as the bridge and sank. The Preston had her topside demolished and soon sank. The Gwin received considerable topside damage.

At 2338 Benham was struck by a Japanese torpedo on her starboard side. As a result of this torpedo hit, the ship rose forward, heeled about 5 degrees to port, then rolled to starboard about 30 degrees, settling by the head and righting herself slowly. The explosion threw up a great body of water which came down on the ship with considerable force, washing one man overboard and injuring several others. Below her main decks her bow had been carried away back to No. 1 gun turret; some forward compartments below the waterline were flooded. Numerous frames and supports broke in No. 2 fire room and the hull was creased on both sides of the ship. Due to the debris forward, the ship could be maneuvered only at slow speeds. She made a slow circle attempting to avoid ships and Japanese gunfire. Because of her badly damaged condition and the fact that the ships close to Savo Island opened heavy gunfire, she changed course toward Guadalcanal. Hugging the shores to avoid observation, she worked her way to seaward and took no further part in the action.

While our two remaining badly damaged destroyers were

clearing the battle area, the battleships engaged the Japanese destroyers Asamuno and Terufuki, the heavy cruisers Atago and Takaro, and, at 2348, the battleship Kirishima, while the Japanese concentrated on the South Dakota, the Washington, disposed of the Kirishima in seven minutes and scored hits on the cruisers. While the damaged South Dakota moved to retire, Washington steamed north in a deliberate decoy move which drew the whole Japanese bombardment group away from her sister battleship and the crippled Gwin and Benham. She escaped damage as her heavy guns turned back the bombardment group, having been skillfully maneuvered clear of the torpedoes launched by two trailing destroyers. The burning and exploding Kirishima was abandoned and scuttled, as was the Japanese destroyer Ayanami.

The Benham had fifteen feet of her bow sheared off by the explosion. Through the gallant efforts of the damage-control crew, stemmed the flood forward, was making slow headway. With ever-worsening seas, the damage was progressive and cumulative, and on the late afternoon of November 15th there was a sickening sway and the entire hull began to divide itself into two distinct sections. Her escort, the destroyer Gwin, received her officers and men and the two floating sections were hurried to the bottom of Iron Bottom Sound by 5-inch salvoes.

In this battle, which took such heavy toll of lives in Walke and Preston, no Benham lives were lost and only seven men were injured.

    I believe that covers the story.

Q: The end of a noble ship.

Interview No. 5 with Rear Admiral Joseph M. Worthington,

U. S. Navy (Retired)

Place: His residence on Gibson Island, Maryland

Date: Wednesday morning, 21 June 1972

Subject: Biography

By: John T. Mason, Jr.

Q: Today we are to have an interesting chapter on your tour of duty at the Naval War College, which came immediately after you left the South Pacific.

Adm. W.: I proceed from Noumea, New Caledonia, on the 12th of November by Pan-American plane, scheduled to go to Pearl Harbor. We stopped in Suva the first night -- incidentally, the other passengers on the plane were all Marine aviators from Guadalcanal, most of whom were taking quinine for malaria.

Q: Which was a heavy affliction for our forces?

Adm. W.: Which our forces suffered from very heavily in Guadalcanal. The quinine kept them alive, apparently, and they tried to get them out of there as fast as they could.

Leaving Suva the following day for Canton Island, this twin-engined plane developed engine trouble and the pilot had to look for a friendly island, hopefully. He circled Wallis Island, hoping to find it occupied by U. S. Marines and not Japanese.

Actually, our Marines had occupied it a couple of weeks before and a defense battalion was there, laying out an airfield. The commanding officer, Colonel Griffin, of the Marines, happened to be the one who commanded the same defense battalion that the Benham had removed from San Clemente eighteen months previously. He gave me a temporary billet in his tent until other transportation should be available.

Q: Was your plane able to determine from the air that it was friendly territory?

Adm. W.: Yes. I'm satisfied the pilot would have continued farther but he had one sputtering engine and did not think he could make Canton Island -- I'm satisfied he would have gone somewhere else, tried to get farther away if the Japs had occupied it.

Q: There aren't that many options, however, are there?

Adm. W.: Not very many, not many islands in that part of the world, really.

While on this island, we had a general alarm that a Japanese attack was imminent, but fortunately it proved false and the Marines continued with their construction of the airfield. Three days later, another Pan-American plane picked us up and stopped at Canton Island one day, then Palmyra, and, finally, Pearl Harbor, where I was again fortunate to find the captain of the yard an old shipmate who gave me a place in his quarters until transportation could be arranged to San Francisco, in this case in a B-24.

Arriving at San Francisco, orders were awaiting me for the Naval War College. This duty I had requested a number of times as a choice for shore duty and I had previously completed the War College correspondence courses in strategy and tactics and international law. Since the course was not opening until January 1st -

Q: This was 1943?

Adm. W.: 1943 - I was able to visit Annapolis, my home, on leave, the first leave in four and a half years. I also arrived there in time for the Army and Navy game, which was played in Annapolis that year.

Greeting me there from the War College was a very fine letter from Admiral Pye, the new president, who also sent me a book Sound Military Decision, which I was instructed to be thoroughly familiar with before arrival at the College.

Q: Who was the author of Sound Military Decision?

Adm. W.: To the best of my knowledge and belief, this was put out and printed in the regime of Admiral Kalbfus.

Q: It was a publication from the Naval War College?

Adm. W.: Oh, yes. It was the text of the War College, and it was my understanding that the author was supposed to be one of several professors. To me it was somewhat of a shock, but I'll mention that text later on. It was particularly a shock to try to concentrate on the philosophy of war after arriving back from the actuality in the South Pacific. But we started in with the command and staff course on New Year's Day. To reach the College there was no bus service on account of snowstorms, so we walked over 2 miles through the snow, but school went on and I found that two and a half months of this five-month course was to be devoted to this Sound Military Decision.

Q: How many were you in this class?

Adm. W.: Thirty officers, from captain down to major in the army or lieutenant commander in the Navy, in the command class and, working with them, about twice that number in the preparatory staff class, in rank from commander in the Naval Reserve to lieutenant, junior grade.

Q: Were these men in a similar situation to yours? Had they been in combat and were back briefly for a respite and to attend classes?

Adm. W.: I believe that is true. I think a large percentage of the group in the command class had seen active duty, either in the Atlantic or the Pacific -- active war duty. As for the preparatory staff class, I believe very few of them, up to that time, had had any active war duty.

The problem of conducting a class of such divergence of students is not a simple one, but this class had been ordered the previous March. The year's command class had been stopped to send people to sea -- this was in March of 1941 -- and this class had been substituted for that to try to get as much out of the War College facilities as was possible.

Other parts of this course were, I thought, very valuable. The strategy and tactics course, maneuvering war games, the plotting, as we did, of forces in our own rooms, then when they reached the state of approaching battle we put them on the big maneuvering board and plotted them there and actually had engagements.

Q: Contrary to experience in the past, did you identify the enemy this time as the Japanese?

Adm. W.: We were mostly interested at this time in the Blue Fleet as against the Orange, or Japanese, Fleet. On the other hand, we had problems worked out of the early actions. One of them was the Battle of the River Platte action of the British against the Graf Spee, which, incidentally, I used to very good training purposes up in the Aleutians later on when we had a similar problem confronting us.

The facilities of the War College were perfectly splendid.

It had a wonderful library, an experienced staff, and a staff that was willing to incorporate new things as fast as possible. But you can see the problem, for instance, when we tried to throw in radar. The rule books for the War College maneuver board at that time had not been brought up to date for radar because we didn't know what radar could do, but we did actually work it into problems on the game board. Captain J. J. Brown was very helpful in that. You could tell him what you thought the radar would have done in these conditions and with the help of somebody who'd been working with it, he'd work it right into the problem. It was disconcerting to some of those participating because they didn't have it in their rule books.

Q: This is where they were going on the experience of students to further the teaching?

Adm. W.: That's what we had to do. The same way with the carriers. Some of the carrier problems I did not feel were as realistic as they might have been. The damage assessed to them was not as great as it should have been. We knew from experience already what the Japanese carriers could do. This is something that takes place gradually.

One more item I want to touch on and I'd like to record this. Every member of the command and staff class had to prepare a thesis before graduation, and we commenced working on this maybe after two months.

Q: A subject of your own choice?

Adm. W.: The choice was assigned, and I want to get that on the record here. It's rather long: Policies and conditions leading up to the present conflict between Japan and the United States, including notation of the parallels between the opening of the present hostilities and the opening of the Russo-Japanese War (1904).

The various officers produced a varied thesis.

Q: You all wrote on the same subject?

Adm. W.: The same subject. That is, they produced from what data they could get.

Q: You didn't attempt to break it down into sectors?

Adm. W.: Not at all. This was a requirement for graduation. Actually, I put a great deal of time on this because I was interested and I had some background information for it. I'm going to quote just one sentence, the last one, from the thesis: [Referring to the Japanese] "They openly repudiate all the moral concepts of modern civilization as soft and decadent and pride themselves on their brutality with which they propose to cow the world."

I was trying to compare the Japanese and the way they treated our prisoners at that time and were trying to cow the world, as Hitler was doing on the other side of the Atlantic.

The next part of the course -- I have pretty well covered

Worthington #5 - 249

this preliminary course, except to say that, to me, it was great value working with the members of the other services. In my case, a teammate was Lieutenant Colonel William Jack Blythe of the Army, who was an experienced G-2 officer for the Army and from this war college was assigned to the 82nd Airborne Division. By exchanging information between us and working out these problems, I think it was mutually beneficial.

Near the end of this course, I was told that I would remain on the staff as gunnery officer and assistant for tactics, relieving Captain Randall Dees. So, as soon as my thesis was in, he assigned me to his office in the archives.

Q: What was that decision predicated on?

Adm. W.: I think personally Captain Dees wanted very much to get to sea and he knew that he would not be released unless he had a relief that Admiral Pye would approve. Admiral Pye was satisfied and that was it. The only conflict I had was that Admiral Ingersoll had -- and I knew this -- already requested me for duty on his staff in the Atlantic Fleet and I much preferred going to sea duty. This brought up an interesting question but I could do nothing about it.

Q: Did you communicate with Ingersoll?

Adm. W.: Yes, I did. I had a letter drafted to him but the day I was to mail this letter Ingersoll hoisted his flag in the

Constellation down at the War College pier, so I immediately dropped in to see him and told him of my predicament, and he waid, "Well, don't be concerned about it in any way at all because we cannot do anything about it. Admiral Pye is a friend of mine and I'm not going over his head, but I still want you on my staff and I'm sure you will be here in due course." I believe he had no idea my reporting would be nearly ten months later.

I went to work on this staff job with a great deal of interest because it was a splendid job, as far as shore duty is concerned.

Q: I think also that you would welcome the opportunity to impart to these people at the War College some of the wartime experiences that you had?

Adm. W.: It was very interesting doing that, and for that reason I believe it would be helpful in here to give a short list of presentations to show what area I was trying to cover. If it's too long you can delete it, but here it is.

Q: You did this in lecture form?

Adm. W.: Lectures, yes. We called them presentations there because at that time everything presented, given to a class, had to be presented. There was no such thing that I can recall as an off-the-cuff lecture. Everything was written out and prepared ahead of time and checked ahead of time and then delivered to the class. Of course, there were question periods that couldn't be prepared.

Q: All the material presented had to be approved by the authorities?

Adm. W.: It had to be worked over and approved and rehashed many times. Unfortunately, it was very difficult to get a change from an old presentation to a new one, but that's what I did with each one I had.

The first one was the Battle of Midway. Next, the employment of battleships. The torpedo in naval warfare. Unity of effort. Strategical intelligence, Operational intelligence. Weather and its effect on naval operations. Use of the move and gunfire sheet. Amphibian operations in the Solomon Islands. The mine in naval warfare.

These presentations were given to the command and staff class. The short, two-week class composed of Air Force generals and colonels who had two weeks at Orlando, two weeks at Armed Forces Staff College, two weeks at the Naval War College, and I think two weeks at Leavenworth. I should correct that and say some of these presentations were given to that group because, looking at it now, I couldn't possibly have given this many in the short time available.

Q: It's quite a range of subjects, and you presented all of this?

Adm. W.: Yes, that was my assignment. I was given the lectures and the one on weather and its effects on naval operations almost killed me.

Q: I would think from your list of subjects that there were many new factors that entered the picture with the war in the Pacific, and you say that it was difficult to get agreement on presentations differing from the established ones in the past.

Adm. W.: Maybe I overstated that because I do know that, generally speaking, when I submitted changes they were accepted. They went to people like the tactical department, strategy, and Captain Brown, and Admiral Bright, who now lives in Annapolis. They were happy to get the changes, but it took a lot of reworking.

The most interesting thing to me about the lectures was the length of the question periods. I tried very hard to keep them down, the lectures themselves, to forty-five minutes. The one I inherited on weather and war was two and a half hours, so it took some streamlining to get that down. But the interesting thing was the question period. That group of Army Air Corps generals and colonels, many of them ten or fifteen years younger than I was, asked fascinating questions about these lectures and were completely flabbergasted by the gunfire from a 16-inch battleship and the fact that we could put it pretty close to the target. It seemed to, from the type of questions they asked, open up a new vista to them, and I believe it helped later on when they went back to staff duty, which they did in many cases. They went

Worthington #5 - 253

from this course to their staff afloat, Air Force, Army, or Marine.

Q: In the preparation for your lectures and preparation for the question period, you drew on your own experience, but what sort of input was there from the Navy Department in Washington, the battle reports and so forth that were coming in from engagements in the Pacific? This was available to you?

Adm. W.: I was the one officer at that time -- and you'll see that in my final report and recommendation -- charged with reviewing the battle reports, Atlantic and Pacific and the Mediterranean, and incorporating things that developed into these lectures and into the war-game problems, and I found it to be a stupendous task but I did the best I could in the time I had.

As an example, maybe it's not too soon to put in the recommendation that I gave to Admiral Pye later on, the battle force presentation. One other assignment I had was revision of the War College publications. For example, the various editions of fleet tables, the Blue-Red Fleet. I didn't do anything with that because the British were printing one outside at the time, but the Blue Fleet was constantly bringing our own table up to date. Black, Gold and Silver I can't really remember, probably Italian, I'm not sure. But the Orange Fleet was the big job I had. I have a note here that the Blue Fleet 1944 master copy corrected to date, actually March 1944.

Q: This is the operational units?

Adm. W.: Yes. Every operational unit that we knew of in the Blue Fleet as they came into commission we put them into the tables. The tables were printed. It was a book about half an inch thick and we printed them every year. Captain Dees had approximately finished the Blue Fleet when he was detached and so we got that printed very shortly.

Q: It was constantly changing, wasn't it?

Adm. W.: It was constantly changing, our own fleet, from building and putting ships in commission, which is very had to keep up with. We had all the corrections. But the Japanese we had to get from intelligence reports. I had the Japanese Fleet as near -- I've got a note here "completed as of March 1944," and in that, incidentally, I had the Musashi and Yamato down with 18.2-inch and an asterisk because we didn't know then what they had but information indicated that they probably had and I took a chance on the tables that indicated that they had the 18.2 inch guns.

One other assignment I had was of interest. I mentioned the revision of the gunfire maneuver rules which were submitted for approval in December of 1943. That was my responsibility. And finally I was assigned the applied mathematics panel -- War College representative on the applied mathematics panel for the National Defense Research Committee. This proved most interesting because that was a very-high-pressure panel in the Department. It was a national defense group and they had taken under their wing revising the fire-effect curves. We had developed gunnery curves to show at what ranges your ships would be most effective against the ships of the enemy, and we'd developed some very fine curves. The practical problem was if they ever got into action could they maneuver the battleships at a favorable range to enemy battleships. As far as I know, even though our ships had these curves, I know they tried to use them, the captains, there were so many other factors in the range at which you fight a battle that I'm not sure how much they ever accomplished with them. I've seen nothing to prove one way or the other.

This mathematics panel worked on those and also we worked with the readiness division of Admiral King's staff.

Q: This meant you had to spend a lot of time in Washington?

Adm. W.: No. Actually, just for meetings. I'd fly to Washington or take a train to Washington and a train back the same night to attend the meetings with ComInCh. The panel did their work I believe in New York, this research panel. They were all over the country. Some of them were in Washington. They took our ideas. They spent a day with me up at the War College looking at what we had and a day for this meeting in Washington, then they went ahead and produced their effort, which brought out this wonderful maneuvering board for the War College which wasn't placed in effect till after the war, as far as I know. They put all this on machines and computers.

The preliminary results we sent to our battleships and cruisers as possible -- not to be overemphasized. Then we'd expect greatly improved results from radar ranges and spot, greater range of fire in our new installations, improved patterns in armor and greater life in ships. But that was only our belief at the time. I can't say from knowledge what happened, how effective it was.

Q: Admiral, how many were on the teaching staff at the time?

Adm. W.: Twenty-eight.

Q: You say that there were twenty-eight, including the administrative staff?

Adm. W.: The entire staff, yes.

Q: The reason I ask is because they seemed to overburden you with all sorts of tasks. What were the others doing, those who were involved in teaching?

Adm. W.: Captain F. S. Steinwachs was the head of the department of operations with seven assistants and, as gunnery, I was one of the assistants, listed in this case, as second to Captain Bright, senior assistant.

In the strategy section there were two captains and one commander. The tactics section, three captains. Correspondence course, a commander and a lieutenant. Department of intelligence, the head of it was -- also economics, policy, and international law, and he had three colonels and captains and two commanders as assistants. Then there was a captain for the secretariat.

Q: As you made those various breakdowns to the teaching staff, it seemed to me that the subjects you presented cut across the whole field, so what were the others doing? What were they involved with?

Adm. W.: Actually, they were both carrying on the War College routine and regular problems. I mean, the head of the Department of Operations, you see, because what I wrote they saw it to review if they saw fit or just pass it on.

Q: Your presentations were based on actual war experience?

Adm. W.: Mostly, yes. All were based on war experience, I would say. On the list I gave you I don't believe there's a single one that's not war experience and I think that's the reason I was given them.

Q: The others, then, were involved in the more routine and established presentations?

Adm. W.: Yes. It's quite difficult -- and I found this out later, at the Industrial College of the Armed Forces -- to break up a long, indoctrinated staff and policy to suddenly change it all to meet wartime conditions. In peacetime, you can take this over a period of time, you're geared to a slower pace, geared to a year's course or you're geared to three years for the staff and faculty. We were having a staff and faculty that had been trying to get to sea, to get into combat.

Q: Yes, but if what's being presented is outdated by the new developments in wartime, what's the sense in presenting it?

Adm. W.: Well, I agree with you. I thought some of it should not have been presented. At the time, I had some clashes about things. For example, one of them was a splendid lecture on weather and war but it lasted two and a half hours. You have to streamline. I felt that the things to point out you could do very quickly. You could point out the Battle of Midway and the effect of the weather very simply, and the Battle of the Coral Sea, the Battle of the Eastern Solomons. They were our three big air naval battles and they were all greatly affected by the weather.

Q: And there were lessons learned in each case?

Adm. W.: Yes.

Q: So this reflects on the material that was presented from past years and was carried on?

Adm. W.: The material, I felt, was brought out from maybe German studies. They were great weather experts. There was much in there that I personally felt was not necessary and should have been changed and cut down.

There's one more thing I want to mention here and then I'll stop. I think I've been critical enough really.

We had an operation and order form and this book _Sound Military Decision_ had that form in there. Well, I looked at that preparing for my final paper on one of these battle problems. I was called in and told that that was not in accordance with the War College's _Sound Military Decision_ and if I didn't do it over again in accordance with their book, I would be flunked the course.

Q: Oh, this was while you were still a student?

Adm. W.: Yes. So I said, "Well, I have one statement to make, and that is a request that I may have a talk with Admiral Pye," which you are allowed by Naval Regulations -- you can go through channels to the commander.

Admiral Pye said, "What is this problem, that you do not agree with the staff on an operation order in _Sound Military Decision_?"

I said, "Well, Admiral, I believe that the operational form used by the commander-in-chief, U. S. Fleet, commander-in-chief, Pacific Fleet, and Commander-in-chief, Atlantic Fleet, is the form to be taught at this War College now, not something that was written prior to the war. If it was the proper thing to have, I feel sure that these high commanders would be using it instead of their own."

Admiral Pye said, "I agree with you fully and that section of the book will be rewritten," and he rewrote the book himself.

Q: Why did it take a confrontation, though, on the part of a student to provoke this? Why wasn't it an obvious thing to begin with?

Adm. W.: I guess people might say that I'm a controversial individual at times, but having worked under the people I worked under they wanted things done and they wanted things done right, and they were not adverse to changing something if they saw there was a better way.

Q: Didn't this invoke a feeling of frustration on your part and the part of others who had been involved in the war and had come back to the War College?

Adm. W.: I think so. I think very much so, but it did seem to strike me more so. The others just went along with the War College form, which was the simple thing to do. As far as I know, they did.

Here's a comment which I think I will brief. The head of a department at the postgraduate school at the Naval Academy wrote me about the use of the same publication, <u>Sound Military Decision</u> -

Q: While you were at the War College?

Adm. W.: At the War College. In my memorandum I said briefly it is unfortunate you have to teach something from it in twenty short lessons. However, that being the case, I made him some suggestions but I did say in this: "The naval directives should be of considerable value to you. I would use it until the new book is available." Admiral Pye had nearly completed it. It was exceedingly well written and much more understandable, and, consequently, of greater value than the edition he had. I've never seen Admiral Pye's new book but I was told -- I knew what he was writing, he was writing it all the time I was at the College, so I'm sure that he did get that straightened out all the way through and bring it up to date.

Then a comment about the plans and I said the best plan I'd seen as of that date was the North African campaign, and that was Admiral Hewitt's plan.

Shouldn't this be taken verbatim? It's not long but it's the recommendation I made upon detachment? I think it's a good summary.

Q: Yes. This was a summary after you'd completed your teaching stint there?

Adm. W.: Yes, on my detachment. I'd drafted it previously but waited for the detachment date, and I handed it to Admiral Pye personally.

Q: Is it expected that a man will present his recommendations at the end of his tour there?

Adm. W.: I do not believe at that time they asked for any.

Q: This was entirely voluntary on your part then?

Adm. W.: To the best of my knowledge, they did not ask for any, because I found from later experience at the Industrial College when a student makes recommendations they involve an awful lot of work by a lot of people and frequently they have something that's been discarded in the past. However, this was before my tour as Director of Education at the Industrial College and I felt very strongly about this. This was to the President of the Naval War College, 20 March 1944, via the Head of the Department of Operations and the Chief of Staff:

> Subject: Recommendations for improving War College courses of instruction
>
> 1. It is my earnest conviction that the value of the War College to the Navy in this war can be enhanced by effecting certain changes to the present courses of instruction. The following recommendations are respectfully submitted:
>
> (a) Include in the course one complete amphibious problem. This would require a minimum of four weeks. Two weeks might be diverted from the present course on international

law for this purpose.

(b) Include in the study course war instructions revised, general tactical instructions, current tactical orders, and doctrine, U. S. Fleet. Insofar as practicable, adhere to these publications in all chart and board maneuvers.

(c) Assign at least two additional officers to devote their full time to study and analyze action reports as soon as received in the archives and present lessons learned therefrom to the combined classes as promptly as possible. Make out schedule flexible enough to permit this. Experienced officers available for limited service only could do the valuable work of making these studies.

(d) Have each historical presentation given by the member of the staff who has made the most complete study of that particular action and repeated by the same officer as long as he is a member of the staff.

(e) Hold a staff conference at least twice a month presided over by the president for the purpose of (i) having open discussions of War College problems; (ii) assisting in coordinating the work of the staff.

(f) Have each officer reporting for duty at the War College who has recently returned from a battle area present a short, informal talk upon latest developments with which he may be familiar.

(g) Shorten the tour of duty for members of the staff

physically qualified for sea duty to eighteen months and replace them with officers from combat areas.

I presented that to Admiral Pye upon departure.

Q: What kind of reception did you get?

Adm. W.: He thanked me for it and I believe he assured me that there would be changes. He'd already told me that he was revising that publication.

Q: Were you able to have your family with you while you were there?

Adm. W.: Oh, I forgot to mention getting married, didn't I? Yes, I was allowed the weekend off in October -- October 22nd 1943 -- to leave for Cambridge, Massachusetts, where I married Katharine Cram, and returned Sunday. The long delay of my getting from the staff of the Naval War College to the staff of CinCLant was very fine for me for personal reasons, as we had a nice place to live in Newport at the La Forge Cottages. However, the uncertainties of this period were rather unusual.

I was actually detached in December and turned over all my lecture assignments to other members of the staff and departed on a few days' leave to carry out orders to CinCLant staff, when Admiral Pye returned from his leave and directed that I be recalled till a relief was available on the War College grounds, which he had been promised by the Chief of Naval Personnel, Admiral

Jacobs. So, this did enable me to spend the next two months working on the review of the battle reports and helping with the corrections to the tables without any interruption with classes or lectures on my part.

Again, the departure was rather unusual for on the 15th of March the War College received a dispatch from the Chief of Naval Personnel, referring to his previous dispatch and saying "Hereby detached" and I was able to leave within that day -- I was detached that day.

Q: And your relief was on the grounds?

Adm. W.: No, he was still in the Pacific, but they made some informal arrangement that I was to get together with him at a later date for one day and turn over, which was quite unnecessary.

Q: Before you close this chapter, may I ask one other question that occurs to me? The student body was comprised of Army men as well as Navy -

Adm. W.: Army, Navy, Marine.

Q: How did the Army men in particular react to the fact that some of the material being presented to them predated World War II?

Adm. W.: I think some of them reacted the same way I did. They did not appreciate it too much. Especially they did not like the great many hours on that <u>Sound Military Decision</u>. That was very difficult for all of us.

Q: Do you know whether the same thing was occurring in the Army War College?

Adm. W.: At that time I believe it probably was, but I do not know. I'm sure it was because the Army War College was much slower getting up to date in those days than the Naval War College. From what I saw of the two back at the Army Industrial College in 1933 they were still working on what I would call nuts and bolts of logistics at that time. Then they got really going after the war and they developed something, but they had some splendid officers working on it. It takes time to develop a curriculum and to revise it with the changes in weapons that were developed during the war. We learned some things awfully fast, and we had to to survive.

Q: You tell me that during your period at the Naval War College you also went down to New York occasionally and delivered lectures to the Advanced Intelligence School, which was under the aegis of what? ONI?

Adm. W.: I can't tell you, honestly. I would think so. The Henry Hudson Hotel in New York was where they had their classes and their students.

Q: What sort of material did you present to them?

Adm. W.: One of them was the Battle of Midway, another was Guadalcanal amphibious operations, another was on naval intelligence, the strategical intelligence and operational intelligence. I believe those were probably the four subjects covered. I have no record of exactly which ones were there, except letters, but, generally speaking, they were the ones on the War College list that seemed to be of most interest to them. They picked them out. They had a list of all of our War College lectures and they picked out the ones they wanted.

Q: Did anything come out in these lectures about our prowess at that time in the field of communications?

Adm. W.: I'm sure that all of my lectures have something in them about communications because I felt that communications had been a bugbear since my early days as communication officer of the Memphis, communication officer of the Tutuila -- some of the messages do not get through.

Q: No, but I was thinking about our ability to read some of the Japanese codes and the basis for the success at Midway. Did this come into your lectures?

Adm. W.: Absolutely not. We would never have been permitted. If I'd known anything about it. I don't believe I knew anything about this Japanese code until after the war. I'd read things in magazines and newspapers and what not. But the Navy did a fantastic job of keeping that security, and that's why I like to mention the fact, as I mentioned it earlier, I had a Japanese typewriter -- I knew that much about it, I knew we were copying it, but I mean the development of it.

Q: I was thinking, in presenting the Battle of Midway, it almost seems requisite to present this aspect?

Adm. W.: Well, I presented the aspect of it that we had information, but how we got it was something else, and if they asked me I would say I do not know.

One of these came up the other day. A review of both Smith and Morison on the Battle of Midway, and the message that I mentioned in every one of my Midway lectures that I felt was a very important one during the war. On the 3rd of June when our patrol planes reported Japanese forces advancing from the southwest, and I believe the message may have said "Japanese main body." My recollection is that as soon as we got the message reporting this Japanese main body, we received a correction in the Benham over the voice circuit from Admiral Fletcher, "That is not the main body, that is the landing force. The main body is farther to the northwest." Both Morison and Admiral Smith give a different version of that same message, that is, as to its origin. I think it's reasonable to suppose now that Admiral Fletcher received his correction instantly from Admiral Nimitz, who received it through the code, or Admiral Fletcher already had the information from Admiral Nimitz where they were, and when this message came from this plane he immediately made the correction to his own forces.

I felt that was one of the most important decisions at Midway, to keep our people on the track and not let them get diverted by the approach from the southwest or by the approach from the Aleutians, I mean from the force up there.

I believe that covers that.

Q: Admiral, from your personal experience and knowledge of Admiral Pye, I wonder if you would give me a word picture of him as President of the War College, as the chief administrator there?

Adm. W.: Briefly, my observations of Admiral Pye as President of the Naval War College were all most favorable. I believe that he recognized soon after assuming the presidency that there was much to be done in the way of bringing courses geared to longer terms in peacetime to more realistic courses geared to the war operations with which all graduates were soon to be confronted afloat.

I know that he worked long hours at the College, in his office, writing, attempting personally to get some of his great knowledge of the problems of grand strategy in war and of fighting ships in the fleet indoctrinated into the courses as fast as it was practicable to do so. He insisted on bringing more officers from the fleet, Atlantic and Pacific and Mediterranean and Asiatic, to the College staff to obtain from them all possible new developments afloat, in order that graduates might be more familiar with the problems that were to confront them. One of his first tasks, which he took upon himself to do, was to read, write, and bring up to date the current edition of <u>Sound Military Decision</u>, particularly with respect to fleet directives.

Personally, I was delighted at the opportunity to work under Admiral Pye's guidance. I had tremendous respect for his ability. I had observed in the fleet his splendid performance as Commander, Battleships, in the big prewar fleet activities which we held, and also as Commander, Battle Force. In earlier tours of duty I remember his work as Commander, Destroyers, Pacific Fleet, and I have understood that one of the war plans instructions which was more or less the bible in the fleet for many years was a product of his brilliant mind.

Q: Well, you were detached from the Naval War College and your next duty was with Admiral Ingersoll, this long-delayed assignment on his staff in the Atlantic. You reported to him, according to the biography, in March 1944?

Adm. W.: I reported to Admiral Ingersoll the day following detachment from the Naval War College, and he greeted me with the words, "I thought I would be seeing you soon!" So, not knowing any of the background, I said, "What happened, admiral?" and he said, "Yesterday I met Admiral Denfeld in the Navy Department when I was visiting Admiral King and he inquired as to how you were doing on my staff. My reply was 'I have not seen him yet.'"

That brought forth the detachment!

The job that had been awaiting me and had been performed by others for some time was assistant operations officer on the staff of the commander-in-chief. This assignment involved writing the operation orders, almost always dispatch orders, to all combatant ships under the jurisdiction of the commander-in-chief, including cruisers, occasionally a battleship but not very often, destroyers, destroyer escorts. But most important of all the hunter/killer carrier task groups. This was the most exacting and important responsibility that I had ever encountered.

At that date we were engaged in the buildup for D Day in Normandy and pushing our forces across the Atlantic just as fast and as well protected as it was possible for us to do. The setup in the Vixen, flagship of the commander-in-chief was typical of Admiral Ingersoll's methods of operating. He had a very small staff close to him, and other members who could perform their functions ashore were so stationed. In this case, he had his chief of staff, his current operations officer, two assistant operations officers-- one for the amphibious forces and auxiliary forces, a communications officer, a small communications staff afloat, a Marine intelligence officer but, generally speaking, the intelligence was received from the commander-in-chief in Washington (Com Tenth Fleet). The supply officer, chaplain, medical officer, all had offices in Norfolk, where they could better perform their respective assignments.

Q: That was his land base, in Norfolk?

Adm. W.: His land base. I neglected to mention the most important of his staff afloat, in my opinion, and that was his materiel officer, whose desk was right adjacent to mine and we had instant communication as to availability of ships and the work to be done on them, and, in my opinion, this was of inestimable value in properly utilizing the forces afloat.

The Vixen moved from port to port along the Atlantic coast in order that the commander-in-chief could visit with his various commands, the operational command in Norfolk, the destroyer base in New London -- I mean in Casco Bay, the submarine command in New London, and see his subordinate commanders from time to time, confer with them and their problems personally.

Q: Was the Vixen set up as was a typical command ship in the Pacific later?

Adm. W.: The Vixen was in no sense a command ship, as such. The Vixen was a converted yacht of less than 4,000 tons but did have facilities, communications facilities, for transmitting afloat while at sea, if urgent, but excellent landwire communications which were available every stop the Vixen made except, possibly, Argentia and San Juan. She was a small ship and had small facilities, very crowded facilities for the staff. But in this way a larger ship that had been flagship of the commander-in-chief, Atlantic Fleet, the Augusta, was sent to Europe, where, the Admiral felt, her guns could be put to better advantage.

I might add that the visits to these various ports were a great help in my work because I had an opportunity to talk personally to the operations officers of the various type commands. In the case of New London, Captain Barchet first, and then Captain Dempsey was the operations officer for the Submarine Force. In Casco Bay, Captain Francis McCorkle was operations officer of the destroyers, and I had almost daily communication with the latter officer.

Let us look into the problem of supplying escorts, which was the vital part of CinCLant's responsibility to get troops and supplies across the Atlantic safely.

Q: These were convoy escorts?

Adm. W.: Convoy escorts. Convoys departed out of Boston, New York, Philadelphia, Norfolk, Charleston.

Q: What about Halifax?

Adm. W.: Halifax joined up at times and also farther south to

Aruba. I might state that these convoys were entirely the function of the chief of naval operations, the commander-in-chief, Admiral King, under his division of Convoy and Routing. The commander-in-chief issued all orders to the convoys through their respective sea frontiers, if necessary, but for forming up and departing their sections frequently joined off Norfolk for the trip across the Atlantic or off New York for that part of the Atlantic. The function of CinCLant was to see that each of these convoys had their proper escort from the Eastern Sea Frontier line -- actually, these convoys formed up off the entrances to the various harbors. Commander, Sea Frontier, had patrol planes and escorts for covering his area. It was a matter of tactical means how escorts joined them on deployment.

For example, a convoy would leave Norfolk for the European theater, in this case there might be 90 to 120 ships in the convoy -

Q: Merchant ships?

Adm. W.: Merchant ships -- and usually the troops were sent on faster ships. These convoys would be escorted with maybe 18 escorts but towards the end of that year we got down to about 9 for a convoy of 100 ships, which was very light escort under the conditions.

At the same time we used small groups along the coast - the coastal convoys were handled by the Commander, Eastern Sea Frontier, but when they got farther to sea, like to South America, then CinCLant had to step in. We had oil convoys from Aruba across to the Mediterranean and we had those convoys to cover on the escorts.

Q: When you had a convoy of 90 merchant ships, they would be strung out over how wide an area?

Adm. W.: Well, their front -- they tried to use columns -- I'd have to give you figures on that but there was probably 1,000 yards between columns and ten columns, so that's 10,000 yards wide, and the depth was less, but that's about it. They steamed in convoy columns and tried to get the depth reduced and the escort ahead as much as possible. We also had to have escorts trailing them because the German submarines would come to the surface and attack them from the rear.

In this particular year we were quite successful with our convoy escorts for two reasons. One was that this year of 1944 that I'm speaking of Admiral Ingersoll had eleven hunter/killer groups operating in the Atlantic. There might be two in port and the other nine at sea at the same time. They were placed not with the convoys but in support of the convoys so, generally speaking, you had one that could search ahead and get rid of the submarines that might be lurking in the way.

Q: Were they jeep carriers?

Adm. W.: CVE carriers. Several were converted tankers like the *Sangamon* class, the *Santee*, the *Bogue*, then we got into the *Guadalcanal* class.

As soon as CinCLant received notice of a submarine whose position was located by our land-based direction-finders which went in to ComInch, we would order the nearest CVE carrier group to attack and destroy. Then we looked for the second carrier, knowing their fuel condition and how many days they had left before they had to fuel somewhere, we would have a second CVE carrier group ready to take up the search if the submarine was not destroyed by the time the carrier had to leave the area. In one case, I remember, one of our carriers south was chasing a submarine toward South America and then to South Africa and was worried about the fuel situation. By the time he crossed the area of the Atlantic Fleet and then the South Atlantic Fleet, the carrier was turned over to her commander who chased the submarine on down -- he finally wound up in South Africa. He got the submarine. He was staying with it. He knew he could put in at some place, either South Africa or in the middle part of Africa to get fuel.

Q: What comprised one of these hunter/killer groups?

Adm. W.: Generally one of the larger antisubmarine carriers that had been converted from tanker hull and had tremendous fuel capacity. The escort consisted of a destroyer for flagship for the escort commander and four or five escorts.

Q: One carrier and the escorts?

Adm. W.: Yes. By this time we were getting destroyer escorts in and they were very good for antisubmarine warfare and, working with the carriers which could fuel the destroyer escorts, except those like the Guadalcanal (Kaiser class) did not have too much fuel capacity.

Q: Were the Canadian corvettes available to your command?

Adm. W.: My recollection is that we had very few of them available to us. They might escort something out of Halifax but when they joined up in the Atlantic, Canadian escorts returned to port.

The troopships we tried to send over at high speed. The "Queens" did a lot of troop-carrying because they could make 30 knots. That's really too high speed to do any escorting.

Q: They weren't escorted at all, were they?

Adm. W.: Only when Churchill was aboard or someone like that. That was a gesture because the escort could only take them partway into the Atlantic and then turn into Argentia or some place for fuel.

Q: Did the system prevail at that time wherein the convoys were escorted by the Atlantic Fleet to the chop line and then taken over by the British?

Adm. W.: All the orders issued to the convoys, in our case, to the escort commanders, were upon reaching the chop line to report to Commander, Naval Forces, Europe, who, in turn, might have them report to Commander-in-Chief, Mediterranean. The chop line was the end of CinCLant's responsibility.

Q: And where was that actually? Was it in midocean?

Adm. W.: Oh, much farther than that. No, it was north of the Azores. Roughly, I think, about 800 miles off the Irish coast. That was based really on getting it under the Coastal Air Command for search and British authority.

Q: This meant close coordination with the Royal Navy, then?

Adm. W.: Oh, yes. Every order issued by CinCLant to these escorts was "upon reaching the chop line, report to whoever was in command," whether it was Commander, Western Approaches, or farther down to CinCMed.

Q: Did you have cognizance over the convoys to Iceland and then on to Murmansk?

Adm. W.: Yes. That Iceland group was before my tour in CinCLantFlt, but I know CinCLant had the same situation of escorting them to, I think, Iceland. They changed that once or twice.

Q: What sort of arrangement did you have with Admiral Hoover down in San Juan?

Adm. W.: Admiral Hoover covered the search area. There was first Admiral Hoover and there was also Admiral Griffin down there, too. Admiral Griffin was commander in San Juan in 1944. When they got within his coastal area they were under his jurisdiction.

CinCLant was very careful about the ships being under the jurisdiction of the proper area commander, although I have known times when he intervened. One time one of these ships was ordered sunk; the destroyer put up a wonderful fight in the battle across the Atlantic. They kept afloat twenty-four hours and were only 400 miles from the British coast. We intercepted a dispatch to say "Sink damaged destroyer then proceed to port." We sent off as fast as we could a dispatch saying, "Do not want that ship sunk," with copy to ComInch. Well, the ship got to port. It was one of those cases of, we thought, acting too rashly, but, here, when a crew has fought for twenty-four hours to keep the ship afloat and is making good progress, not to give him a chance to make the rest of the journey was pretty bad for morale.

Q: There was a British command on Bermuda. How did that tie in with the situation?

Adm. W.: We had a British command down there and we also had an area command there. We had a training command down there and an air station. We had the responsibility for the searches from Bermuda. You see, we had leased bases there.

Q: What about the existence of German raiders in that year? Were there any in the Atlantic any more?

Adm. W.: I have no recollection of any German raiders in the Atlantic in 1944. They had them pretty well placed under control by that time.

One interesting episode of many in the Atlantic and I will not dwell on it very long because it's been pretty thoroughly written up, and that is the Guadalcanal capture of the S-505.

Q: By Commander Gallery?

Adm. W.: Yes. I think it's been thoroughly covered except perhaps from one angle, and this is my personal reaction from the position of CinCLant staff. When we received the message that he had the S-505 in tow and was at a point in the Atlantic almost equidistant from the Canary Islands, the West Coast of Africa, and Bermuda, it involved some problems because we had some information of other German submarines in the general area. And figuring it out that presumably the Guadalcanal had effectively deactivated the German submarine's torpedoes and of course its demolition charge, but at the same time one of the escorts had been damaged and had no effective sound gear, and, as I recall it, there were two other employable effective escorts, and this was quite a long journey. So we did what we could. We ordered a tanker and two escorts I believe from two other Atlantic convoys -- I know from one, from the westbound convoy -- and a fleet tug, and some type of tender, all to converge on the Guadalcanal, which was directed to proceed to Bermuda. That was made primarily for security reasons. We wanted to know what she had aboard and didn't want the knowledge of her capture divulged to anyone. Both CinCLant and ComInch put out immediate orders that no information was to be divulged. Actually, this succeeded. The tug took her in tow very shortly, in a day or two, and we had reinforced escorts. There were no untoward happenings and she made a safe arrival in Bermuda.

I remember CinCLant visited the submarine once later that summer, but the security was fantastic and the information obtained was fantastic. The Germans didn't realize it until long after.

Q: Would you tell me about the much-touted information that came out from ComInch daily on the location of German submarines in the Atlantic? This was a tremendous help, was it not?

Adm. W.: This was an inestimable help. The Germans reported their positions frequently at sea and our direction-finders ashore were able to zero in on them and report the positions of these various transmissions. They, in turn, were re-transmitted from ComInch's office in Washington to the forces afloat. They were extremely accurate, and generally CinCLant had enough killer groups available in 1944 to immediately get after them.

Q: This was something the Germans didn't suspect?

Adm. W.: I believe they were unaware that we were receiving -- similar to the Jap situation on the codes. I don't know why they didn't know, because we did some intercepting prior to that in World War I, I think. Some of the direction-finders worked, but they were not very good.

Q: Did the Germans themselves have a highly developed direction-finder system?

Adm. W.: They did for the defense of Germany and I'm sure they did afloat, but they were so insistent that their submarines report their positions back to the Admiralty. It happens so often.

Q: What was the reason back of this? Has that been divulged?

Adm. W.: I haven't seen anything, except that the Admiralty operated on that basis of knowing where their ships were and being able to give them orders regardless of whether they came up to receive. Those were their orders and they were slow to change, until too late. It was a very effective intelligence system.

Q: Were there any extremely interesting events that occurred during the time that you were associated with Ingersoll in the Atlantic?

Worthington #5 - 283

Adm. W.: One of them has already been pretty well described I think by Morison. One of the submarines had been depthcharged to the surface. The crew were trying to jump over and climb aboard, one of those that came up and wanted to surrender, and the crew of this destroyer resorted to mess cups to fight them off. They were not at all friendly toward them.

Q: They didn't want to receive them?

Adm. W.: They blew them up, after all the damage they'd done to other ships. I've forgotten what ship this was -- the Buckley was the destroyer involved. They had no interest in helping the Germans after all the Americans they had killed at sea.

Q: This period of duty covers the whole time when we were sending supplies over for the invasion of Normandy, which was the climax of the Atlantic effort, was it not? You have there a story, which is more or less a summary of the efforts of the Atlantic Fleet in this whole operation. I wonder if you would read it, with the date, into the tape?

Adm. W.: This is Atlantic Fleet press notice dated 17 June 1944 and I think it is of great importance for the fact that a press notice in the Atlantic Fleet in the entire year 1944 was a rarity:

> The following editorial which appeared in the Washington, D. C. Star of 15 June 1944 is quoted as being of interest

to the fleet.

"Since the start of the war in the Atlantic, the United States Navy has played a role not nearly so dramatic as that of the Pacific Fleet but its task has been nonetheless vital and difficult. The fact that our Allied troops are now battling their way forward in France can be credited to it in no small measure, for with its guns and air arm it made possible the safe arrival in England of the great American expeditionary force and the vast quantities of American equipment committed to defeating Hitler in Western Europe. Probably the best way to measure the achievement is to recall how terrible the U-boat menace once was and to relate to this the fact that since January 1942 up until D Day, the hard-working and valiant Atlantic Fleet convoyed a total of 7,000 vessels, only ten of which were lost to the enemy and not one of them a troop ship. The record speaks for itself. To the officers and men of the fleet and to Admiral Ingersoll, their Commander-in-Chief, who has been in Washington recently, the whole nation has reason to say thank you and well done."

Q: You said that it was a rarity to have any press notice on the actions of the Atlantic Fleet. Was this a set policy?

Adm. W.: I feel sure it was a policy of the commander-in-chief. He felt the place for press releases was with the commander-in-chief in Washington and not commander-in-chief, Atlantic -- that is my belief of how Admiral Ingersoll felt. I'm sure Admiral King would have had no objection to anything that Ingersoll might release.

To continue: After the D Day operation and things had somewhat quieted down in the Atlantic, although our hunter/killer groups were still operating at full strength, the Vixen made a cruise north to the various bases that have been mentioned earlier, New London, Hampton Roads -- no, correction, New London, Newport, Boston, Casco Bay, Portsmouth, and Argentia. This was the desire of the Admiral to be familiar with the present situation at the various bases and, while in Argentia, met one of our hunter/killer groups commanded by then Captain A. B. Vosseler.

Proceeding south, the Vixen stopped in Norfolk, then on to Bermuda, visited Trujillo Ciudad, and the commander-in-chief and his staff were entertained by that great dictator, infamous dictator, I should say. Then on through the various islands in the Caribbean to Trinidad, where Admiral Ingersoll received orders to fly to Washington for a conference with Admiral King.

No one there had any inkling of this meeting or what would happen next. The Vixen continued her cruise under the chief of staff, Rear Admiral W. K. Kilpatrick, and visited Aruba, then started her journey back north to Hampton Roads and Washington.

In Washington -- one little item before the last visit to Washington, a happening in the hurricane of 13 September was distressing to all. The destroyer <u>Warrenton</u> escorting the beef-boat <u>Hyades</u> foundered off the Bahamas, losing all but 66 of her gallant crew. The lesson to be learned from this tragedy was that hurricane area weather reports must be sent afloat from a single coordinating station, and after this the Weather Central in Norfolk was established. The tragedy is partly attributed to the conflicting nature of weather reports received by the <u>Warrenton</u> in the vicinity of the Bahamas at that time.

After arrival in the United States, we learned of Admiral Ingersoll's prospective detachment. I was privileged to witness this ceremony in Admiral King's office in Washington. Without dwelling at length on this, I would like to comment on this rather unusual ceremony. Admiral King issued orders to Admiral Ingersoll which I have never seen before or since, and I believe these should be appended hereto. Prior to the presentation, Forrestal introduced my good friend Hanson W. Baldwin as the Navy's best friend and severest critic. When Admiral Ingersoll thanked Secretary Forrestal for these orders and the responsibility they vested in him, Forrestal replied, "I would not have issued such orders to anyone else."

Q: And what were they?

Adm. W.: The orders were:

Worthington #5 - 287

8 November 1944

From: Secretary of the Navy.

To   :   Commander Western Sea Frontier.

Via :   Commander in Chief, United States Fleet and

            Chief of Naval Operations.

Subject: Functions of Commander Western Sea Frontier.

Reference: (a) General Order No. 174 of 2 June 1942.

            (b) SecNav ltr. Op-OEB-MD, Serial 26102 of 12

            Feb. 1944.

    1. Upon the assumption of the duties of Commander Western Sea Frontier by Admiral R. E. Ingersoll, U. S. Navy, about 15 November 1944, the duties of that officer are hereby enlarged in order to afford more effective support for United States Forces in the Pacific Theater. They shall comprise:-

    (a) those set forth in reference (a) and elsewhere relating to Commanders of Sea Frontiers;

    (b) the control and coordination of all naval activities and functions on the Pacific Coast, including the 11th, 12th and 13th Naval Districts. To this end

        (1) the Commandants of the 11th, 12th and 13th Naval Districts will be directed to report to the Commander Western Sea Frontier.

        (2) all agencies of the Navy Department (including Marine Corps and Coast Guard) located and operating within the 11th, 12th and 13th Naval Districts, but not assigned to those districts, will be directed to report to the Commander Western Sea Frontier.

        (3) Reference (b) is hereby cancelled and the appropriate duties and personnel are accordingly transferred to the Commander Western Sea Frontier.

    (c) the performance of such duties as the Commander in Chief, Pacific Fleet, and Pacific Ocean Areas may direct.

    2. In carrying out the duties herein prescribed, the Commander Western Sea Frontier will have the status of a Deputy Commander in Chief, United States Fleet, and Deputy Chief of Naval Operations.

3. Commander Western Sea Frontier will report to Commander in Chief, Pacific Fleet, and Pacific Ocean Areas, for duties as set forth in paragraph 1 (c) above.

4. Subject to such instructions as may be received from the Commander in Chief, United States Fleet, and Chief of Naval Operations, the Commander Western Sea Frontier has authority to place existing agencies of the Navy Department (within the limits of the 11th, 12th and 13th Naval Districts) in the organization of the Western Sea Frontier as may be best suited for the performance of the duties set forth in paragraph 1 above. He is accorded discretion as to when this shall be done in the development of the organization.

5. All provisions of the Navy Regulations, Bureau manuals, etc., which are in conflict with the foregoing are hereby placed in abeyance.

(Signed) Forrestal

Interview No. 6 with Rear Admiral Joseph M. Worthington,

U. S. Navy (Retired)

Place: His residence on Gibson Island, Maryland

Date: Wednesday morning, 19 July 1972

Subject: Biography

By: John T. Mason, Jr.

Q: Well, as usual, it's good to see you this morning, Admiral. I believe that you're going to begin by giving me a word portrait of Admiral Ingersoll, with whom you worked on so many occasions and with whom you've maintained a very close friendship through the years. Would you go ahead, Sir?

Adm. W.: My observations of this brilliant, modest, and great naval commander are made in the sincere hope that future naval officers find inspiration and encouragement in studying the character of Admiral Royal Eason Ingersoll. Previously in commenting on Admiral Ingersoll, I wrote as follows:

> As an ensign on the Nokomis "no one could have been finer to serve under than Captain Ingersoll. He had all the fine qualities that our Naval Academy textbooks spelled out for a great naval commander and, in addition, that wonderful qualification of modesty, and with it all a

deep friendliness to younger officers which was a real inspiration."

Q: Admiral, I hope you're going to spell out what these wonderful characteristics are that the Naval Academy textbooks relate?

Adm. W.: I will attempt to do so after these many years -- leadership, understanding, confidence, familiarity with the problems of the Navy, the ship, and the individual, courage, quietness and steadiness in emergencies are some of them. While aide and flag secretary to Commander, Cruiser Division Six, in the <u>Minneapolis</u> "while operating at sea, the Admiral had extremely long hours on the flag bridge or in the flag plot and what little rest or sleep he could get was in the emergency cabin. Under the Admiral's magnificent leadership, all of us tried to do our level best at all times. It was such a privilege to work for him, we performed our duties as a closely knit team."

After his detachment, "I never expect to meet a finer naval officer than Admiral Ingersoll."

Another quote: "I can assure you that the Navy is in splendid hands with Stark and he could find no better advisor than Ingersoll. I sincerely hope the President and the new Secretary of the Navy will take Ingersoll's advice. He is the genius the country needs right now. There is no time for amateurs."

And quote again: "He is the most unassuming and informal

soul I've ever known. I surely wish him well in Washington with a tremendous task before him. I miss Admiral Ingersoll a great deal and his family. He's one in a million. I shall always be truly thankful for my cruises with him. I am constantly told how much Admiral Ingersoll is missed and also of the magnificent way he commanded the heavy cruisers out here in Hawaii."

And now from his successor, Commander, Cruisers, Hawaiian Detachment, Rear Admiral John Henry Newton:

"I am delighted to see Admiral Ingersoll sent where he is needed (Assistant Chief of Naval Operations). Any admiral can handle a cruiser division."

As assistant operations officer, staff of CinCLant:

"Admiral Ingersoll was a marvelous commander under whom I've served twice previously. His small but highly competent staff do the most perfect teamwork and cooperation within his staff."

I've had the very great privilege of serving under the command of many fine and great naval officers, some of whom I've known very well. I truly believe that Admiral Ingersoll is the finest of all and the greatest naval officer our Navy ever produced.

Q: Admiral, I wonder if you would mind thinking up some illustrations of some of these points? Your laudatory remarks are very good, but the historian would want some specific incidents which illustrate his leadership and his ability to command this kind of love and respect from his men. Can you think of anything that would do this?

Adm. W.: Well, as captain of the survey ship <u>Nokomis</u> operating off the north coast of Cuba -- operating independently, I might say, he took a personal interest I believe in every officer and man in his crew. He knew them. He made a point of calling them by name, of asking after their welfare, of seeing that they were properly taken care of.

I observed him when he was in command of the cruiser <u>San Francisco</u>, which he placed in commission as commanding officer, and he said "Take a stroll around the ship," and we did just that, from the top to the bottom of that ship, up in the fire-control foremast, down in the hull, and in every place we went practically he called the officer or man in that area by name. He made a point of knowing them. He made a point of knowing what was happening in his ship, and, when I mentioned this in this particular ship, he said -- and I was thanking him for showing me this big ship -- and he said, "Oh, I make this inspection every day. It's part of my job."

When he was commander of the cruiser division, the cruisers in the Hawaiian Detachment, everybody admired the way he handled the division in tactics and knew what was going on in each of his ships. I will give an example of this.

We were having a rather difficult gunnery practice called a duel and two of the cruisers were firing this offset. It was quite an elaborate practice, and I had worked as his gunnery operations officer to lay it out. The camera people -- the ships had cameras in certain places, the planes were towing targets in certain places and photographic planes. An hour before we put to sea to start this practice, the captain of the Astoria sent his communication officer over and said, "I want you to explain to the Admiral that this practice is unfair to my ship and should not be fired this way." So I took this officer in to see the Admiral and I told him what the problem was and what the protest was, which he repeated, and he looked over the chart I had and I said, "Admiral, ships have to fire in certain directions, the cameras can't take the pictures in the sun -- or they couldn't in those days -- and this is the only way you can possibly fire this practice at this time with the sun where it is." He looked at the situation and analyzed it. His mind is brilliant. He came back and said, "Tell Captain Turner that the practice will be fired as ordered." That's all there was to it.

But to know enough of these things when we were having fast maneuvers, sometimes a little too fast to get your maneuvering board worked out, he could take his cruiser division into position by eye. He never criticized his staff. We made a mistake here and there but he said, "I believe I would have done it this way." He put tremendous faith in his staff. We would want to send something, say, this ship or that ship was doing poorly, and he'd say, "I believe that captain knows what he's doing." It was that type of leadership, understanding other people and not interfering. One of his remarks to me was, shortly after he hoisted his flag, "You know the hardest thing for the admiral to do is to keep out of the hair of the captain of the flagship." And he did just that. He stayed in his cabin, his staff worked out the details, and the mail was brought up. He would not fool with any mail at sea, unless it was some urgent letter. But when he was in port at a convenient time and after I'd had time to go over everything and bring it up to him, he'd look it over.

But he used his staff to the fullest. He used his captains to the fullest amount. He was thinking of bigger problems. He was thinking ahead, of war plans, and things like that.

Q: As you reflect on it, you served with him when he was still a captain and later on when he was in command of a fleet, did you see any gradual transformation in the man? Did he grow in wisdom?

Adm. W.: Well, he was a commander at the time he was captain of the Nokomis and I always felt then that his mind was working way ahead of his time in the field of captain's or admiral's duties and responsibilities. He was a great reader. He had his hobbies, which he used to divert himself from his current problems, and his mind was clear when they came up. But I never saw that his mind wasn't ahead of his time, or ahead of his job -- that was my impression. Besides developing methods in the surveying of Cuba and with the cruisers, he was thinking about how to better use cruisers. He didn't think we should have planes on cruisers. He thought that there should be small jeep carriers. We didn't have any under construction then. That was one of the things. A cruiser was no place for planes.

And he was always thinking of the logistic problems of a cruiser in the fleet. As soon as we went to Hawaii the first thing he did was to dig into the problems of that base and what they could supply and how they could be developed to supply a much greater outfit.

He interchanged personal letters with a great many people. I never saw them but I know from the gist of things that they were talking about future plans. You see, he had served in the Office of Naval Intelligence, in the Division of Fleet Training, and as Director of War Plans, and later as Assistant Chief of Naval Operations. All of that was thinking of the future and basically if war would come against Japan. I thought at the time that it was unfortunate he could not have had the Pacific assignment because of all of his years in that work, whereas the Atlantic was entirely different, just as important a job and it had to be done, but King had the Atlantic job, and knew what it was, and he knew who he could get to do it.

I could go on a lot on this but I don't know how much is appropriate.

Q: Well, you spoke about another illustration, which I think is a very good one. It had to do with the Torch operation. Would you repeat it, Sir?

Adm. W.: Yes. The commander-in-chief, Admiral King, issued a rather complete operation order for the invasion of North Africa, known as the Torch operation. The Commander-in-Chief, Atlantic Fleet, having received this order, stated that it covered what was necessary from the point of view of the commander-in-chief and issued merely a letter of instructions to Admiral Hewitt and from that combination of the commander-in-chief's order and the Commander-in-Chief, Atlantic Fleet's letter of instructions, Admiral Hewitt drew up his complete plan for the invasion of North Africa. Admiral Ingersoll was not going to put anything more into the paper work than was necessary to ensure the success of it, and this letter would largely pertain to crossing the Atlantic safely.

Does that cover it?

Q: Yes. Well, now, shall we go on. In January of 1945 -- January 15, as a matter of fact, you took up your duties as Commander of Destroyer Squadron 57 in Alaskan waters.

Adm. W.: I assumed these duties in Dutch Harbor. In this squadron were Rowe, flagship, and also Smalley, Stoddard, Watts, and Wren in DesDiv 113. Bearss, flagship, John Hood, Jervis, and Porter comprising DesDiv 114.

Shortly after relieving Captain Stewart of Destroyer Squadron 57, I shifted the flag to the relief flagship Watts in order that the Rowe could proceed to Pearl Harbor for additional antisubmarine training, which was not available in the Aleutian area. I reported further to Rear Admiral John McCrea, Commander, Cruiser Division 2 and Task Force 92, and to Vice Admiral Frank Jack Fletcher, Commander, North Pacific Force.

Shortly thereafter, this task force proceeded westward, stopping off in Adak for additional fuel and supplies, and went on their first bombardment mission on 9 February -- sortied for extensive sweep of the Kurile Islands and bombarded Matsuwa Island.

Q: Was this the overall purpose of the fleet being in this area, to carry on bombardment?

Adm. W.: To carry on periodic raids of the Japanese installations in the Kurile Islands and, of course, defend that approach, should the Japanese make another approach via the Aleutians.

Q: Was there any thought of them doing this?

Adm. W.: Not at this late date. They'd already been driven back. We'd captured Attu, but they made an earlier start there, and this was just to put more pressure on the Japanese from the north. The force was only a small force. It was an old light cruiser division and a squadron of destroyers, and our planes were merely for search purposes, the planes that we had up there.

Q: You had no carriers with you?

Adm. W.: No carriers.

On 9 February sortied for the offensive sweep of the Kurile Islands and bombardment of Matsuwa Island. Made a night approach on 11 February to bombardment position, enemy radar was encountered and searchlights were seen on the horizon, distance 24 miles. H hour was first postponed, then canceled, due to the early disclosure of our forces and the heavy seas building up in the area.

I might add that this operation of night bombardment in a hostile territory with no air protection necessitated that we run in at high speed after dark, conduct the bombardment, and then make a high-speed withdrawal. If the seas became heavy, our withdrawal was slowed down and there was greater danger of the Japanese land-based planes overtaking us. So it was a hit-and-run affair all the way through.

Q: Did you have excellent navigational charts of that area? It seems to have been rather dangerous.

Adm. W.: We had good charts and we had good gunnery plots for these night bombardments of shore installations and airfields and some fortifications.

Q: You had specific targets, then?

Adm. W.: Oh, yes, we had good targets charted -- you might say grids -- and these bombardments were made on these grids and radar plots.

Q: How did you come by the information on the location of these targets? Was this intelligence?

Adm. W.: This was our intelligence, which had been built up for several years, and the intelligence was furnished us by Commander, North Pacific Force, whose base at this time was in Adak. Previously, he'd been at Anchorage, at this time he was shore-based at Adak.

On 16 February, the ships sortied for a sweep of the Kuriles to bombard Kurabu Saki, on the southern end of Paramushiro Island. Approached bombardment area in calm seas through frequent snow squalls and, after firing 4,214 rounds of antiaircraft common ammunition commenced retirement.

Shortly after midnight, 19 February, enemy plane formation in two groups was detected on radar on approaching course. No attack was made on this force, which entered Massacre Bay on the 20th.

Q: Would you mind telling me about the base at Adak at that time?

Adm. W.: There were two bases. The base at Adak had been built up for the operations of a fairly good-sized force and they had, at that time, stores and anchorage, but storms rather frequently interfered with our operations and we had to put to sea, but we had buoys and we had some docks. But we were always concerned that ships at a dock would have to get under way in a hurry when these storms came up.

Q: Were these the williwaws?

Adm. W.: The williwaws. In my squadron I had issued permanent orders for ships to get up steam and have boiler power based on the wind. As the barometer dropped, the winds came up and we were getting up more power ready to proceed. If the winds got up to 30 knots any captain was authorized to put to sea without any further instructions. In some cases, if a ship was moored to a buoy it would prefer to steam to the buoy. My flagship did that once or twice, with full boiler power ready it steamed to a buoy during the storm.

Q: Tell me what sort of warning did you have when one was coming and what was its strength?

Adm. W.: A 5- or 10-knot wind would get up to 30 knots, maybe, in half an hour and from directions which you could not forecast. They were certainly the worst storms that I have ever been in, at least the most exasperating ones, because a typhoon and a hurricane you can generally forecast and generally avoid. With the williwaws you've got to get ready to move -- you can watch it on the barometer. The barometer will go down.

Q: Are they cyclones?

Adm. W.: Yes. You can see it. The barometer will go down and it will go down so quickly. It's the only place I've ever been in my life where you can actually see the barometer move, just look at it and see it go down.

Q: It's cyclonic in nature?

Adm. W.: Yes, it's cyclonic in nature. To me they're terrible things! The wind comes in sudden cold gusts from the north.

Q: How long does one last?

Adm. W.: Maybe 12 hours, 24 hours. Not long. But it's the suddenness of picking up and their intensity.

Q: Is there a great deal of rain with them?

Adm. W.: Not necessarily.

Q: It's largely wind?

Adm. W.: Largely wind, but the seas build up, of course, tremendously. It's a very nasty storm to work with, particularly in destroyers. Even the ships we had tied up to the docks, we were very much concerned that they would not be able to get away without damage to the docks, but those that stayed were able to get cordage from the Army doubled up on moorings and stayed successfully.

The more advanced base was Attu, and we had space there for getting fuel and ammunition, and anchorage, and mooring buoys. That was much closer to the enemy. But generally we operated from, first from Adak as our rear base, and then on to Attu where we filled up before going on to the raids. But there was a lot of ice and snow there all winter, and that was very uncomfortable.

Q: What about fog?

Adm. W.: Not so much in winter. Fog is in the other seasons. During my several months there that winter we did not encounter very much fog. I'd like to go into this weather business a little bit more because it's something we got into in the next raid and the one after.

On 2 March DesRon 57 ships got under way for training exercises. On 8 March sortied from Adak and arrived Massacre Bay the next day. On 14 March this task force sortied from Massacre Bay to make a sweep of the Kurile Islands and bombard Matsuwa Island. Made approach in a calm sea undetected and shortly after midnight conducted bombardment. Returned to Massacre Bay.

The following week, 20 March, ComDesRon 57 and Commander, Task Force 92.2 in Rowe with ComDesDiv 114 in Porter, Smalley, Wren, John Hood and Stoddard sortied from Massacre Bay for an offensive sweep and bombardment of Surabachi Wan area, Paramushiro Island.

Rather than go into this, I will describe this operation.

Worthington #6 - 303

Q: Yes, that's better because some of these details are in the operational reports and there's no sense in repeating that.

Adm. W.: In this case, this was the first opportunity I had had of making an independent sortie for an offensive operation against the enemy, and everything seemed to be going to perfection. Visibility was unlimited in the afternoon, which was unusual up there, and about four o'clock in the afternoon I ordered the squadron to take antiaircraft disposition because the only danger there was enemy aircraft. This was a circle disposition antiaircraft and increased speed to 25 knots. The next order was that bombardment will be conducted as scheduled at 2200. Within the hour we started to observe flickers on the water and I thought there were some cans thrown overboard but you didn't know what ships up in that area were throwing them. As we got closer, at 25 knots you're moving pretty well, these flickers got bigger and bigger and we noticed that they were chips of ice and no ice was indicated in our weather reports and meteorologists said no ice fields had been seen in this area for thirty years. But within an hour we were in icefields. By that time I was saying "How do I get out?" And I ordered just one signal, two signals: one, follow the motions of the flagship, and two, slow speed to 15 knots, then 10 knots.

In roughly an hour and a half we snaked our way through between -- I still call them fields, but they projected above the water maybe four to six feet, which meant a pretty good size amount of ice below the water. And just by Providence we were able to get out. I tried first going to southward and then got into worse fields. I couldn't go westward because it was all fields, and I finally got out by snaking around to the north and to the east.

Q: What sea was this? The Bering Sea?

Adm. W.: Yes, the Bering Sea, because Paramushiro Island was on the edge of it. But we were first thankful to get out of the icefields, and second safely without damaging the ships, the propellers or anything else. We were tremendously disappointed at not being able to fulfill our first independent mission.

Q: Did you have any specific knowledge about icefields and how one operates in icefields? Had this been a part of your background?

Adm. W.: None whatever.

Incidentally, I missed one part of this episode. We had two planes, long-range planes, scouting ahead and they reported visually, steamed by us on their return to base, "Everything clear for night bombardment." The next day or two days later when we returned to port at Adak, I reported to Admiral McCrea and he was naturally quite shocked. He'd sent out a bomabardment mission and no bombardment. So when I explained the situation to him he was completely aghast, so was Admiral Fletcher. Fletcher immediately sent out photographic planes. I have some quite interesting pictures of those ice floes. The planes reported that the floes extended for 200 miles from that coast, way south. There was no place our ships could have gotten anywhere near it.

There was a lesson learned, but learned the hard way.

Q: These ice floes appeared rather suddenly, did they?

Adm. W.: No one had ever reported them. As I say, they were many miles south of where the meteorologists figured them to be. No one has ever explained to me how they got there that year, but they were there and I have the photographs to prove it. The meteorologists missed out on this forecast.

Q: It does point up the lack of knowledge that the Navy had about ice and ice conditions and how to operate in ice conditions?

Adm. W.: We learned a lot about that, and that's why we had a lot of this south pole work after the war. One of the skippers of this squadron, E. A. MacDonald, who commanded a South Pacific expedition to the south pole -- he was one of the skippers of these ships and that's where he saw his first ice, I think.

I believe we've covered enough on the ice episode and returning to Attu and Massacre Bay first, of course, and then Kulak Bay, Adak.

Early in April we received orders to prepare for an expected

Worthington #6 - 306

sortie of the battleship Yamato. So the cruiser division -- these ancient light cruisers -- and the destroyer squadron drilled at sea quite a bit in preparation for intercepting the Yamato, should she head east. Intelligence reports indicated she was sailing but we did not know whether she would head south for Okinawa or head east. There was a very strong indication she would head east for San Francisco in the hopes of making a raid on the United Nations Conference that was just opening up for the President.

Q: With her 18-inch guns!

Adm. W.: With her 18-inch guns. The other force to intercept was the Bonhomme Richard and her small destroyer screen operating out of Hawaii.

This was an interesting operation and training. As you might have gathered, it seemed rather futile for these ships to try to stop the Yamato with her 18-inch guns and her 6-inch batteries, but we did train for it and we used the squadron which I took out several more times for drilling division torpedo attacks, what we called the three-point attack that I'd learned under Admiral Conolly. Also it was similar to the game-board problem we'd worked at the War College with the cruiser Graf Spee and the British cruisers Achilles, Exeter, and Ajax, who were able to get in and knock out the Graf Spee by the three-point attack. As I say, we drilled faithfully on that and then the Yamato headed for Okinawa and was sunk by our carrier air and also our submarines got in on the act. My division of the squadron, that is, DesDiv 113, of five ships was ordered to Hawaii. We had lost quite a number of men and destroyers at Okinawa and DesDiv 113 was sent to replace some of the ships that had been sunk. I believe by that time more than five destroyers had been sunk at Okinawa and our people were very much conerned about it.

We proceeded independently to Hawaii, had some excellent drill on the way, because every night I had a surprise firing, and had one of the ships fire star shells or turn loose balloons for target, and all the ships were supposed to take it under fire without any further orders, which meant that all the condition 2 watches had a chance to control the guns. So we were pretty well drilled in antiaircraft fire on the way to Hawaii.

Q: May I interrupt and ask a question about the Yamato?

Adm. W.: Yes.

Q: In the postwar period when Japanese records were discovered, was there any indication that she had contemplated going to the U. S. coast?

Adm. W.: Not as far as I know. I don't know. I never heard anything more about it. I never looked up the Yamato after that. But I assume we had fairly good intelligence information. It would seem that they wouldn't have conducted this preparation had they not had that information.

Q: Her demise was something of a suicide venture in itself, wasn't it?

Adm. W.: Yes, but we were sinking their ships with our air bombardment in Japan. I'll have more about this later on when we get to operating off Japan when many of her ships were knocked out by our planes.

11 May sortied Pearl Harbor screening the Ticonderoga en route to Ulithi. Rear Admiral C. A. F. Sprague commanded Carrier Division 2 and the task group, and was embarked in the Ticonderoga.

On 17 May the air group made a strike on Taroa Island, Maloelap Atoll in the Marshall Islands group.

Q: What was the island again?

Adm. W.: Taroa Island, Maloelap Atoll. One torpedo-bomber was ditched and the crew of three picked up unhurt, one each by the Stoddard, Rowe, and Smalley as their parachutes hit the water.

I insert this notation with particular interest because I have never seen a more beautiful performance by three ships rescuing a parachuting crew with no loss of minutes. You know, a falling parachute is hard to stop a destroyer right alongside, and these three captains did it beautifully and they had a trained swimmer in each one of them to swim out with a line to the crew member they were rescuing.

Q: This indicates a very great concern on the part of our fleet for the rescue of flyers who were down?

Adm. W.: Oh, there's no question about it. We did all kinds of things. We did it on the day of Pearl Harbor and well before Pearl Harbor in training, and that's what my first destroyer did a great deal of. Of course, we didn't have much of this in the Aleutians because the water was too cold for anybody to stay alive in and we didn't have many planes up there. We made every effort everywhere to save personnel. If we lost the plane that was one thing, but don't lose any personnel.

On 20 May DesDiv 114 -- that's the other division of my squadron, bombarded Suribachi Wan, Paramashiro To; they were still in business up there. This task unit was dissolved at Ulithi, and Commander DesRon 57 in Rowe, Stoddard, Smalley, Watts, and Wren reported to Commander, Fifth Fleet, Commander Task Force 51.

Q: This was Admiral Spruance?

Adm. W.: Admiral Spruance -- Admiral Hill didn't come in till later, I think. Admiral Turner was still Amphibious Commander. He was relieved about this time. Hill was there when we got to Okinawa. To show the ships were in action pretty quick, on the 24th of May the Watts shot down one Rufe-type enemy plane while on picket station off Okinawa.

I don't want to give the details of all these picket stations, but the five ships of DesRon 57 and DesDiv 113 were assigned to picket stations continuously from the day they reported until things were almost over when we departed on the 16th of June. They changed the assignments somewhat in order that a squadron commander or a division commander would have on picket station at least one fighter-director destroyer. So when the Rowe went out I would have command of the group on picket station and would have assigned to me a newer type destroyer with a fighter-director, like the Frank Knox, the Benner, and the Lowry, and normally we had four destroyers augmented by four landing ships, small, or gunfire-support ships, which, although slow, were very useful.

Upon arrival at Okinawa, I reported to Commodore Moosbrugger and also to Rear Admiral Hill, who was just assuming command of the Fifth Fleet amphibious forces off Okinawa. He'd just relieved Turner.

During the night of 24-25 May Wren in company with Cowell and Ingersoll destroyed from 1 to 14 Japanese boats, shot down 4 Japanese planes while on way to Picket Station No. 16. They caught these boats at their source.

Q: What were they? Speed boats?

Adm. W.: Yes, those suicide speed boats like the kamikaze planes. They made a killing that night.

Q: Tell me about that picket station. How far off the island were you stationed? This was an outpost?

Adm. W.: They varied and I do not have here, I've been trying to find one for you, a map of those picket stations. They're generally in any of the plans on Okinawa but I haven't been able to find one. They varied. There were some close in -- when I say "close in," maybe fifteen miles and there were some out thirty or forty miles. They were placed with a view to Admiral Spruance's original plan for Okinawa, which was to have pickets -- originally there was supposed to be one destroyer, but when the Japanese kamikazes started knocking off the one destroyer they increased the number to four and then the gun ships helped. But they were placed in certain directions. It's hard to describe this, but then basically there were some stations in all directions around Okinawa. I had stations both northwest, northeast, and west, I remember distinctly. They placed us on the directions in which they expected the planes might be coming in. They knew where the Japanese bases were, their plane bases for the suicide planes. Also in order to be close enough to help protect their anchorage.

I believe I mentioned before that there was great use of smoke in this organization at Kerama Retto, my fueling area, and at Hagushi Anchorage itself, and when an attack was coming on they just turned loose these smoke pots and the place was just completely smoked in. I think that was very effective.

Q: But the results were a hindrance to the picket ships, weren't they?

Adm. W.: They were far out. They were way beyond, and the smoke was in close. The picket ships did not make smoke, as far as I know they did not. We were prepared to but we wanted to see the planes to shoot.

Q: Exactly.

Adm. W.: And we also -- these radar picket stations had fighter planes under their control and for a while they based on, I think, Yontan airfield -- Marine fighter planes. The minute we got reports of planes coming in, we'd call fighters out to help us.

Q: They were land-based?

Adm. W.: Land-based, and they did an excellent job.

Q: You didn't have jeep carriers with any of the picket units?

Adm. W.: No, not with the pickets at all. They had a separate function. They had the function of furnishing air support to the transports in the area, in the base, but they were not on picket station. They were kept farther away, or rather in a different direction.

One example of how assignments were shifted around. ComDes 57 was directed by Commodore Moosbrugger to take charge of the antiaircraft and defensive screen off transport area at Hagushi with the following units, nine destroyers. In other words, he assigned any squadron commander or division commander in all the groups there to these specific jobs, and they might last a few hours or many hours.

Q: That was a very flexible situation?

Adm. W.: Flexible. What he did in this case was to take my picket station group plus another group that was, I guess, coming in and put them on this job because you want everybody in the antiaircraft screen. This was in the daytime, right off the transports, and a supply ship was still unloading. There were not many transports there.

On June 4 Stoddard patrolling off Picket Station 9, Smalley 11, Rowe with Lowry and Guest on No. 5. Lowry was made fighter-direction ship for this station.

Shortly after relieving ComDesRon 45, the senior officer at the picket station No. 5, all units were directed to report to Com Group 31.19 for escort duty in connection with typhoon plans. This was a rather interesting assignment. Taking a group off the picket station, dash off to the entrance of Buckner Bay, and escort all the ships departing to safety from the typhoon, having no idea what ships were there, no idea who was departing, and arriving after dark, the only thing I could do was to arrive off the entrance, set course east, speed 15, and tell all ships to report to the convoy commander whoever it was -- there was a battleship commander mixed up in it and there was a convoy commander mixed up in it. Actually, we did just that, head east, because the only thing I was concerned about was to get the ships clear of land.

Q: Did you have weather information on this typhoon? Did you know about it?

Adm. W.: It was coming toward Okinawa, but you never know which way they're going to curve. We knew the rate it was coming toward Okinawa, and the only time element I had was to get them off shore as quickly as possible, and I did just that. By that night, on the radar screen I counted the number of ships, so I knew the number of ships actually following to sea. About midnight or after midnight the convoy consisted of convoy commodore and seven big transports.

So we steamed east and west. What we actually did after midnight the high command ashore gave us word that the typhoon had turned and the ships could return to port.

Q: These transports were loaded with troops?

Adm. W.: In the process of unloading, whether they were loaded or unloaded I don't know. They were all anchored in the big Buckner Bay area and they had a convoy commodore. But I never found out till later who the ships were we were escorting or what they were supposed to be. At any rate, the next day we were ordered to cease and return to picket station.

Q: Did other ships take your place on picket station?

Adm. W.: No, there wasn't anybody. In this case, they were trying to save the ships in port. You see, they had no screen for them, so they had to sacrifice the group on station 5. We must have left the small craft there, LCSs, four of those, which wasn't very good for them but they had to furnish some adequate screen for the convoy.

That bay was Nakagusuku, later named Buckner Bay.

I believe I should describe here the system used in patrolling the picket stations, at least the one that I used. You've got the problem of fast destroyers and slow support ships. You keep your destroyers steaming at too slow a speed and you just cannot get them up to speed desired fast enough, so the system we outlined, and I know one of the squadron commanders at least used it, was to direct the small ships to steam in column at right angles to the angle of expected attack of the Japanese planes coming in. In that way they had their maximum armament, rockets and machine guns and 40-mm., bearing on the low-flying planes, which they tried to do. They steamed back and forth past this point to the end of the picket station at 12 knots. The destroyer group, four destroyers, took station parallel to the pickets and timed to pass the center point of the station a mile or two miles away at the same time the small ships were steaming destroyers at 15 knots, or 18 knots. They overlapped the pickets. In that way, they were able to keep at higher speed and, at the same time, furnished mutual support with their bigger guns for the small ships.

This worked out pretty well because the small ships got the low-flying planes and as soon as the destroyers could get into position they were over them with their bigger guns, and when we got to high speed during the attack the planes were going after the destroyers, not the small ships -- so if they increased speed beyond that, 25 or 30 knots, they had a clear run to fire. We also had the small ships sort of protecting the rear flanks.

In the one attack that we actually had there it proved effective. On 7 June my picket group came under attack by two Vals. Both were shot down and no casualties suffered by our ships. We were again right off picket station No. 5. In this particular case, we got up speed by voice signal, increased to 15, 20 knots, 25, and 30 knots, and as soon as we reached 30 knots our captains had all had instructions to maneuver independently. When the attack got in close, they could maneuver their ship any way they saw fit to defend their ship. We maneuvered on turn signals to try to keep the attacking planes on a beam so all our guns could bear. In this case we were quite successful. By successive turns we followed these planes as they came in, originally, from ahead, trying to get around on our beam, we kept manauvering so they could not attack us from astern where there were only two guns to bear. By this time, we had all turned, had all guns bearing, and we shot them down before they reached the ships. So it was an effective maneuver and no one was hit, so we were quite lucky.

Q: Actually, the pickets bore the brunt of the aerial attack, didn't they?

Adm. W.: They did in this respect. Initially, you see, they were attacking the transports unloading at the anchorage, but they found that the pickets had their own fighter protection and their fighter-directors. They knew as soon as the pickets got word, the planes would be coming out, and so they started picking off the pickets and were very successful. There were twelve destroyers sunk off Okinawa, which is a lot of ships, and some of them with very heavy losses. One of them, I remember, was right inside the anchorage there. That was the Twiggs, Commander George Philip Jr. in command.

Here's another, returning from picket station No. 5 to Kerama Retto for fuel and, on the way, the Lowry spotted a Japanese boat and picked it up eight miles south of Okinawa and captured seven Japanese soldiers trying to escape from Okinawa.

Q: A most unusual thing, wasn't it?

Adm. W.: Yes, they usually committed suicide. I guess they thought they could reach their own islands, not knowing Kerama Retto had been occupied.

I believe this pretty well covers it.

Q: Would you talk about the kamikazes? They reached their height at Okinawa.

Adm. W.: The kamikazes were the most effective weapon, I would say, of the Japanese Navy and air in the latter part of the war. They caused trouble early in the war. We had things similar to that rather early in the war. Their effectiveness was if they could get in, the exploding gas tanks as well as their bombs -- the gas tanks would explode, the bombs would cause trouble, and they'd set very severe fires. The Japanese built up this kamikaze corps for the defense of the empire, having been very effective in their operations with the fleet. So many of our ships were hit by them, and off Okinawa they did a great deal of damage, but at this time they were all land-based and they were one-way planes. In other words, all they needed was enough gas to get to the target and they didn't give them enough to get home, if they had a capacity for greater range. They did a tremendous amount of damage.

While we were there the Mississippi was hit by a kamikaze on the 16th of May just before we were ordered to Leyte Gulf. Kamikazes are terrible things and, even though we had fighters way out, combat air patrols, they got through. At Okinawa they had to knock out the pickets otherwise the planes would get them before they could hit their targets.

Q: Did you have any experiences with your picket group and kamikazes?

Adm. W.: They were kamikazed, as I've just described. These

two that were shot down were definitely kamikazes.

Q: Were there any that came near enough to cause damage to your ships?

Adm. W.: They would've if we hadn't shot them down, yes. They got to within a couple of thousand yards. We could see them plainly, but they were still heading right for the stern of the ship. There again our ship was doing 34 knots, maximum speed she could make, and in a turn movement. They could point their kamikaze at the ship but then you're making high speed on a turn with all guns firing at the attacker. They would have had us if we did not have high-speed maneuvering. The pilots, of course, after they caught fire, could no longer control them, but he pointed towards the ship and he was finished.

Q: What effect did this type of tactic have on the morale of your men?

Adm. W.: Delight when we shot them down. It boosted our morale. We figured we could take care of them. We heard so many reports about how dangerous they were and we'd seen all these badly damaged destroyers right in Kerama Retto at the time there were two or three badly damaged destroyers. We were briefed at Pearl Harbor, you're taking a squadron out there but you'll never get them all back. I said, "I intend to get them back." When I said twelve destroyers were lost, there were a great many more very seriously damaged.

Q: This must have had some bearing on the attitude of your men. They must have been apprehensive?

Adm. W.: They were apprehensive, but they'd been through this Aleutian business of night bombardment and it had had certain harassing effect, and we'd had planes overhead but they hadn't been close. We never knew how many planes overhead, actually. I would say the morale, as far as I could observe it, was that all they wanted to do was shoot down one Japanese plane. They knew what damage they'd done to our own people in the destroyers, battleships, cruisers, everybody -- the carriers -- had all been hit by them. I thought they were pretty well steeled for this thing and they were ready, and the fact that one close attacked -- we had reports on them many times and we reported them and the fighter-director shot down more than one. I have a report here that our fighter-director shot down six or eight of them.

Here's a report on the two and three-quarter months' fighting on land in which the picket boats went to battle station 150 times and averaged almost twice a day. Sometimes, a full alert lasted many hours. Twelve destroyers were sunk, twenty-one were damaged -- that's an earlier figure. I'm sure there were more than that damaged. The naval loss at Okinawa was 4,100 men. Antiaircraft batteries took a toll of 490 Japanese planes -- that's just anti-aircraft batteries. So it was a grim picture, the whole thing.

Unless you have some other question you want to bring out about Okinawa, I think we might go on.

On 16 June ComDesRon 57 in Rowe with Smalley, Watts, Stoddard, and Wren was ordered to escort Mississippi, which had been kamikazed, to Leyte Gulf.

Q: Was she terribly badly damaged?

Adm. W.: She was damaged considerably but she stayed there well after she was damaged. She stayed for several weeks after she was damaged, actually.

Q: What kind of speed was she able to make?

Adm. W.: She could make her proper speed. She was making about 15 knots on that trip, maybe 20. But she stayed because she'd been hit several times. The Mississippi had taken it right rough. She stayed on in connection with the bombardment of that Shuri Castle. She only arrived early in May. She was one of the late battleship arrivals. I think she came up from northern Luzon where she'd also been damaged. They repaired her and sent her on up so her 16-inch guns could help bombard that Shuri Castle.

Reporting to Leyte Gulf to ComTask Force 38, Vice Admiral John S. McCain, Commander; Task Group 38.4, Rear Admiral Radford, Commander; Task Group 38.4.5, and Commander, Task Flotilla 3, Commodore John Higgins.

On 1 July Task Force 38 sortied from Leyte Gulf. Now I'm

going to try to brief these operations off Japan because we steamed north and the Third Fleet was conducting these bombardments -- air bombardments -- off Japan about every fourth day.

Q: And your destroyers were escorting -

Adm. W.: They were screening. Well, there were four task groups with carriers, battleships, cruisers, and destroyers, and, in this case, we were in Admiral Radford's task group, but they operated simultaneously with targets designated by Commander, Third Fleet, who was Admiral Halsey in the Missouri.

9 June, high-speed run in and launched attack on the Tokyo area.

Q: 9 June?

Adm. W.: 9 July, I'm sorry. Just as an aside, Smalley sank two Japanese mines. We sank many mines on this screening duty. That was one of the destroyers' jobs.

Q: Did you meet with any heavy air opposition on the part of the Japs?

Adm. W.: I wouldn't say heavy air but one of the men on my flagship was killed on the 14th of August in one of their last attacks, the CAP didn't quite get him in time. He shot him down but the bullet came through and got this fellow. One of those sort of freak attacks. No, I know of no damage to the Third Fleet task force at this time. We had the planes in the air, our own CAP and the four carrier task forces.

Q: You really had control of the air?

Adm. W.: We had control of the air, and right over to the target pretty much. We were knocking aircraft out on the airfields. That's what a lot of these bombardments were.

Q: And there wasn't really any danger from the Japanese Navy, was there?

Adm. W.: Not at that time, no. We just had the power.

Q: So it was a one-way operation?

Adm. W.: It was a one-way operation to beat them into submission, and about every fourth day we would retire to the logistic support area to take on more planes, more pilots if we needed them, more fuel, and supplies -- all the ships. The logistic support under Admiral Beary had everything in that big support group of jeep carriers with planes, an ammunition ship, all kinds of supplies.

Q: And how far off were they standing?

Adm. W.: One day's steaming. Just to give you an example: We made strikes on the 11th of July and we were at the replenishment area by the 12th of July. We made some more strikes on 13 July --

we were only a day's steaming from launch point.

The logistic support people also had a carrier for their own protection and a screen. They were an independent unit that had everything believed necessary at the time. But they fueled the entire task force in this case from 6 o'clock to 1400, eight hours -- fuel, provisions, ammunition, everything we needed -- then went back to another station.

Q: Tell me, was the kamikaze threat over with at this time?

Adm. W.: No, not entirely and that's why we're going to get into the next step.

Instead of being a radar picket off Okinawa with a fixed station, we were sent out as radar pickets. In this case, what we called a Watch Dog Station. In this case, bearing 320° true, a distance of 40 miles from the fleet guide, in a position bearing from the fleet guide depended on the bearing from which the fleet was expecting attack by the Japanese. In other words, if we were attacking on the bearing of 320°, the chances are we would expect the Jap air attack somewhere on that bearing because we were attacking their airfields and we expected them to be alerted, or whatever the fleet commander thought was the most likely point for the kamikazes or other planes to attack from. This was 40 miles out, which was about the limit of our voice transmissions. And the same again, we had the warships, including the radar pickets, specially designed fighter-director ships, and we had our own fighter planes on call from the task force. We had some attacks out there but not generally.

The order was fixed for these ships in the North Honshu-Hokkaido area. Then Halsey switched back and raided southern Hokkaido, then he switched back to Honshu.

Meanwhile, in July Halsey was sending in battleships for shore bombardments at various places on the shore where there were industrial centers mainly. We hit one at Muroran. In this particular raid, the air attack was 14-15 July, the force lost nine aircraft and three air crews. In the surface ship attack, "The battleships and lighter units fired more than 1,000 tons of projectiles into the industrial transport and harbor area of Muroran, doing a large amount of damage to steel plants, iron-works, blast furnaces, coke ovens, chemical plants, and the general city area."

This information came in dispatches we received the following day, after our photographic planes had photographed the results of the bombardment and put out results in a fleet communiqué.

Q: Was this a new procedure, to issue a broadside estimate of the damage accomplished?

Adm. W.: Well, it was the latter part of the war and they were trying to get out public communiqués to help out at home as well as fleet morale. Early in the war, we weren't able to tell much of anything.

Q: So this wasn't done earlier?

Adm. W.: But Halsey's Third Fleet at this time thought they had to show what was being accomplished, and I think it was very wisely done.

Here's another Watch Dog Station on 265° -- enemy planes all around the compass to 320°, up to the northwest to 265° west. And after the raids we withdrew and joined the task force when they retired to the support area. After dusk starting back in because our planes had landed.

Here's another, the bombardment of Hitachi.

We had to keep our big ships busy. I mean it's very discouraging to see the antiaircraft ships screen carriers unable to bombard ashore with the guns and get some exercise in big gun shore bombardment.

Q: And it was another way of keeping the pressure on the enemy?

Adm. W.: Yes. Here's an interesting item, I believe.

On 22 July proceed to launch strikes on Japan, and the next morning DesRon 57 was ordered to carry out a night anti-shipping sweep around Ogasawai, in the Bonin Island, and bombardment of Omura Town on Chichi Jima -- anti-shipping sweep conducted, no contacts, conducted night bombardment, 100 rounds of 5-inch, no results observed, rendezvous with task force the next morning, proceeding to launch air strikes on naval shipping at Kure, Japan.

An interesting thing about this night bombardment to show that all is not as easy as it looks, intelligence reports I was given for this area to bombard, the little item was, "Many mines laid by our Army Air in this area in March, location is not known."

Q: Take your chances!

Adm. W.: Take your chances going through with five ships! Anyway, we came out all right.

Q: What kind of merchant shipping was under way at this point, small ships?

Adm. W.: Small ships, yes, coastal ships trying to supply the other islands.

Incidentally, I was reading somewhere -- Admiral Dyer's The Amphibians Came to Conquer -- the other day on this surrender to one of our ships after the Japanese surrender that there was a naval station with 5,000 naval men on this Chichi Jima, of which 5,000 surrendered and 9,000 Army and they had guns, too. They never opened up on us, though. I guess they thought they'd better not reveal their location.

Now here's a dispatch on 24 July air strikes on the Kure and Kobe naval bases: "Eighteen enemy planes shot down, twenty-one destroyed on the ground, and forty-three damaged. Heavy cruiser Tone left burning, also light cruiser Oyodo. Two battleships of Ise class damaged, also large aircraft carrier Amagi. Simultaneously cruisers and destroyers of Third Fleet bombarded Kushimoto seaplane base."

This all shows -- you see, their battle fleet was immobile then withdrawn to home bases, and we were trying to get them destroyed and be sure they stayed that way.

Here's another strike on Kure and more damage to the Haruna, and Ise, cruisers Tone and Aoba escort carrier Kaiyo, all three were damaged and sunk. Haruna is now resting on the bottom. They were really knocking what was left of their air out which many times makes me think we had them licked before the A-bomb episode.

On 29 July we shifted over to another task force, 38.3, for one night, while their destroyers were on bombardment mission.

On 1 August shifted command pennant from Rowe to Watts. Rowe had propeller shaft troubles and was sent back to Leyte Gulf for repairs, and the Taylor was sent to join my unit.

Incidentally, on all these replenishing expeditions, the jeep carriers towed target planes and we all fired antiaircraft exercises.

Q: You didn't get enough actual exercise, so you had to have practice?

Adm. W.: It was Halsey's idea, I'm sure, just keeping everybody on their toes. But on every replenishment, it was part of the exercise to get all the antiaircraft firings possible, somebody's towing a target out there and you fire a practice when target came within a safe bearing for you to shoot. He'd fly them around the whole task force.

9 August made an air strike on northern Honshu and Hokkaido.

Here's one: Japanese Grace-type airplane was shot down by Combat Air Patrol near the Wasp, while attempting a suicide dive on that ship. That's the only attack I can recall during those operations. Robert E. Caya, machinist's mate, third, lost his life during this engagement.

10 August, continued air strikes on northern Honshu and Hokkaido. Wadleigh and Norman Scott reported to ComDesRon 57 for administrative purposes.

12 August -- see how close we're getting to the day and everything's going on just as if the war was going to go on a long time. Task Force 38 retiring on southeasterly course for air strike on Tokyo. Nicholas, O'Bannon and Buchanan assigned to ComDesRon 57. All that meant was I had three more ships to fit in the screen in the area that the screen commander, Commodore Higgins, assigned to my ships.

ComDesRon 57 in Watts, Stoddard, Wren, and Frank Knox on Watch Dog station a distance of 40 miles bearing 300° true from Task Force guide.

It was 12 August now, combat air patrol shot down five enemy planes. Rejoined unit task force during the night.

15 August, task force began air strike on Tokyo area at 4:15. At 7:15 all air strike planes were recalled. The war was over.

Among voice radio messages received during the day were

Commander, Third Fleet -- you've probably seen this quoted elsewhere but I copied it down, "All snoopers are to be investigated and shot down not vindictively but in a friendly sort of way."

Q: I've seen different versions of that.

Adm. W.: That's my copy of it from the scene! Then there were these messages of congratulations from everybody. I don't think you want those in here, do you?

Q: No.

Adm. W.: Task Force 38 steaming in an easterly direction, 16 August.

Now, we start moving around again. Still operating combat air patrol. Then an interesting thing happened. I received a confidential letter informing me that Destroyer Division 115, Metcalf, Shields, and Wiley, had been a unit of Destroyer Squadron 57 since 1 July 1945, by the Pacific Fleet organization. I'd never seen any of them and I'd never had any report of them! No harm, apparently, was done.

Q: What do you do when you get a message like that?

Adm. W.: I didn't do anything. I said, if they're not in sight of me or they don't report for duty, I'm not going to worry about them. If Admiral Nimitz' order says they're in my squadron, maybe they are. I got messages from them later, when they wanted to get detached!

Q: Well, they could have been off fighting somewhere.

Adm. W.: They were working and I was simply too busy to keep up with them.

In these operations after the 15th of August, this task group made reconnaissance flights over Tokyo and on the following three days each flight -- and the reason they did that was that they were also looking for prisoners, detection of prisoners, because we were greatly concerned that our prisoners might be further harmed and we kept up our air flights over Japanese territory where the enemy was rumored to have prisoner camps.

Q: Was there any cessation of effort during the period when the atomic bomb was being dropped?

Adm. W.: We still operated the same. As I mentioned, we launched an attack on the 15th of August. No, as far as I know, we operated the same before and after the A-bomb. But, actually, they were licked by that time, I've always felt, and I think some of our postwar findings indicate that.

Q: Tell me about your reaction to the atomic bomb.

Adm. W.: I was truly thankful that it had been dropped at the time for the simple reason that I wanted to see the war over. I thought we'd sacrificed enough lives. Our people, not having started the war, and purely in self-defense and after the very dastardly deed of attacking Pearl Harbor while peace negotiations were presumably going on in Washington, I felt anything to end the war should be done and save our lives.

Q: That, plus the fact that you anticipated with almost certainty the bloody slaughter if we attempted to land?

Adm. W.: That's correct. Another landing. Having witnessed part, at least, of the Okinawa business where our Navy suffered 5,000 lives, the largest Navy loss in the war, I believe, at Okinawa, and other serious losses we had in some of the earlier operations, I felt it was time to stop and the sooner the better.

Q: And when the bombs were dropped, this was the real stopper?

Adm. W.: Yes. I felt very strongly that the Emperor would give in as soon as the message got to him of what had happened and presuming we had plenty more.

Q: Which we didn't.

Adm. W.: No, we didn't! He might have thought that, though. Hiroshima one day and Nagasaki a few days later. He had no way of knowing how many more we had, I don't think.

Q: Then came the signing of the armistice, the capitulation of the Japs. Where were you stationed at that time?

Adm. W.: Our task force was designated as Group 38.4 and designated to remain at sea to fly reconnaissance planes, photographic planes, in an endeavor to keep a check on our prison camps until they could all be released. Rear Admiral T. L. Sprague was now our task group commander.

The flying operations were greatly reduced, but still it required a single task group, to be on the safe side.

Q: Were your units imbued with the feeling that you couldn't trust the Japanese?

Adm. W.: I personally was certainly fully imbued with that feeling and, to the best of my knowledge, the units I worked for, under, or with had exactly the same feeling. In fact, I do not even trust them now. There's something in their characteristics that I've observed over a good part of a lifetime. I think they have to be watched. But, at this time, there wasn't any question about watching them. These flights were careful, checking, trying to get the prisoners out, and locate them so that our people on the ground could do something.

We finally entered Tokyo Bay for a weekend I think on the 10th of September, and then were withdrawn from that area, the task group departing for Eniwetok 18 September for training exercises and some time of recreation.

We returned again on the 13th of October with a new task unit. The Bennington was the carrier and Captain T. H. Robbins was the task unit commander. We operated partly out of Sagami Wan anchorage, which is a bay just below Tokyo.

Q: What was your duty then?

Adm. W.: Still on the alert for any activities that might develop. We wanted primarily to be ready.

Q: But they'd already shown all the evidence of laying down their arms?

Adm. W.: That is correct, but we couldn't send everybody back at once and I think as fast as we could we started withdrawing candidates and sending those who'd been there longest.

Q: Had Magic Carpet begun at that time?

Adm. W.: Yes, I'm sure it had begun before this because we started losing officers and men in the latter part of September when we were at Eniwetok. And it was drastic. It was based on points and ships had to give priority to those with points and the Navy people who were most urgently needed. In my case, I lost out of a staff of four the two senior officers immediately.

Q: That must have been pretty demoralizing, wasn't it?

Adm. W.: The worst thing was the doctors. We had no doctors. There was only one left in the squadron. And other things. It was quite demoralizing, but I sort of put a hold on the ships regardless, just to keep enough on board to get the ship safely back to the United States port. I didn't know when we were going, but I didn't think it would be reasonable to hit a ship so badly that they couldn't safely operate at sea. It was pretty drastic.

Q: I would think that certain of the men who were eligible to go home would feel some kind of obligation to the units they were serving in.

Adm. W.: Many of them did, yes.

Q: I mean a doctor, for instance, just picking up and going home and leaving the men without medical attention.

Adm. W.: A good many of them did. I just know that we were pretty hard hit at the time.

We went back for further operations off Japan. We joined Admiral Sprague east of Japan. It was my division, that was all they had at the time, then Division 114, which was up in the Aleutians, was on its way down and they helped in accepting the surrender in the northern islands with the North Pacific Force. They were supposed to come down to join us. But this Task Force 53, the Eastern Japan Force under Rear Admiral J. Carey Jones -

Conditions were so bad in Tokyo Bay at this time, late October, you might say the pollution was so bad that I requested Admiral Jones' permission to take the squadron to sea for four or five days to clean out the ships' tanks, make fresh water in all the tanks. Not much is said about it, but when I was ordered aboard his flagship, as I recall it, a large percentage of his crew were laid out with dysentery. There were a great number of ships, you see, in Tokyo Bay.

Q: It was water pollution, and not air pollution?

Adm. W.: Water pollution -- a horrible situation. The worst I've ever seen anywhere in the world, except maybe China.

Q: You mean oil and oil slick and all that kind of thing?

Adm. W.: Filth. You see hundreds of ships at anchor in a harbor close together with all their outgoing sewage mixed up with the city, I suppose whose drainage system, too, went into the bay. It was a very serious situation. At any rate, we avoided it -- I think we avoided it by those four or five days at sea.

Q: The Navy didn't do anything but dump its debris in the sea, in the bay?

Adm. W.: That's all they could do, the overboard discharges. There was no other place to put it. You could pump everything clean at sea, but it wasn't only the Navy, there was the merchant fleet, a tremendous merchant fleet. But in this late October I believe this action prevented much illness other ships in Tokyo Bay had experienced.

Then, for the last time, on 2 November the task unit was dissolved and I was relieved by Captain Edward N. Dodson on the following day and immediately arranged earliest transportation to the United States, preferring to take an oil tanker, the <u>Millicoma</u>, with the first stop San Francisco than risk the chance of being detached on a priority basis en route by air. And I was able to get immediately from San Francisco to the East Coast. I called up the detail officer and was authorized to proceed to the East Coast.

Q: You must have been rather relieved to be relieved of command at such a juncture when the men were disappearing and all that?

Adm. W.: I was relieved in one sense, yes, because I was awfully glad to get home, but I was deadly anxious to have the opportunity to bring the squadron back to the East Coast of the United States, as I knew my orders would get us back before Christmas, and the division flagship, Div 113, was destined to be in Philadelphia Navy Yard for decommissioning and Division 114 at Charleston. I would have been very happy even with reduced personnel to at least bring the nucleus back to the United States. As it was, though, I was fortunate in getting this tanker and getting to my wife's home in Cambridge by the day after Thanksgiving, with a little help from Western Sea Frontier staff, my old shipmates and Admiral Ingersoll's group.

Q: They were your friends!

Adm. W.: Oh, yes. Call up and get these orders. The detail officer was the operations officer just relieved when I left the Vixen, when I left for the Pacific, Captain Converse. He said, "I don't know where you're going, but you come on to the East Coast and we'll find something."

Q: Now, when you returned home, you obviously had some leave?

Adm. W.: A few days, but just a few days. I stayed a few days and visited -- moved my family from Cambridge and made a short visit to my family in Annapolis, and reported to Washington for assignment, hoping to enjoy a few days' leave.

To make a long story short, I requested duty on the staff of the National War College. I figured that might be appropriate after having had the Industrial College duty and the Naval War College duty, both staffs, and hearing about this new institution.

Q: And the fact that Harry Hill was setting it up!

Adm. W.: I knew Harry Hill had it but I didn't know what was to happen. At any rate, I requested the National War College for duty. I'd talked to the new detail officer by this time, my old friend Roland Smoot, and he said, "You are going to the Army Industrial College." There's been tremendous pressure on us to get someone with experience, a graduate in that field, and that is where you are going, and you will report tomorrow morning."

Q: Smoot's a very forceful man.

Adm. W.: Well, they'd put the heat on him for weeks to get someone over there. And the next morning I reported to Brigadier General Donald Armstrong, U. S. Army, and he said: "Come on. Come on into this meeting. We're having a gathering of our industrial advisors, some of the most prominent people in industry in the States."

Remember, I had not been near the Industrial College since graduating in 1933. I got into the meeting and, at the close of the meeting, General Armstrong said, "I wish to inform you distinguished gentlemen that present with us today is our new director of the department of instruction." Well, I shuddered -

Q: Did you look around to see who he was?

Adm. W.: Me. Yes, I looked around! So, that was it. At any rate, the problems were manifold. In the first place, a new course was starting on the 6th of January and I asked what the curriculum was. "Oh, we do not have any." So I said, "Who's going to provide a curriculum?"

"If you don't do it, nobody else will." And so you can imagine the confusion, but at least we were able to put up the semblance of a curriculum.

Q: Had it not been functioning?

Adm. W.: It had closed at the beginning of the war. Most people were sent to field duty, the active troops, and they had a small group there teaching renegotiation. They'd been in operation for about a year, teaching renegotiation of war contracts, which had really relatively little to do with the real function of the Industrial College. So we dug in with what staff we had.

Q: This was a new beginning, then?

Adm. W.: This was a brand-new beginning following World War II and a new concept, really, of what we should be doing. But we were able to produce an abbreviated -- it was a six months' course, five months really, January to June -- curriculum, and there were a great many people ordered there with a lot more experience than I had in the field of industrial mobilization, you might say, or industrial planning or that type of warfare. We put a course on the table on the 3rd of January and divided them up into groups in various fields with the idea that one of these groups would work up this particular field with a view that it might be incorporated in the ten-month course that would start the following September.

Q: The first course was only six months and then you planned - ?

Adm. W.: We'd expand it into a larger. Well, we'd expand these groups. It was a rather exasperating period.

In the brief time available, the preliminary course was divided as follows: Organization and administration; manpower, production; purchase and distribution; foreign resources. The experience of the officers in this short course enabled us to prepare a very good outline for the next year's full-length course.

Q: How many men did you have enrolled for the six-month course?

Adm. W.: Approximately fifty.

Q: And how closely did you follow the pre-World War II curriculum as to breakdown of subjects?

Adm. W.: I would say that we did not follow too closely the pre-World War II curriculum. For example, we added things which I think were quite important. Besides purchasing, we had the distribution of supplies, and in foreign resources we went into rather complete detail. We used what we could of the earlier course but tried to expand on it in the knowledge that had developed during the war.

Q: This was World War II knowledge that was being incorporated?

Adm. W.: Yes, we tried to get the brand-new things. There was this board of industrial advisors led by John Hancock who submitted a report to the Secretary of War, in which he urged that the college be joint, Army and Navy. This was finally placed in effect by the Secretary of Defense, James Forrestal, in April. That's when it became a joint college. This was rather interesting. In the process of these meetings with the staff of the National War College, Admiral Hill, General Gruenther, and General Landon, and their civilian, Hardy Dillard, the dean of the University of Virginia Law School, and with the Industrial College, General Armstrong and myself.

Q: What was the idea of making it joint?

Adm. W.: To see whether we should or should not work the two colleges together in use of the auditorium -- the National War College had a series of national policy lectures and a splendid auditorium. We used to use their auditorium for their lectures, but also for our own lectures. The one thing I believe I was instrumental in accomplishing in this respect was to convince the Army that we should attend National War College lectures and work our own lectures in in addition. Now it's not academically sound, I'm sure you would probably say, and other educators say the same thing, but I felt so strongly that this college should have the benefit of these high-pressure lectures on national strategy and they could work in these industrial problems.

Q: The specialized ones?

Adm. W.: The specialized problems on the side and the industrial policy and economic mobilization plans.

Q: That seems to make sense.

Adm. W.: To me, it just made sense. I had a battle to get that across but we succeeded.

Q: What was the objection to it?

Adm. W.: The objection was in the Secretary of War's office. I pretty nearly got crucified up there. There was a captain -- Kenneth Royal was the Secretary at the time, and he had an administrative assistant, who was an Army captain suddenly made general, and he wouldn't have any part of anything the Navy suggested, anyway. But I literally had to get that across and through and went over his head, really, to the Secretary of War to get this thing through.

So I made up the first curriculum and lecture schedule and I used the one that Admiral Hill had and inserted ours in our own courses. That was the beginning. Our people liked that, the students there, and it then became quite interesting. And, incidentally, all that summer I worked with the staff of the War College. Our class later attended all those lectures. It didn't start till September, so I had a good chance to know their staff and work with them, and it turned out quite well.

The next thing that happened. It was a question of status for the Industrial College, where did it stand? Where did Leavenworth stand? Where did the Armed Forces Staff College stand? I'd been studying to put the level -- it had to do with rank and preference and things like that, assignments, and so forth, at the top level. We succeeded pretty well. We got some fine naval officers in the student group and were working toward that end eventually. Kenny was Under-Secretary of the Navy at the time,

W. John Kenny, and he was appointed chairman of this ad hoc committee, and it had the Assistant Secretary of the Army and Undersecretary of the Air Force, Lieutenant General LeRoy Lutes was the deputy chairman. It was a pretty high-powered board to consider reconstitution of the Industrial College of the Armed Forces.

Well, the factors that came up were: was it to be a purely logistic place and specialize on a smaller scale, as it had before the war, on purchasing and what not, or was it to be on a long-range national planning level where you could plan for the whole picture together. We finally had this ad hoc committee, of which I was made the secretary, which almost got me fired, and came up with a solution. The Mission is worth quoting:

> "To prepare officers of the armed forces for important command, staff, and planning assignments in the National Military Establishment and prepare selected civilians for important industrial mobilization planning assignments in any government agency: . . ."

This was the thing that caused the real battle, the paragraph which stated:

> "The Industrial College is an educational institution. As such, it will not engage in investigation studies, or activities which would place the college in the status of the staff agency or executive agency of the joint chiefs of staff. . . or any other governmental agency."

The Munitions Board tried to use the students when I was

there, every spring, to help their planning, because Secretary Forrestal had only allowed 100 on the Secretary of Defense military staff and 100 on the civilian staff, so they tried to use the students of the Industrial College, and every year I'd battle that one.

Q: Thinking that they would in turn benefit by this experience?

Adm. W.: Thinking they would benefit by it, but primarily to do their pick and shovel work. So we got this worded in this charter, ad hoc committee report, to give it a charter which would place it under the Joint Chiefs of Staff, increase the rank of the commandant to be the same as the National War College, flag or general officer -- the policy of the establishment to make graduation from both the Industrial College and the National War College compulsory for all officers being groomed for higher key positions in the national military establishment, and the joint chiefs of staff, with the guidance of the Munitions Board, effect modifications of the curriculum consistent with the charter. In other words, by the new charter the joint chiefs of staff were responsible for all educational institutions on the top level in the military establishment, and we were able to get the new mission of the college placed under the jurisdiction of the joint chiefs of staff. The logistics people didn't want that, the Under Secretaries of the Navy and the Army.

But by September we had gotten approval by Secretary Forrestal on the mission, which gave the college equal status with the National War College on the educational level and left the student enrollment numbers at the discretion of the joint chiefs of staff, and put them with a mission where they could conduct top-level national planning, to prepare people for top-level national planning. This was placed in effect in the fall of 1948, and in the final draft on the thing we had to increase the rank of the deputy commandant, to parallel the National War College, to flag officer, so that gave me an out to get to sea. But they didn't want to let me go. Finally, the did and I was able to get a good sea command.

Q: Tell me what happened prior to World War II to the courses in logistics and what have you, which were on a lower level, what happened to them and what happened to the type of preparation they provided?

Adm. W.: To the best of my knowledge, they proved quite useful. They worked on their own national mobilization plans before the war. You remember when Roosevelt was having a terrible time with Congress, trying to get a draft act passed?

Q: Yes.

Adm. W.: Word got out that we had national mobilization planning for war, so these plans were shelved, as it were. They were supposed to have been destroyed. Actually, some kind soul hung on to them and they were put back in use pretty quickly, and they were the basis for some of our war logistic planning, when they were allowed to use them again. But there was a political time there when mobilization planning was horrible -- planning for war was horrible. After all, we'd changed our war plans division in CNO to strategic plans and international planning. I'm not downgrading what they did. I think they accomplished a great deal with their plans. I think in one of the earlier talks on the Industrial College I gave you a list of the kind of people they produced and what they were doing. So they all had big logistic jobs. We had some of them out in the Amphibious Force.

Q: The gist of my question was, with this new setup and the elevation of the status and so forth, what happened to what had been done or attempted to be done prior to World War II? Was this incorporated?

Adm. W.: Yes, we incorporated it. We reviewed it all and incorporated it in the best way we could into new studies, but we tried to make, I would say, more advanced studies than they had previously. You see, this board of advisors they had down there, people like Ferdinand Eberstadt, John Hancock, Dr. Edward A. Fitzpatrick, who was one of the top manpower people during the war, Stanley F. Teel, J. Carlton Ward, Jr., all these people were the very tops in the U. S. national advisory group as well as the college.

The October 1941 class was a very young class of lieutenants and captains; more experienced officers had been ordered to sea or field duty.

Q: So you didn't throw out what was in being prior to World War II?

Adm. W.: Oh, no, we realized we could not do the type of thing that had been -- I mean, for instance, when I attended in 1933 we were counting nuts and bolts, as it were, and we didn't do any of that. We were trying now to plan about the use of all the national facilities on an all-out national effort, rather than as -- purchasing was part of it, yes.

Q: War was a new ball game, so to speak.

Adm. W.: Oh, yes, it was a national effort, that's what it did.

Q: Well, you learned in World War II?

Adm. W.: Yes, we figured we had to do it, and then the people in these classes -- if you looked through this January to June class, we had people from all services who had had experience in logistics abroad and here, and then we got the top people in the Army and Navy who came down, as well as a civilian group.

Q: You had civilians from where?

Adm. W.: From the various departments of government.

Q: As students?

Adm. W.: We didn't have them as students until later on. That was the next step, after my time. We had one State Department student. Now they've got a State Department deputy. They've tremendously expanded the place with a tremendous new building that outshines the National War College building and makes it look like an old monument, with all new equipment, and they do some of their planning. They're teaching them to use computer planning. They have a number of those courses going on at the same time. They rent these GE computer services.

But the intricacies of getting this thing going, to get that charter through once we had it drafted -- I processed it through the Navy, that was no problem because I knew I had Admiral Carney behind me and Admiral Denfeld so that was simple. But the Army had a very laborious way of going through it. We had a colonel on the staff who was a very live-wire, interested colonel, and he knew how to get to the top people in the Army. By the time we got to the charter they had the Air Force commandant, so we had no problem with the Air Force.

Q: You had no problem with them?

Adm. W.: No, we had an Air Force commandant!

There were so many people who came down to help. General Hershey came down every year. From the time we first met a manpower problem, he'd come down and give us a talk, when invited, and he'd even come down to seminars. I talked to him a year or two ago at one of our reunions over there. He did a fantastic job on the matter of personnel, and he said, "There's one way I tried to straighten it out during the war when I suggested, 'Let the Navy and the Marines fight the Pacific War and the Army the European War. You'd get no problem with feuds who does what!'" He said they didn't like that. He is a genius, that fellow.

Interview No. 7 with Rear Admiral Joseph M. Worthington,

U. S. Navy (Retired)

Place: His residence on Gibson Island, Maryland

Date: Tuesday morning, 1 August 1972

Subject: Biography

By: John T. Mason, Jr.

Q: Admiral, this chapter today begins with your tour of duty on the cruiser Rochester in the Atlantic. You left the Industrial War College for this assignment.

Adm. W.: This was a most fortunate piece of luck to me, for large commands were very few in the Navy at that time, 1948, and the number of officers available for such commands were many.

Q: So the competition was great!

Adm. W.: Yes. The Navy was at a rather low ebb in active ships during this period. I received my orders and was detached in November 1948 and was sent first to the amphibious warfare school at Norfolk, next to the damage-control school in Philadelphia, and finally to radar school in Boston.

Q: These consumed just a matter of weeks in each place?

Adm. W.: Several weeks. It consumed about a month at the three schools, and I relieved Captain Gordon Crosby in command of the

Rochester in Boston Navy Yard on December 16, 1948, in a snowstorm.

Navy Yard work in addition to the regular three-month overhaul phase involved an improvement in the antiaircraft installation of a new type of GE directors valued at about $6 million in the currency of that day. We finished this work shortly after Christmas and held post-repair trials early in January.

Q: I assume this is one reason why you went for these refresher courses at the three schools, in order to be prepared for the new equipment being installed in the Rochester?

Adm. W.: That is correct, and the Navy's efforts to give these refresher courses, to my mind, were one of the finest things we developed during the war. I'd been through the same series of courses at Pearl Harbor on the way to command DesRon 57. I had no time for any when I went to command the Benham. These courses brought you up to date on the equipment you had. The radar installation, for example, in the Rochester was such a tremendous improvement from what I'd experienced in the squadron, and that was a great improvement on what we had in the Benham.

Q: We were cashing in on our World War II experience?

Adm. W.: We were cashing in on it. The Rochester, I may add, was completed after the war, so she had no wartime record and had been commissioned two years when I was fortunate enough to assume command.

Q: In addition to the skipper being sent off to these specialized schools, were some of the other officers assigned to the Rochester?

Adm. W.: We made a practice of sending officers over to every school we could get them into, and men, the fire-fighter school, for example. They had them in the yards. They had them in the Boston yard, Philadelphia had some -- wherever we happened to be, we took advantage of getting as many officers and as many men through these up-to-date schools.

We had our post-repair trials off Rockland in early January. This was my first opportunity to handle this fine ship at sea and under varying conditions and, as was expected, we found a snowstorm off Rockland -

Q: This was in Casco Bay?

Adm. W.: No, this was Rockland -- not too far from Rockland, Maine, and not far from Casco Bay, but it's where the measured miles were laid out for these trials. This was a very valuable day as far as I was concerned and it gave us a chance to see something of the officers and crew. I did not know a single officer or man in this command when I reported for duty. I was very fortunate in having an extremely able executive officer, Alton Parker, who had a brilliant war record and was perfectly competent to command the ship, should it be necessary at any time. The other officers were very fine. We had a crew of 1,100 men, but on the Reserve cruises we picked up an additional 600. So on each Reserve cruise the ship was being used for this year, we sailed with about 1,700 officers and men.

The next change in our plans involved installing the helicopter deck, so we went into the South Boston Navy Yard, removed the catapults, and installed this new deck.

Q: This was an innovation, wasn't it?

Adm. W.: This was one of the first helicopter decks in a cruiser -- I believe the Columbus had one about that time -- and we were to have a very interesting time developing the use of a helicopter.

Q: What was the intention of the Navy in installing it? What use was the cruiser to put it to?

Adm. W.: For scouting, for gunnery spotting, and much more easy to handle than the planes, which took up a great deal of time and effort, and weather conditions made them not always easy to recover. This was to prove a great interest to me particularly and to the Navy from our various reports.

We moved on from the Boston yard for refresher training at Guantanamo in March, stopping by Norfolk en route where our helicopter was flown in from her home station at Lakehurst, New Jersey. We did not have a regularly assigned helicopter. We had one report to us for each cruise. This enabled the helicopter group to train more pilots in operating from cruisers and also gave us more experience in handling them.

Q: When you had a helicopter on board, how many pilots did you have?

Adm. W.: We had two.

Q: And a maintenance crew?

Adm. W.: And a maintenance crew, but most of the maintenance was performed at Lakehurst because they went with us for a two weeks' cruise.

On the trip to Guantanamo we held a full-power trial, which was most successful and it was very encouraging to me to find out that the ship was doing the things she was supposed to.

Arriving at Guantanamo was a new awakening. As operations officer on the Atlantic Fleet staff, I had ordered a great many ships to refresher training. Never before had I realized what an ordeal it would be. The group in Guantanamo was quite competent, but they did things in refresher training that I felt were highly undesirable in the way of disabling engines without warning so you'd know how to react and work on three engines or two engines -- things of that nature, and they were not as experienced personnel as the ship's officers themselves. I had a most experienced engineer officer, gunnery officer, damage-control officer.

So I felt that my time at Guantanamo was more or less keeping peace between the ship's officers and the training command. But they did a good job. We profited by it and we survived it. Fortunately, at the end of this six-week period, the division commander, Rear Admiral James H. Foskett, flew down from Washington to observe our last group of exercises, including gunnery, antiaircraft firing, surface firing, tactical exercises, and all the general exercises we could perform. And fortunately for us they went off beautifully. For example, I requested a relief utility plane flying the targets, saying I was sure that one target would not be enough to complete the practice. I did everything I could with the training command to supply the reserve plane. I had ideas what this new antiaircraft equipment we had could do. What it did was automatically knock down the first target with the first three rounds, so we couldn't fire the rest of the battery.

We called for a second plane, knowing there'd be a delay of two hours, so we swung right around and fired the long-range practice against surface targets. We wore battle dress for this, helmets and everything, equipped with gas masks if needed, and this surface practice went off beautifully. The division commander was very much pleased with the performance of the ship, which was very fortunate for us. At the same time we had on board about eight or ten prominent visitors sent down by the Secretary of the Navy, so it all turned out for our good. Admiral Foskett returned to Norfolk with us and the ship returned to Philadelphia, as we were supposed to have two weeks in port and get another admiral's inspection and then go off on another Reserve cruise.

I might group these Reserve cruises because they were similar in nature.

The first was made out of Philadelphia for Panama the 25th of April, falling in with the battleship Missouri at sea, and Captain Page Smith, of my class, was the commander of the unit going to Panama and return. We had a very fine cruise, did practical drills together, fired star-shell duels together, fired battle practice at a raft as we steamed by Guantanamo -- we didn't bother to go in, and had a little visit in Panama. That was the first of these Reserve cruises.

The second one was the 22nd of May and started from Newport. Meanwhile the Rochester's home port had been changed. Kingston, Jamaica, was the port of call, and we returned. There, we operated with a carrier group at sea, but for the port of call found the other ship in port was the newly commissioned Newport News with Captain Roland Smoot in command, and it was very pleasant for me to be able to make official calls together with Captain Smoot in governors' official parties and everything. Kingston was a very fine port at that time. We returned to Newport.

The next cruise was from Newport to Bar Harbor and return, over the 4th of July. In this we had an unusual incident. Arriving off Bar Harbor, whose harbor is not very large, there was a Canadian frigate anchored right at dead center in the middle of the harbor, so I saw no reason to take the Rochester in in a close situation like that and steamed north of Bar Harbor, where they had a nice anchorage, and anchored. This brought a protest from the officials ashore and I said: "Well, as soon as the Canadian frigate saw fit to move to one side of the harbor or the other, I'd be happy to move back into it." And we did that and had a very pleasant stay there, although it was politically inspired. There were a lot of political speeches and fireworks and parades and what not.

Q: In what connection was it political?

Adm. W.: Senator Owen Brewster of Maine was up for re-election and he arranged this fine affair.

Returning to Newport from this trip, on the 1st of August we made a fourth Reserve cruise to Sydney, Nova Scotia, and return. In this instance, we joined with a carrier task force at sea and maneuvered with them en route. Our port of call was Sydney, and also the commodore's flagship, the Spokane, was assigned to Sydney.

We had an interesting experience on this Sydney visit. The Rochester was assigned a berth alongside a Sydney dock where the depth of water was less than 20 feet and the Rochester drew 24 feet. Well, I brought this to the attention of the Canadian authorities by a surge of dispatches and made no progress whatsoever. When we arrived in Sydney Harbor, a pilot came aboard, a naval commander, and said he was directed to take the Rochester alongside the dock. I said, "We will not go alongside the dock. Where shall we anchor?" He said, "I have no authority to anchor you anywhere," so I said, "Well, we'll anchor here," and there we stayed. By that time, I'd exchanged messages with the commodore, Beverly Harrison, and he said he would tie the Spokane alongside the dock and although the Spokane was a much smaller ship it was a touch-and-go situation. She could get in alongside the dock and then she might be on the mud and have difficulty when she got out again.

It so happened, at the end of the visit, I waited four hours outside of Sydney Harbor while the Spokane was getting away from the dock with a little tug that didn't have enough power to even help her, and the wind was on the dock and she just couldn't get anywhere.

Q: Why were the Canadians so adamant about it?

Adm. W.: I'd say they're stupid. That's all I can say. It made me furious but I had no way of protesting. I had enough experience with ships and depth of water and I refused to go in any depth of water where you couldn't take the ship. I know from experience that a ship squats when you put power on -- you learn that early in the Navy, and when they squat they'll pick up mud, mud will get in the condensers. They put the West Virginia on the ground in Hampton Roads and the Missouri aground in Hampton

Roads later on -- any number of Navy ships that's happened to, but the Canadians show no interest. All these dispatches that I sent -- I sent them to the Commander, Second Fleet, and to my division commander, so they knew I was trying to operate through channels.

But we had a nice visit in Sydney. The most interesting to me was a trip inland to the fortress of Louisburg, which was very famous in our early history and at the time when it was pointed out, it was attacked by these rugged New Englanders in the rear during winter, dragging their small guns over the frozen swamps was one of the lessons of history that the British might well have learned at Singapore if they thought back a little bit because the Japs came over to Singapore where they weren't supposed to be able to come. That's the way the New England Yankees captured the fortress of Louisburg. They went inland and dragged their guns over the ice. It was very interesting and made a good historical point of interest. Have you seen that?

Q: No.

Adm. W.: If you're driving up that way I think it's worth seeing. At any rate, the local people were most friendly to us and we had a nice reception aboard the Rochester, which invited practically everybody, and they volunteered a bagpipe band for the reception, which we used. It rather surprised and startled some Americans who happened to be visiting in that area and came aboard the heavy cruiser to hear Scots bagpipes playing. All in all, the visit was successful. The Reserves liked their training, and we returned them to Newport.

One more Reserve cruise and the last was in September in the Narragansett Bay area and the port of call was New York City.

On all these cruises we paralleled the work of the Reserve officers with whatever officer on the ship they were trying to learn about.

Q: They were on standby?

Adm. W.: Standbys. If they were gunnery officers, they worked with him; if they were training for engineering officer, they worked with the engineer; and the same way with the lieutenants and down the line. We had Reserves with each of our regular officers, and in that way I believe that they learned faster. We allowed them to handle the ship at sea when conditions warranted, but we were always up there to guard against tactical errors and so forth. We let them do a great many things, as many things as possible, and they all seemed to appreciate that.

Q: Did they come from all over the country?

Adm. W.: They came from all over the East. As far as I know, as far West as they came from was Ohio, but from anywhere along the East Coast, I believe, except maybe the far South.

Since our home port was being changed, we picked up the Reserves at wherever the Navy Department had ordered them to.

We just arranged it so we could be there rather than change their big schedule, because orders to 500 officers and men each time had to be handled pretty well in advance.

Q: Tell me, Admiral, coming back to the helicopters again on the Rochester, was the Coast Guard in any way interested in the operation of these helicopters during that time?

Adm. W.: I do not recall, but I'm sure they were getting interested in them very early because they saw the use.

Q: But I meant did they have observers on the Rochester?

Adm. W.: Not to my knowledge at that time but they could certainly see us operate in each one of these ports with the helicopters when we were on a cruise and some of the other assignments to the Rochester.

I might add that the Rochester had returned from the flagship of the Sixth Fleet in the Mediterranean, Admiral Sherman's flagship and she was beautifully equipped for that. She was one of the big flagships at that time with a big admiral's cabin and a captain's cabin that was almost as big, and she was equipped with everything else for a fleet flagship's entertainment. But in view of the shortage of ships in the Atlantic, the Rochester had to be assigned to this Reserve duty and one of our smaller cruisers was assigned as flagship in the Mediterranean, of the Sixth Fleet.

Now, some of the other assignments of the Rochester I might touch on in here.

In June we were assigned to represent the Secretary of the Navy at Nahant -- no, at Swampscott -- for the annual meeting of the Society of Electrical Engineers. This might be indicative of the condition of the Navy at that time, but I had received a copy of the Secretary of the Navy's letter a month previously that the Rochester would be there for these visits and sent an officer up there to see the boating situation. He told us that the nearest place we could count on landing boats was Nahant, which was two miles away. And the only dock at Nahant was a very small boat dock. So, in presenting this to the Atlantic Fleet commander, they ordered a landing ship, dock, to meet me at Nahant and they would provide the boats for taking the people, as many as wanted to see the ship, in and out. It was extremely fortunate they did because there were 1,500 electrical engineers at this meeting and some of them were pretty prominent people.

Q: This was a public relations job, then, for the Rochester?

Adm. W.: A public relations job, but still, with these preliminary arrangements made, I still had no orders. So, the day before I sent a message to Commander, Second Fleet, the Navy Department, and the division commander, who was in Europe, and said unless otherwise directed, the Rochester would proceed to Nahant for the American Electrical Engineers meeting, as indicated in the

Secretary of the Navy's letter. I never heard any more, so we got there.

The meeting was extremely interesting. There was the outgoing president of the American Society of Electrical Engineers, the incoming president, Dr. Killian of MIT was one of the speakers, and they visited the ship with great interest. I think we had several hundred take the trip down to Nahant and go out in these boats to visit the ship. We had a continuing series of visits, and I had a group of them aboard for dinner the last day there. We showed them the operations of the helicopter on rescue operations and things like that to show something besides the routine.

On return to Newport, we saw a burning fishing boat, the Fan and Mary, so that gave us an excellent chance for our fire and rescue party. We put the bow of the Rochester to windward and used our fire hoses, our foam extinguishers, and our whale boat, and put the fire out. The crew did not want to leave the boat because of the salvage value and we stayed with them until the Coast Guard cutter took them in tow, and then proceeded on to Newport.

The next unexpected visit was to Marblehead for the tercentenary of the city of Marblehead. That was another public relations assignment. It was very pleasant. The city fathers did everything to entertain. I took my wife, and her friends there entertained all the time that was available, at the Yacht Club and in private homes. Admiral Theobald was there, my first destroyer commander out in prewar Pearl Harbor. He entertained us and also came aboard and his wife came aboard on the next to last day we were there. He was most agreeable and I think he was delighted to get back aboard a ship again, as he inspected the ship.

One of my interesting visits was when I had instructions from the admiral to be sure and call on Mr. Crowninshield. He was a descendant of one of our first Secretaries of the Navy and in his family were several Secretaries of the Navy. His house at Marblehead was just a naval museum. It was fascinating. He had things from the early ships, logs, and pieces of instruments. It was a regular naval museum and he was just as courteous as he could be.

Getting back to Newport, I had taken aboard for the division commander a beautiful new admiral's barge. We picked it up in New York and carried it aboard, but it was so big we had difficulty in handling it, and it had to be the last boat in and the first boat out, so with our airplane crane which was still there and which we also used to put the helicopter in the hangar on occasion, and a storm came up off Marblehead on our departure and it was with great difficulty that we got this barge aboard and back to Newport and delivered it to the admiral, who was there at that time. He was very much pleased with it.

There, we had exchange of calls and he had a chance to look over the ship. This should have been his flagship but the duties assigned to her made it impossible.

Next orders were to be inspected by other admirals in Newport. Admiral Shoeffel was the task force commander we were supposed to be operating in but so far we had never seen him, not even at sea. But he was able to look over the ship and he did appreciate our gunnery, as he was one of our gunnery people in the years back.

Our next orders were to prepare for an amphibious expedition to Labrador. We first went down to Norfolk for conferences with Admiral Wright, commander of the Amphibious Force, Atlantic, and Admiral Thackrey, who was to command the expedition. Then we went down for rehearsals, mostly in the training area down there, but we had drills on the fire support doctrine and so forth. There were many briefings.

We finally sailed for Cape Porcupine, Labrador. Meanwhile, I had been able to see the Coast Guard survey after they'd been up into Labrador and made some preliminary surveys, and had gone over the various channels and everything which were not previously too well charted. So we were pretty well prepared in advance.

On the expedition north everything went as expected, except going through the straits of Belle Isle the Rochester had a rather unusual casualty. When our compasses passed $55°$ north, we tried to reset them and our gyrocompasses were frozen beyond $55°$ north, so we had to pass through the straits without the aid of our gyrocompasses. But we had no difficulty really, as I immediately signaled the destroyer ahead of us to take formation guide and used our radar ranges and the plotting board to plot our precise position as we went through. So we actually navigated by radar in broad daylight and regular compass, and by the time we'd gotten clear of the straits we'd gotten the compasses unfrozen and back up to speed; it took a certain length of time to get them back up to speed again.

Q: What caused them to freeze?

Adm. W.: They'd never been used -- you see, you set them in changes of latitude, but they'd never been moved that far up. Presumably, it should have been done in tests in the Navy yard as a matter of testing, but it had never been prescribed as far as we knew. The ship had never been that far north. Normally, a ship when you move it certain degrees of latitude changes settings every two or three degrees change of latitude.

The straits of Belle Isle were of great interest because on my midshipman cruise a British cruiser went on those same rocks. They're pretty tricky straits to go through in fog or without radar or modern equipment.

Moving up to Cape Porcupine with the amphibious group, the Rochester and some landing craft fired the preliminary D-minus-1 shore bombardment. Prior to that we'd sent a submarine with underwater demolition teams to survey the area we were going to fire on and also the area we were to anchor in to get a check on them.

Q: This was entirely our operation? The Canadians were not involved?

Adm. W.: Oh, no, no Canadians at all. They knew about it and gave us permission, of course. It was a pretty barren area and you wouldn't expect anybody, but they were notified to be sure there would be no hunters or anything like that. We also used our helicopter for the same purpose, to check over that there wasn't anybody in that particular area.

We went on the D-minus-1 day bombardment, then D-day was the landings, which were handled from the Mount Olympus, the amphibious flagship, and her boats and landing craft. We had some special landing craft on this expedition, and this was of particular value because this was the first time we had ever operated in northern country in modern times, that is, since the Alaskan invasion -- I mean, the Aleutian Islands invasion. It was the first time we had operated our troops, so they were all inexperienced in amphibious work in cold climates. The Marine Landing Team camped ashore for ten days in the snow and ice and everything.

General McGee was in command of the Marine unit, a brigadier general. He was in the Rochester and used our helicopter for considerable reconnaissance duty.

Just before departure, we were told to investigate Hamilton Inlet, some 30 miles to the northward, and it so happened the amphibious people went on up ahead in one of our light carriers. Duerfeldt was in command of that carrier. The Rochester brought up the rear, entering the channel in the dark. This was just to try out the anchorage and see how a ship would make out in there. Well, it was a pretty rugged anchorage. The Rochester's chains held all right. The carrier had difficulties in the anchorage.

The next day we returned to Cape Porcupine, and looking at the charts and looking at that channel we came through, we went back by the other direction, where there was a little more room! We had nothing else to interfere. I believe that pretty well covers that Cape Porcupine expedition, except the helicopter was not equipped for all the flying, of course. This was, you might say, the Model T Ford of helicopters, no all-weather instruments to speak of. It depended on the pilot being able to find himself, and also no antifreeze and things like that. We learned a great deal from this expedition.

Q: Helicopters at that stage were fairly vulnerable, weren't they?

Adm. W.: Absolutely vulnerable. As I recall, they didn't carry any guns unless it was a rifle or something. They were very lightly equipped.

Q: And prone to accidents?

Adm. W.: And prone to accidents. I flew in this one to make a call on the Commander, Air Station, at Quonset Point. It was very nice for me. It was a ten-minute flight and I landed on his front lawn. He was rather surprised, I think, but, being an aviator, he didn't mind.

On the return trip everything was going beautifully and after we cleared the Labrador area the admiral released the Rochester to return to Newport independently, at which I was delighted because it was the ship's home port and the crew hadn't seen their families very much. But we got only a few hours' away before the orders were canceled by higher command and we were sent back to escort the LST flotilla. So instead of going back at a respectable speed we went back at a crawl pace. But I was glad we did because they had need of our doctor on part of the journey home in one of the ships. We got back in a respectable time.

All in all, I think the expedition was most successful. One of the things that we did preparatory to this trip was to enclose the open bridge. The Rochester was designed with a conning tower that theoretically you were to fight the ship from and an open bridge that had some instruments. And, of course, it was envisaged that you worked from the combat information center with your radar, but I pointed out in one of my reports that no commanding officer since the ship was commissioned had ever really operated the ship from the conning tower, except on the battle problems. The visibility was so poor and handling at close quarters with docks and things you had to get where you could see things. So I was authorized to enclose -- make a temporary bridge up above. This was used up north and was very successful. We connected a line to our own steam heat.

So, upon our return, the first order I got was to dismantle the temporary bridge structure. I fired back on that "urgently request that bridge be retained for further testing," and it was granted. I questioned the captain who had the ship in Korea a couple of years later and asked him was the bridge still around. He said it certainly was and they'd have been in bad straits without having it. That temporary bridge was still being used five years later.

The ship returned from Labrador and was given New York for a liberty port, after stopping at Newport and were told to pick up some ammunition to fire a 5-inch gun practice off Bloodsworth Island, down in the Chesapeake Bay.

After New York, we went down to the Chesapeake Bay area, fired this exercise, and, on the return from that exercise, we arrived in the York Spit Channel after dark and we encountered an Army dredge which cut across us but fortunately our backing power saved us and we made it through all right.

Then we put to sea to prepare the ship for distant duty. We did not know what it was at that time. We thought it was the Mediterranean. At sea that night everything was going beautifully and I was sleeping in the emergency cabin, open sea, steaming singly, and I felt a severe jolt and inquired of the officer of the deck, "What did you hit?" He was a new officer of the deck and he said, "Nothing, Sir."

Well, I bounded up on the bridge in my pajamas. We were at sea off Ocean City, Maryland. By that time I could hear a scampering up on the forecastle. The officers from the forward quarters of the ship were all coming up on deck. By that time I'd established communication with the lookout on the forecastle and, putting lights down, observed a whale impaled on the prow. The whale was really impaled. We slowed, stopped, and finally were backing at two-thirds speed before we could get the whale disentangled. I had grave concern that the bridge might have been damaged, I mean the prow of the ship, on entering port put over divers and found no outward damage. But I'm sure there was one whale on Ocean City beach the next day. It was a rather unusual experience, to say the least.

Q: Whales don't usually ply, do they, in that - ?

Adm. W.: No. I've seen many, many of them at sea in destroyers and other ships and up in the whaling country, up in the Aleutians, and around there, and spouting off Japan, but never close to shore. All I can say is that this whale must have been resting on the surface, asleep, or something when this big prow came under him. I've only heard of one other instance in the Navy and that was a big aircraft carrier many, many years ago. That was written up in the Naval Institute Proceedings.

Arriving in the Boston yard, we did everything possible to prepare the ship for distant duty. Captain Irving Duke was ordered as my relief and to report on the 21st of December in Newport. Meanwhile, he was in Boston at the radar school and he was able to come aboard and look over things with me. No one, in my opinion, could ever have been a finer officer to relieve someone else than that man. We had the formal inspection when we got to Newport, went ashore, and he said, "I don't need to see anything more. I'm perfectly happy with the ship and everything that's turned over to me." It's a pleasant way to turn over a command.

I might add one more thing to the Rochester's cruise. In battle efficiency she was rated that year second of the cruisers --

Q: Second of the eleven?

Adm. W.: Of the eleven cruisers in the Atlantic and third, counting the battleship Missouri, which was first. The Fargo was second, and the Rochester was third -- that's the cruisers of the Atlantic Fleet, final results of the battle efficiency competition in 1949. [See appendix 13.]

Q: You were relieved of command of the Rochester and your next tour of duty sounds like an extremely interesting one. You went to Washington to be in the internal affairs division of CNO?

Adm. W.: International affairs.

Q: I mean international affairs.

Adm. W.: Office of the Chief of Naval Operations, International

Affairs Division, and assigned as Assistant for Joint Chiefs of Staff matters and Armed Forces Policy Council Liaison Officer.

Q: What does that mean?

Adm. W.: These duties required the closest cooperation with the Strategic Plans Division of the Office of Naval Operations and the Joint Strategic Survey Committee of the Joint Chiefs of Staff. I experienced many painful crises cutting down national defense under Louis Johnson and building up under Marshall. These daily crises were in connection with the Armed Forces Policy Council liaison officer duties. This required preparing the Navy Department's position for the meetings of this all-powerful Armed Forces Policy Council, which the then Secretary of Defense was using as a tool to reduce our national defense as rapidly as possible.

Q: Who served on this Policy Council?

Adm. W.: The Secretary of Defense, Louis Johnson; the Secretaries of the Army, Navy, and Air Force; the chairman of the Joint Chiefs of Staff; the Chief of Naval Operations; the Chief of Staff of the Air Force; and the Chief of Staff of the Army.

Q: Were they all in agreement on this great reduction in the armed forces?

Adm. W.: The interesting method of Johnson's operations was to give extremely short notice on proposed action at the meetings, which were generally held, I believe, on Tuesdays. In other words, receiving an agenda maybe Monday, late, or Tuesday morning on items to be discussed, it would be necessary for me to communicate by telephone with the most likely officer in the Navy Department to be familiar with this particular item. As an example, one meeting I remember, at noon I received a notice that a proposal to amalgamate Bolling Field and Anacostia for economy reasons was to be considered at that meeting. I was able to get the Navy admiral most familiar with it at the time on the phone and get a brief position which I hand-carried to Admiral Sherman, who read it on the way up to the meeting with the Secretary of the Navy.

This is just one example of many things that were done.

Q: Didn't the membership rebel at this method? It seems to me that some of these matters were of great importance and deserved greater consideration?

Adm. W.: These matters were of great importance and deserved a great deal of consideration. Fortunately for the Navy, the then Chief of Naval Operations, Admiral Sherman, was extremely competent to cope with the various problems on very short notice insofar as interests of the Navy and national defense were concerned. He had the additional difficulty of briefing Secretary Matthews, who was very slightly familiar with any of these problems but had the common sense to lean heavily on Admiral Sherman's able advice.

Insofar as the complex of the Armed Forces Policy Council

work changed with the advent of the Korean War, it became diametrically opposite. Secretary Johnson had returned to his native West Virginia and General George Marshall had been made Secretary of Defense, and from that time on the problems that came before the Armed Forces Policy council were handled with much greater preparation than before and understanding.

Q: This turnabout reflected the attitude of the President himself, did it not?

Adm. W.: Yes, with the advent of the Korean War he had to reverse the policy of slashing down our defenses to one of building them up as rapidly as possible.

Q: But, going back to my original question, didn't some of these men, men like Admiral Sherman, speak up in opposition to this hasty policy that Secretary Johnson pursued?

Adm. W.: Admiral Sherman spoke up most ably on many, many occasions and had the brilliance to say things that would be listened to, if not carried out. It was my assignment to read over the minutes of the Armed Forces Policy Council meetings in the Secretary of Defense's office and verify them to the extent that the Navy's interests were concerned. And it happened on more than one occasion that Admiral Sherman was quoted as saying a certain specific thing. I would copy this down in the belief that he didn't say any such thing and take it to him personally, and he would see that that record was properly corrected.

It was amazing to me how in a meeting of that nature with good recorders things could be so twisted and had I not been very skeptical I would never have picked up these things and been very careful about reading the minutes of these meetings. As for what the other services did for their part, I do not know. I know they were hesitant to speak out very much. The Navy had recently had the harrowing experience of having its own chief retired for speaking out and I believe that fact may have given the incumbent chief a stronger footing that it might not look too well politically if two successive chiefs were eased out for disagreement.

Q: The minutes from these meetings became a part of the permanent record, but were they used more immediately for any purpose?

Adm. W.: Well, theoretically, my reason for reviewing them was to be sure that I recorded exactly any decision that was made that required action by the Navy and pass it on to the individual in the Navy who would have the action. My assignment was merely to relay.

Q: So that it was implemented?

Adm. W.: So that the various things were implemented. Of course, in the case of the correction, it had to go to the Secretary of Defense and going back it had to go through the Secretary of the Navy -- the Chief of Naval Operations and the Secretary of the Navy, and he had to take it up with the Secretary of Defense.

Q: One other question in that connection. Was there any difficulty in getting the minutes revised to more accurately reflect what Admiral Sherman had said?

Adm. W.: To the best of my knowledge, he had no difficulty in getting anything corrected which he felt was a matter of substance. He had a tremendous ability to persuade when he was right and he knew he was right. I must say Secretary Matthews, seemingly, supported him to the limit, as far as I know.

Q: Now, you're going to talk about your other hat?

Adm. W.: The purpose of reviewing Joint Chiefs of Staff papers in this division was for the international implications of the various documents. In doing this, we had to work very closely with the Strategic Plans Division of the Office of the Chief of Naval Operations and also with the Joint Strategic Survey Committee of the Joint Staff. Our assignment was to prepare either a recommendation for approval by the Chief of Naval Operations or a recommendation for changes in the document as drafted. These documents would be sent to the Army, Navy, and Air Force from the Joint Staff for consideration and the position to be taken by the head of each service on the specific document.

With this prepared recommended change, if approved by the Director of International Affairs -- while I was there it was Admiral Orem, Thach, and then Austin -- and then on to the Assistant Chief of Naval Operations, either Admiral Gardner or

Admiral Fife or Admiral Struble, DCNO for Operations, and on to the Chief of Naval Operations, who, if he approved the document as written, signed an endorsement on it. If he approved the changes proposed, he signed the changes. It was rarely, in my time, that the Chief of Naval Operations did not accept the proposed action that had passed through his chain of command, as it were, from International Affairs and on up to the Deputy Chief and Vice Chief. It had a lot of reviewing before it got that far, but the initial work was done here.

Then I'd attend the meeting with the Chief of Naval Operations and we'd try to reconcile his changes with the changes proposed by the other services. In that way they had to reach an agreement or divide on the paper. A tremendous effort was made to reach agreement, but this was right difficult in those days, particularly when it came to matters involving forces of the three services. Each of the other services felt that there should be much less Navy, more Air Force and more Army, and that's where the big crises came with the Joint Chiefs because it split them.

Q: Can you give me an illustration of a paper that went through the hopper at this time?

Adm. W.: Papers on action in the Korean War. One was a review of the recall of MacArthur. I may say that every dispatch pertaining to the Korean War and the Far Eastern Commander who, in that case, was General MacArthur, had to pass through the

International Affairs Division as well as others. Every dispatch and order. In reviewing this thing, I picked out this one because the particular people had not really realized just how things had been, I don't believe, till they saw this review.

He was recalled by the President. The Joint Chiefs of Staff Strategic Survey Committee were told to make a review of all the orders exchanged between them and, in this particular case, during that period, which was two years, I believe, this rough document, flimsy, was referred to our division for review and comments. Having to be there at the time or assigned to it, I'm not sure, but at any rate I worked all weekend going over the draft review of the Joint Strategic Survey Committee, and then took it up with Strategic Plans the first thing Monday morning. My review was rather short and to the point, and that was, to the best of my belief, the Joint Chiefs of Staff had not given General MacArthur any orders. He told them what he intended to do and they generally approved it. Something along that line is what was hand-carried up to Admiral Sherman that morning, and that was the last I heard of that particular document. I think they met and approved it. They naturally concurred with the President because MacArthur disobeyed his orders. They couldn't do anything else. But the nature of the thing was so hard to believe that when you look at the fact that General MacArthur and the Chief of Staff of the Army, General Collins -- when MacArthur was Chief of Staff of the Army, General Collins was a 2nd lieutenant, and General Vandenberg,

Chief of Staff of the Air Force, was a few years junior to that, it's not surprising that they had two votes for him on most things. That's my opinion whether or not it was recognized.

But Admiral Sherman handled all those things amazingly and he moved forces. He saw things happening -- you've probably read this elsewhere, I'm sure -- but when the Korean Wonsan evacuation was in dire straits, Admiral Sherman ordered the amphibious forces in the Pacific out in that western area for training purposes. So by the time Wonsan was desperate, they were available to order in there. He did this on his own initiative. He was thinking ahead. I believe I mentioned earlier about the battleship Missouri. He ordered the Missouri out there just as soon as she got back from the midshipmen's cruise. I prepared a draft to get her out there and put the midshipmen ashore here but they did not approve of that. It was held up for weeks, but the Missouri turned out to be very valuable in Pusan with her 16-inch guns.

There were many other things that came in, naturally, in this International Affairs Division, but I have tried to touch the high spots of the bigger problems. A lot of these things were assigned to joint boards and committees. I was on one of these joint committees with the three services. Louis Johnson had ordered action abolishing -- to see how many committees could be abolished in the Defense Department. I found a tabulated list of over a thousand and decided that it would be quite a long project to abolish all those committees.

Q: There wouldn't be anything left of the Department!

Adm. W.: That ended it for the time being.

On the protocol question, too, for some reason I was made the Department representative on how many high-ranking foreign officers should be received each year, that is, of the rank of the Chief of Naval Operations. The Navy wanted a very limited number, the Air Force wanted a great many, and the Army wanted a great many. Well, I negotiated this paper with the other services and battled back and forth, and finally I drafted one which I figured Admiral Sherman would put through. This was policy for the Secretary of Defense on inviting high-ranking foreign officers. I believe it permitted three a year with the rank of Chief of Naval Operations for each service. The last clause in that was that any official visitors that the Secretary of Defense desired of this rank would be welcome out of funds provided by the Secretary of Defense! And to my amazement they got that phraseology through. The document was never approved by the Secretary of Defense, but three years later I was called by somebody that my name was on the document to know about the present status, and I said:

"Well, it has never been approved by the Secretary of Defense, but I'm unofficially informed it is followed religiously by all three services, that it was approved by their respective Secretaries."

If the Secretary of Defense didn't approve it, the individual services did.

Q: Operating as they did once upon a time, before the Department of Defense was set up!

Adm. W.: Yes. Well, a little more than that. The three services were coordinated on this document, and it kept it somewhat under control.

There were many others. One of the papers brought to the Joint Chiefs of Staff by one of the other services was to set up a special division, Army, Navy, and Air Force, to direct control of defensive sea areas. I investigated a little bit for the Navy and then made my report at the next meeting. The Navy was unalterably opposed to this, the setting up of this extra organization, as in our case they saw no need for it at the present time. It was handled by a lieutenant and in his absence, the duties were performed by a WAVE ensign -- and they wanted to set up a committee of officers from all three services, a captain or colonel heading each service section. It was an example of trying to expand. Some of those were unreasonable.

Q: What I was about to ask was, was there any difference in freedom of expression on the part of the various service heads in the Armed Forces Policy Council and the Joint Chiefs of Staff? Did they have greater freedom and greater leeway in really expressing themselves in the Joint Chiefs, in contrast with the other, which seemed to be under the domination of the Secretary of Defense?

Adm. W.: I would believe that they had much greater freedom in expressing their own views among their military opposites, who had a military background and understanding of their reasons, whereas the Secretary of Defense and the civilian Secretaries are only familiar with the problems for a short period of time and take more interest in the domestic political values involved. I believe that to be the case.

Q: So, when a consensus of a military opinion was sought for the benefit of the President, it was much better that it came from the Joint Chiefs than from this special council?

Adm. W.: That was true at the time, when the Joint Chiefs were respected by the President and the law still permitted an individual chief of staff to present his case to the President, as was the case, I believe -- as far as I know, the last one to do that was -- the law might have been changed after that -- Admiral Burke when he was Chief of Naval Operations. He presented his case directly to General Eisenhower. He might have been invited to do it over certain matters. I don't know. He would be the one to straighten that out. I'm certain that he did, under certain conditions. But that law, I believe, has been changed.

Certainly they couldn't under McNamara. They couldn't get near the President unless the President invited them to one of his Sunday lunches or Tuesday lunches, and that would be generally the Chairman of the Joint Chiefs of Staff to be the one to present the views supposedly of the Joint Chiefs of Staff, as he saw it. I believe in those McNamara years, from all I've been able to read, the military head did not have direct access very often. I believe that is different now. I think they do get called on from time to time.

I was detached from duty as Assistant Director of the International Affairs Division on August 5, 1952, and reported the following day to the director of the standing group of the North Atlantic Treaty Organization, at that time under the direction of the Secretary of Defense. I was extremely fortunate in reporting to Vice Admiral Arthur C. Davis, who was Deputy U. S. member of the standing group at this time and under whom I had served happily previously.

I was assigned to the long-range planning team of the NATO standing committee.

Q: There was a great deal of relationship between your previous assignment and this, wasn't there?

Adm. W.: It worked in very closely with the work I had been doing the previous two and a half years, and that background was of inestimable value to me in doing this work.

The long-range planning team consisted of U. S. Army, Navy, and Air Force members and similar opposite numbers from the other members of the standing group, Great Britain and France.

Q: Where were the headquarters?

Adm. W.: At this time, the standing group was located in Washington and the military representatives' committee met in Washington, in the Pentagon, with meetings in Paris several times annually of the entire military committee.

Our first assignment in this team was to redraft the strategic concept for the defense of NATO, taking into consideration the admission of Greece and Turkey. I found this extremely interesting work and enjoyed very much the members of the team of all nations, who I felt were extremely capable, at the same time had to represent their national views. One of the most interesting members of this team was Colonel Michel Fourquet, French Air Force, who later became the last French commander in Algiers and still later Chief of Staff of the armed forces of France under de Gaulle.

Our duties in this team were to brief the military representatives, in our case it was, first, General Bradley and, later General Collins, prior to attending meetings in Paris. Working with these two, directly under these two, was most interesting to me and I was extremely fortunate in working through Admiral Davis who, generally speaking, was the local coordinator of this group between meetings, locally in charge as a military representative rather than the military committee.

One particular assignment that I had on this long-range planning committee was consideration of our atomic responsibility in these same plans, at the same time having very strict guidance by the U. S. law as to what information I could divulge. I had to be continually on guard in this particular work. My French contemporaries never offered any problem whatsoever and accepted whatever statement I put in as to the capabilities to do so and so -

Q: That's rather surprising, isn't it, in the light of French actions?

Adm. W.: It might be considered surprising in the light of French actions, but, at this time, the French military representative in Washington was Lieutenant General Paul Ely, one of the finest French officers I have ever had the opportunity to meet. Upon occasion, I would take a draft paper to him and say, "Well, General Ely, I don't believe you can support this back home," or something to that effect, and he would say, "I do support this and those at home will support it also." He had supreme confidence that he represented his country's best interests and he did not seem too concerned about the political aspects. He later became chief of the armed forces, first chief of staff of the Army, then chief of the armed forces. He succeeded de Lattre de Tassigny in Indochina at the time the latter was assassinated, and, finally, was chief of national defense under de Gaulle. He was a wonderful person.

The British, on the other hand -- our British and Canadian friends -- were everlastingly trying to pry from me atomic information and, to the best of my knowledge, they were not successful.

Q: They had a certain amount of knowledge, anyway, didn't they?

Adm. W.: They had some, yes, but they knew our law, and they tried surreptitiously to get it. One example, there'd been a meeting in Ottawa of the military representatives and Admiral Davis had been our representative. Before I'd seen him upon his return, the British brigadier who was director of the secretariat standing group in Washington had a draft of what happened at Ottawa. I read the draft and in that draft was purportedly the position taken by the United States. I read it and wrote parallel to that paragraph the position that I believed the United States had taken, and I took the two in to Admiral Davis and I said, "I believe this alternative position is what you probably said at Ottawa." And he said, "Yes, scratch the other."

There again, deliberately they were trying to twist our position around, hoping it would be approved by a staff paper and get through up the line. But the paper went through as agreed.

One of the things that came up in NATO repeatedly was this carrier business. We'd just had this unhappy experience in the

Navy of trying to defend our carriers and papers were being brought in to eliminate the carriers from our defenses. The British position was that if we did not have carriers we would have more fighter planes based in England and therefore they were based where they could not leave and be a greater strength for the defense of Britain. It was logical to expect them to believe that. They invariably brought this paper up. I saw it when I was in the Chief of Naval Operations International Affairs and saw it again in this NATO. The paper came to me through the mission. Apparently they did not realize that we had rather close coordination within our department because when I got one of these papers that I thought meant something serious I was able to get five minutes with Admiral Burke, who was then director of strategic plans, and while I was presenting him the story he would be dictating a memorandum which would go right up to Admiral Carney, on to Admiral Fechteler, the Chief of Naval Operations.

I'm merely repeating this for the simple reason that I don't want to see any United States representative in any category ever be caught off guard by international planners.

Q: How could they presume to interject themselves into our domestic policy, I mean the use of carriers, the building of carriers?

Adm. W.: It wasn't so much domestic policy. They'd abolished their own carriers. At the same time, this same policy came from the

Royal Air Force, you see. They'd abolished them in the Royal Navy.

Q: I know they had, but why did they presume to speak for us?

Adm. W.: Well, I dare say the feeling was such at that time that our own Air Force had egged them on. I don't know, but to end this story on the carriers because I feel keenly about this thing, after we slapped it down completely in our job, Lord Ismay who had been chief of staff to Churchill in World War II and was at that time secretary general to the whole NATO organization published an article in our Reader's Digest that was almost paragraph by paragraph the paper they had tried to pass through me in NATO about a year before. He didn't get anywhere privately with the thing or through military sources, so he tried to go to the American public, which I thought was pretty awful. I believe this is worth recording. There were other instances, but I think one or two is enough.

Q: May I ask you a question? You spoke earlier about one of the projects was to revise the long-range plans for NATO in the light of the admission of Greece and Turkey to the organization. Was this a drastic revision, since we then had NATO powers in the Eastern Mediterranean?

Adm. W.: It was not so drastic, except that the plans added these two countries into full status of NATO members, and while working on this particular plan the British opposed including Turkey, merely because they said that their geography showed that Turkey is not in Europe, Turkey is a country in Asia mostly.

Q: Was that because of the relationship between Turkey and Greece, which was always a sore point?

Adm. W.: That was touch and go. Our feeling was that we wanted to make them feel they, both Greece and Turkey, had full military status. They'd already made the full political status in NATO, but full military status for what forces they could contribute and work them right in with ours. Yes, it made some change of our military concept. We had to furnish more arms to Turkey, for Asiatic Turkey, some armored divisions and artillery, and this meant mainly improved weapons and radar, but we'd already done that for the Greeks. The British had replenished for the Greeks, but we did more for the Greeks than for the Turks, much more. So we only had one view and that was we should make them part of the whole plan for what they could contribute and hope they could contribute more.

My experience with the Turks was that they were a very tough aggregation and would fight if they had to. We used to talk about Russia and the dangers from Russia in these informal meetings and this delightful Turkish admiral that I worked with, Ulusan, said, "Well, we've fought the Russians over 13 centuries and they haven't defeated us yet."

Q: How do you spell his name?

Adm. W.: Ulusan -- Azis Ulusan. I had extremely pleasant relationships with both the Turks and the Greeks in all this planning.

Q: Would the two of them sit down together and collaborate?

Adm. W.: Sure. Oh, yes, we sat down at the same table day after day, going over these things, and after we'd redrafted, rewritten, and discussed it, we had no problem there.

I think I've already mentioned some of these people in that NATO organization at the time. I mentioned Paul Ely of France. The representative of Denmark on the Military Committee was Admiral T. J. C. Quistgaard. He was a perfectly splendid officer. He was the top military in NATO at one period there.

Q: How cooperative were the Scandinavian representatives? How willing were they to shoulder equal responsibility with the other powers within the NATO organization?

Adm. W.: That's a very fine question. I had great difficulty in the plans with our Scandinavians. At the time we were very anxious to establish a NATO base in Norway, which would be a big help in our NATO exercises and something on the northern limit. The NATO representative was at that time, I believe, an admiral, but it would make no difference, did not want to let us get any semblance of a base in Norway. It would not have been extensive but we wanted something to help the forces. What they wanted was to have all the advantages of American defense of Scandinavia without taking any of the risks.

Q: Put very succinctly!

Adm. W.: Very succinctly. The same was true of -- well, Sweden was not in NATO, but Norway and Denmark. Denmark was fine. They had a rear admiral on the military committee whose name was Ramlau-Hansen. He was a very able officer and most cooperative in every respect. Never had the slightest problem with him.

On the other hand, Holland's representative was everlastingly blocking us. He wanted -- it reached the point where, for one example, one problem I happened to be assigned was minesweepers. We wanted a certain number of minesweepers for Holland in the setup of NATO and Holland wanted them because they could use them as fishing vessels in peace. We put down whatever we felt was reasonable. I worked on that problem and worked on it for several months, knowing that at the lower level the representative went back with his view. He knew the firm position of the military, but at the meeting in Paris fortunately I'd brought my file on this thing along, which was about an inch thick, and at the meeting in Paris the Military Committee got through all right, but the foreign minister of Holland brought up this question of minesweepers. General Bradley was next to him and Admiral Davis, and Bradley turned to Davis and said, "Will you answer this?" He thought it was on such a low level it shouldn't be answered. So he turned around to me and said, "Captain, will you answer it?"

Unfortunately, I think I spoke too long on the subject but by the time we got through they knew our views about why they shouldn't get any more minesweepers and the question was dropped right there and then. It was most embarrassing. It was a minor military question being brought up by the foreign minister and after he'd been overruled. But, as you know, the Dutch are right stubborn at times.

But the other people were fine. Lieutenant General Cesare Gandini of Italy was perfectly fine in all of our dealings with him.

Then, speaking of colorful characters, Major General Umberto Delgado of the Portuguese Air Force was their military representative, who, on occasion, expressed his views which were rather strong and later history recalls he attempted to overthrow the government -

Q: Salazar!

Adm. W.: Salazar, and he finally was assassinated, I believe, but he was one of the colorful characters there.

The head of the Greek mission whom I thought a great deal of was Aristides Argiropolis.

Q: Was he an admiral?

Adm. W.: A major general. I thought he was perfectly splendid and my latest report on him was that he was condemned to death for treason, and pardoned for being over 72 years of age, in this recent Greek uprising.

I did not mention -- I'd better though -- the British chief of the NATO Council, Air Marshal Sir John Slessor. I mentioned Slessor, but Elliott I haven't mentioned, Sir William Elliott, who was the one fighting the Air Force carrier battle, but fortunately Admiral Davis could handle it without any problem, except he would speak out of turn.

Q: He must have been colorful?

Adm. W.: Oh, he was delightful. The meetings in Paris were delightful. There was a lot of work.

Q: Did you go to the full meetings of NATO?

Adm. W.: Yes, we went over there a few days early and took the fourth floor of the old Hotel Talleyrand for our offices and we had direct communication with Washington and the Pentagon by our own radio circuits, and we had Marine guards from the fleet who guarded these offices. We did our final preparations for the meetings there. The meetings were in the Palais de Chaillot across from the Eiffel Tower. It has since been torn down and they've put up this massive new building. Our group stayed at the Hotel Crillon on Place de la Concorde, but the gatherings where we'd meet in the mornings, maybe at ten o'clock, the Military Committee first, and that would be for several days, and probably the following week would be the whole Council. Although the military were not normally invited to the Council meetings, we were invited to attend in civilian clothes and were merely present to observe.

Nothing very much happened that I can recall at those meetings because by that time we'd presented everything we could. They were on the foreign diplomatic field.

Q: In that period, was General Montgomery giving his annual performance.

Adm. W.: General Montgomery, yes. He was Number 2. General Gruenther was the head of SHAEF and General Montgomery was his deputy and, of course, General Montgomery always expressed his views and they were quite different from some of our views as a general rule. They always wanted to take over control of our atomic capability. The British in all these dealings, in all these setting up of commands, wanted to get the top man. I'll give you this last one which was in NATO. That came into my bailiwick and I had all the plans and all the figures and all that was needed for the NATO use of mines. Then the British suddenly came forth with a request to create the NATO Mining Agency with a vice admiral in charge. I was able to convince our people that the plans were already in existence in NATO. They required no vice admiral to command them, and it was just a waste of another expensive type of organization. And so far it prevailed, but not without some feeling by the British. Prior to my departure from NATO, I got a big made-up certificate: "Honorary Member of the NATO Central Mining Agency." Fictitious, of course, but it really hurt them because their vice admiral didn't get the job.

Q: They had a candidate for it?

Adm. W.: Sure. They told me on a low level who it was and I said, "What in the world are you people talking about?" And they said, "Well, we want to give this fellow the job. He's had long service and he needs the money. Bring him back to active duty and give him this job."

Q: They were at that period then a destructive force in NATO?

Adm. W.: They were destructive all the time I worked with NATO, and the French were so cooperative. That's what hurt me so when the French under de Gaulle withdrew. The French cooperated beautifully with us the whole time I had anything to do with them. In the meetings we knew we had a two to one vote against the British. The question was how to get them to cooperate a little bit.

On 30 June 1954 I was relieved of all active duty in the Navy, and having been specially commended by the executive department for performance of duty in actual combat, was transferred to the retired list with the rank of Rear Admiral. On 1 July 1954 I started work in Cleveland, Ohio, as Resident Engineer on the Ohio Turnpike representing the J. E. Greiner Company of Baltimore, their Consulting Engineers. I remained on this interesting assignment for nine years. In January 1963 my wife, son, daughter, and I moved to our current residence on Gibson Island, on the Chesapeake Bay 12 miles north of the Naval Academy. For the past 12 years I have been a substitute teacher at Marley Junior High School, done some writing on naval historical matters, and drafted a number of letters in support of National Defense. At home I have done considerable gardening and property maintenance, and played as much tennis as practicable.

Q: I want to thank you for all the time and the work that you have put into the preparation for this series. I'm very grateful.

Adm. W.: Thank you, Sir.

Index for

Series of Interviews with

Rear Admiral Joseph Muse Worthington,

U. S. Navy (Retired)

ADAK: see entries under COM DES RON 57; also p. 299; p. 302, p. 305.

ANDERSON, Vice Admiral Walter S.: p. 94-5.

ARMED FORCES POLICY COUNCIL: SecDef Johnson works through the Council to reduce national defense commitments, p. 374 ff; policies change with advent of Gen. George Marshall as SecDef, p. 376; need for correction of navy part of the minutes of the Council, p. 376-7.

A/S HUNTER/KILLER GROUPS: use of them in the Atlantic, p. 271 ff; use of the 10th fleet information on location of German subs, p. 281-2.

USS ASTORIA: se entries under Battle of MIDWAY.

USS ATLANTA: operations in the Guadalcanal area, p. 228 ff.

ATOM BOMB: use of over Japan, p. 331-2.

ATTU: the advanced base (1945), p. 302.

USS BALCH: see entries under Battle of MIDWAY.

BALDWIN, Hanson W.: classmate of Worthington, p. 12; roommates, p. 12-13; p. 28

BALLENTINE, Admiral John J.: stationed at Dahlgren (1924) p. 22.

USS BENHAM: Worthington given command, p. 144 ff; amphibious operation at San Clemente under Commodore Conolly, p. 149-150; training excercises in the Hawaiian area, p. 151-2; plane guard duty with the carriers, p. 152-3; drill in night torpedo attacks, p. 153; operates with the ENTERPRISE at time of Pearl Harbor attack, p. 156-8; aid to the disabled SARATOGA, p. 160-1; refitting at

Worthington

Mare Island, p. 162-3; escorts convoy to Pearl Harbor, p. 163; reassigned to Des Ron 6, p. 166; joins with CV HORNET and her escort for Tokyo raid (April, 1942), p. 167; carries orders from Halsey to deliver Nimitz messages from Kinkaid, p. 170-2; p. 174; (for participation in Battle of MIDWAY see entries under MIDWAY) brings wounded from HAMMANN back to P.H., p. 188-190; repairs at P.H. p. 190-1; as part of revamped DesRon 6 departs Pearl for the Solomons, p. 192 ff; Worthington directs BENHAM torpedoes be re-set for depth after reports from SS patrol people in Feb. 1942, p. 207, participation in operations off Guadalcanal, p. 210 ff; the first night fueling, p. 210-211; fueling situation, p. 212, p. 214; p. 217-8; participation in battle of Eastern Solomons, p. 220 ff; detached to command of Adm. Ghormley, p. 224 ff; escorting HMNZS MONOWAI (transport), p. 225-6; joins the escort of BB WASHINGTON under Adm. Willis A. Lee, p. 229; under a variety of commands, p. 232 ff; re-fueling incident involving commercial tanker and civilian crew in harbor of Espiritu Santo, p. 235-7; Worthington relieved as skipper (Nov. 11), p. 237; story of her final mission and loss on Nov. 15, p. 239-41.

BLAKELEY, Vice Admiral Charles A.: p. 26, p. 28.

BRISTOL, RADM Mark L.: Cinc, Asiatic Fleet, p. 44; p. 46.

BUREAU OF ORDNANCE: Worthington has temporary duty upon graduation - Naval Powder Factory, Naval Proving Ground, p. 20-21.

Worthington

BURKE, Admiral Arleigh A.: p. 389.

USS CHESTER: p. 232

CHIANG kai-chek: p. 69

USS CHICAGO: rammed by the British merchantman SILVER PALM p. 96-8.

CHUNGKING: see references to gunboat TUTUILA.

CINC ATLANTIC: Worthington reports to staff of Admiral Ingersoll (Marc, 1944) p. 270 ff; duties as Assistant Operations Officer, p. 271; flagship - USS VIXEN, p. 271-3; problem of supplying Atlantic escorts, p. 273-4; hunter/killer CVE Task Groups, p. 271; their employment for protection of large convoys, p. 275; p. 283-4.

CIVILIAN CONSERVATION CORPS (CCC): use of naval officers in running the camps, p. 89-90.

COM DES RON 57: Worthington takes over (Jan. 1945) as skipper in Alaskan waters, p. 296; DD ROWE served as flagship, p. 296; periodic raids on Japanese installations in the Kurile Islands, p. 297 ff; other operations, p. 302 ff; icefield in the Bering Sea, p. 303-4; picket ship duty off Okinawa, p. 309 ff; note on DD Division 115 - assigned to ComDes Ron 57 but never reported, p. 330-1; Worthington relieved of command on November 2 - returns to the U. S., p. 337.

CONOLLY, Admiral Richard L.: squadron Commander of DD's in Pacific - flagship the BENHAM, p. 147; - fitness report he made out, p. 148; his conduct of an amphibious operation at San Clemente, p. 149; "close-in-Conolly", p. 149-150; p. 168.

CONVOYING - Atlantic Ocean: see entries under Cinc, ATLANTIC.

CRU DIV 6: duties of the Aide and Flag Secretary, p. 122-3; realistic excercises in Pacific and off Panama, p. 124.

DAHLGREN PROVING GROUNDS: (1924), p. 21-22.

DAVIS, VADM Arthur C.: Deputy U.S. member of the NATO Standing Group, p. 385-6; p. 388; p. 393, p. 395.

DESRON 6: p. 166; also see entries under Battle of Midway and USS BENHAM.

DRAEMEL, RADM Milo F.: Commander, DD's Pacific, p. 155.

DUTTON, Captain Benjamin, Jr.: succeeds Ingersoll as skipper of the Nokomis, p. 33, p. 35.

EASTERN SOLOMONS, Battle of: p. 220 ff; Worthington cites value of this operation, p. 223-4.

EDGEWOOD ARSENAL: Worthington attends chemical warfare school, p. 71-2.

ELY, Lt. Gen. Paul: French Military Representative in Washington (1952), p. 387.

USS ENTERPRISE: p. 152-4; carries fighter planes and marine pilots for reinforcement at Wake, p. 156; her planes launched, Dec. 7, p. 157. flagship of Adm. Kinkaid for landing operation on Guadalcanal, p. 211 ff; Battle of Eastern Solomons, p. 221 ff; damaged, p. 222; pursued by Japanese planes, p. 223; returns to Pearl Harbor for repairs, p. 224.

USS FARENHOLT: p. 228 ff.

FLETCHER, Admiral Frank Jack: for participation in Battle of Midway - see entries under MIDWAY. p. 210; p. 217.

FORRESTAL, The Hon. James: SecNav - his orders for Adm. Ingersoll and his comments on them. p. 286-8. as SecDef, p. 341; p. 345.

FOURQUET, Col. Michel: French member of the NATO Standing Committee Team, p. 386.

GATCH, Vice Admiral Thos. L.: Assistand JAG, p. 111.

GUADALCANAL OPERATION: p. 210 ff.

USS GUADALCANAL - CVE: p. 277; her capture of the German Submarine, S-505; p. 280-1.

GUNNERY E (for excellence): Worthington comments on malpractice in the fleet, p. 92-5.

HALSEY, Fleet Admiral Wm.: p. 155-6; p. 158; enroute for relief of Wake Island - recalled, p. 159; p. 169; Tokyo raid, p. 167 ff; takes his Task Force to the Coral Sea, p. 170 ff.

USS HAMMANN: see entries under Battle of MIDWAY.

HART, ADM Thomas C.: sends navy families home from Far East (1940) - army with a policy of sending them out to the Far East, p. 137.

HAWAIIAN DETACHMENT: set up in 1940 with VADM Andrews as Commandant, p. 127; increasing need for supplies pointed up inadequacy of Pearl Harbor as a fleet supply base, p. 129.

USS HELENA: p. 228 ff.

HELICOPTERS: use of by Cruiser ROCHESTER, p. 354-5; p. 362;

use of during amphibious exercises off Cape Porcupine, Labrador, p. 366 ff.

HENRY PU YI (Hsuan Tung): former boy emperor of China - later Chief of State in Manchukuo, p. 44.

HIRYU - Japanese CV: attack on YORKTOWN and U.S. attack on her - see entries under Battle of MIDWAY.

USS HORNET: with her Task Force in Pacific preparatory to the Tokyo raid, p. 167-8; joins Task Group for Battle of Coral Sea, p. 170; (for her participation in Battle of MIDWAY - see entries under MIDWAY) as part of T.F. 16 sails for Solomons, p. 193 ff.

HUSSEY, Vice Admiral George: p. 166.

HYDROGRAPHIC OFFICE: sponsors three surveying ships, p. 29-31; methods employed in these surveys - triangulation towers, p. 33-35.

ICHANG: see references - TUTUILA.

INDUSTRIAL WAR COLLEGE (Industrial College of the Armed Forces): Worthington detailed there as Director of Department of Instruction, p. 338-350; struggle to develop a curriculum, p. 339-343; becomes a joint Army/Navy College, p. 341; the ad-hoc committee to deal with reconstitution of the Industrial College, p. 343-5.

INGERSOLL, Admiral R.E.: skipper of the surveying yacht NOKOMIS, p. 29-31 p. 33; p. 77; Worthington becomes aide and flag secretary to him as Comdr. CruDiv 6, p. 122; his personal views sought on many fleet problems, p. 126; Comdr. Cruisers Hawaiian Detachment (1940),

p. 127; Vice Chief of Naval Operations (June, 1940), p. 130; promises Worthington a staff job, p. 131; requests Worthington for Atlantic Fleet staff (1943), p. 249-50; Worthington reports in March, 1944 as Asst. Operations Officer, p. 270-2; recipient of praise in Washington STAR for Atlantic convoying job, p. 283-4; a new command (Nov. 1944) - Commander, Western Sea Frontier - ceremony in office of COMINCH - copy of unusual orders, p. 286-8; Worthington's comments on Adm. Ingersoll through the years - with illustrations, p. 289-96.

INTELLIGENCE SCHOOL - Advanced: Worthington lectures there during tour of duty at Naval War College, p. 266-7.

INTERNATIONAL AFFAIRS DIVISION of CNO: Worthington assigned there, p. 373 ff; also as liaison officer with Armed Forces Policy Council, p. 374 ff; reviewing JCS papers for international complications, p. 378-9; review of documents pertaining to the MacArthur recall, p. 379-80; policy on visiting officers of the highest rank, p. 382; p. 385.

JAG OFFICE: Worthington asks for assignment there, p. 111; task of reviewing general courts-martial, p. 112-6.

JAPAN - Coastal bombardment: Third Fleet efforts, p. 322-4; use of DDs on WATCH DOG Station, p. 324 ff.

JAPAN - the Surrender: an American attitude, p. 333-4;

conditions in Tokyo Bay, p. 335-6.

JAPANESE CODES: p. 50-51.

JAPANESE NAVAL TACTICS: Discussion of, p. 218-9.

JOHNSON, The Hon. Louis - SecDef: p. 374.

JOINT CHIEFS OF STAFF (JCS): Strategic Survey Committee reviews all orders exchanged between JCS and General MacArthur, p. 380; practice of greater freedom in expressing individual views, p. 384.

KAMIKAZE: p. 317-21.

KING, Fleet Admiral Ernest: p. 296.

KINKAID, Admiral Thomas C.: p. 170; p. 172; p. 174; p. 211-12; p. 214-5; p. 217; p. 221.

KURILE ISLANDS: see entries under ComDesRon 57.

LABOR PROBLEMS: Guadalcanal area, p. 235-6.

USS LANSDOWNE: p. 228 ff.

MacARTHUR, General Douglas: President Truman recalls him from the Korean command, p. 379-80.

USS MACON - CRS-5: the loss of the MACON off the Pacific Coast, p. 101.

MAGIC CARPET: p. 334-5.

MARSTON, Major General M. W.: Commander, 2nd Marine Division, p. 150-51.

MATANZAS HARBOR: p. 32.

MATERIEL DIVISION - Chief of Naval Operations: Worthington has temporary duty - assigned to study war plans with emphasis on logistics, p. 75-77.

MATTHEWS, The Hon. Francis P.: p. 375; p. 378.

McCLUSKY, RADM Clarence Wade, Jr.: led dive bomber attack from ENTERPRISE on Jap carriers off Midway, p. 200-1; p. 205; p. 208.

USS MEMPHIS: Worthington goes to her from the Nokomis, p. 36 ff; embarks President Coolidge for the Pan American Conference in Havana, p. 39 ff; cruising at eight knots to save fuel, p. 41; MEMPHIS to the Far East, p. 43-52; (see appendix for account of an exercise in the Far East, p. 52).

MIDWAY, Battle of: as seen by skipper of the DD BENHAM, p. 175-92; an overall account of the Battle as prepared by Worthington for a speech on the subject, p. 195-210; presentation of the subject at the Advanced Intelligence School, p. 267-9.

USS MINNEAPOLIS: Worthington attends gunnery school aboard, p. 106-7; reports for duty on her (1938) as aide and flag secretary, p. 122 ff.

USS MISSISSIPPI - BB: p. 320-1.

MITCHELL, General Billy: the attempt of his bombers to sink the old BB WASHINGTON, p. 24.

HMNZS MONOWAI: escorted by DD BENHAM to Sydney, p. 225; orders in poetry form, p. 226-7.

USS MORRIS: p. 228 ff.

NATIONAL DEFENSE RESEARCH COMMITTEE: Worthington becomes
(1943) War College representative on applied mathematics
panel, p. 254-5.

NATO STANDING COMMITTEE: Worthington becomes member of the
long-range planning team under VADM Arthur C. Davis,
p. 385-6 ff; study of U. S. Atomic responsibility,
p. 387; British attitude towards U. S. naval aircraft
carriers, p. 389-90; British attitude towards Turkey in
NATO, p. 391; attitude of the Scandinavians in NATO,
p. 392-3; Holland the question of minesweepers under
NATO, p. 393-4; the British and a proposed NATO Mining
Agency, p. 396-7.

U. S. NAVAL ACADEMY: entrance (1920), p. 3-4; big hazing
incident, p. 4-5; the first cruise, p. 7-10; second
class cruise, p. 13; scholastic difficulties in the
second class year, p. 16-17; first class cruise, p. 18;
teaching in the Department of Seamanship and Flight
Tactics (1931), p. 70-1; additional Academy duty of
Worthington (1937), p. 117; Board of Investigation of
charges against dental department, p. 117-8.

NAVAL RESERVE CRUISES: see entries under USS ROCHESTER.

U. S. NAVAL WAR COLLEGE: Worthington attends command class
(1943-), p. 244-7; Worthington goes on staff of President
Pye as gunnery officer and assistant for tactics, p. 249 ff;
Worthington gives series of presentations to class

Worthington

dealing with experiences gained in Pacific, p. 251 ff; incorporates data from battle reports, etc., p. 253; task of keeping several fleet tables up-to-date, p. 253; the staff in 1943-4 - various duties, p. 256-7; strict adherence to provisions contained in Sound Military Decision, p. 259-60; summary of recommendations submitted to President Pye by Worthington when he left for sea duty, p. 261-4.

NIMITZ, Fleet Admiral Chester W.: takes command in Pacific on New Year's, 1942, p. 159-60; p. 170-2; p. 174. (For entries on Nimitz and Battle of Midway - see MIDWAY.)

NIMITZ, Captain Otto: p. 108-9.

USS NOKOMIS (Survey Yacht): commanded by R. E. Ingersoll, p. 29; surveying the Cuban waters, p. 29-30; p. 32.

USS NORTHAMPTON: Worthington assigned as gunnery officer (June 1940), p. 131 ff; visits to Midway, Johnston Island and Palmyra, p. 133; installation of radar and its proved usefulness, p. 134-5; orders for modernization at Pearl Harbor Navy Yard, p. 138; orders changed to Mare Island for new AA batteries - final target practice using radar and the success, p. 139-40; new installations - new skipper, p. 141-2; flagship for ADM. Taffinder, p. 143-4.

USS NORTH CAROLINA - BB: part of Task Force 16 - first fast BB to join the Pacific Fleet, p. 193 ff; joins formation in Eastern Solomons - her accuracy and value of her presence, p. 222; damaged, p. 224; p. 231.

OKINAWA: ComDES RON 57 operates off Okinawa at end of war, p. 309 ff; escort duty in connection with typhoon, p. 313 ff.

USS PATOKA: equipped with mooring mast for lighter-than-air craft, p. 27.

PAYNE, Captain S. S.: skipper of the NORTHAMPTON, p. 132; p. 140.

PEARL HARBOR: readiness prior to Dec. 7, 1941, p. 154-5; Halsey's interpretation of the order of Nov. 28 for fleet maneuvers, p. 155-6; fleet units enter the Harbor on Dec. 8, p. 157-8.

USS PENSACOLA: Worthington assigned to her, p. 90; gunnery practice off San Pedro, p. 92-3; incident off the West Coast during her cruise, p. 95; comments on high grade of naval personnel in time of depression, p. 99-100; special voyage to return remains of Belgian Ambassador to Antwerp. p. 104.

PICKET SHIPS - off Okinawa: p. 309 ff.

POINT OPTION: an explanation, p. 215-6.

USS PORTLAND: see entry under Battle of MIDWAY.

POSTGRADUATE SCHOOL: Worthington attends - p. 72-4.

PRATT, Admiral W. V.: CNO, p. 79; p. 91.

USS PRESIDENT COOLIDGE: p. 235; sunk in our own minefield, p. 234-5.

Worthington

PYE, Vice Admiral Wm. S.: President of the Naval War College, p. 244; Worthington remains at War College on staff of Pye as gunnery officer and assistant for tactics, p. 249 ff; Worthington argues for modernization of War College procedures - supported by Pye, p. 259-60; evaluation of Pye as War College President, p. 269-70.

RADAR: first installation in the cruiser NORTHAMPTON, p. 134-5; final spectacular target practice before return to Mare Island, p. 139-40.

REEVES, ADM Joseph Mason: skipper of the BB NORTH DAKOTA for midshipmen cruise of 1923, p. 18-19; in command - emergency transit of Panama Canal, p. 102.

USS ROCHESTER: Worthington becomes skipper in Dec. 1948, p. 351-2; installation of a helicopter deck, p. 354-5; p. 362; refresher training, p. 355-6; Reserve Cruises, p. 354; p. 357-8; docking incident in Sydney Harbor, p. 359; visit to Nahant and annual meeting of Society of Electrical Engineers, p. 363; visit to Marblehead, Mass., p. 364; Newport, R.I., p. 365; Labrador and the amphibious exercises, p. 366-70; encounter with a whale, p. 371-2; Worthington turns over command, p. 372-3.

USS ROWE - DD: flagship of DD Squadron 57, p. 296; see also entries under ComDesRon #57.

USS SALT LAKE CITY: p. 228 ff.

USS SARATOGA: p. 160-61.

SAUER, RADM Edward Paul: officer on board the BB TEXAS
(1924), p. 26; p. 37-8.

SCOTT, RADM Norman: p. 233; p. 237.

SHANGHAI: see references to gunboat TUTUILA.

USS SHENANDOAH (CRS-3): flies flag of RADM Moffett - target
towing for gunnery practice, p. 26-7.

SHERMAN, Admiral Forrest: CNO, p. 375; his corrections of
record of the Armed Forces Policy Council, p. 376-7;
p. 380; his great ability as CNO, p. 381.

SOUND MILITARY DECISION: Textbook of Naval War College, p. 244;
subsequent references through p. 270.

SPRUANCE, Admiral Raymond: for participation in Battle of
Midway - see entries under MIDWAY.

STANDLEY, Admiral Wm. H.: CNO and Acting SecNav, p. 113.

SYDNEY, Nova Scotia: incident pertaining to docking
instructions, p. 358-9.

TAFFINDER, Vice Admiral S.A.: uses NORTHAMPTON as his flagship, p. 143-4.

USS TEXAS - BB: Worthington's tour of duty on her (1924),
p. 22 ff; experiments with the ex-BB WASHINGTON, p. 23-6;
use of drill shells to deliver coup de grace to
WASHINGTON, p. 25-6; exercises with USS SHENANDOAH,
p. 26-7; p. 39.

TULAGI: U. S. Marines land simultaneously with landings on
Guadalcanal, p. 213.

USS TUTUILA: River gunboat on the Yangtze - Worthington
reports for duty, p. 53 ff; hits a submerged rock,
p. 54-7; data on the construction of this ship, p. 58-60;
incidents on the river involving bandits and communists,
p. 61-7; turned over to Chiang Kai-chek, p. 69.

TYPHOON: the huge storm that hit Okinawa at end of the
Pacific War, p. 313-5.

USS VIXEN: converted yacht - flagship of CinC, Atlantic,
p. 271-3; see other entries under CinCLant (Atlantic);
trip to the Caribbean, p. 285-6.

WAKE ISLAND: p. 156; p. 159.

USS WALKE: p. 228 ff.

WAR PLANS: discussion of War Plans for Pacific and Atlantic
(1932-3), p. 76-9.

USS WASHINGTON (ex-BB): used for bombing tests (1924), p. 24;
tests with depth charges, p. 24-5.

USS WASHINGTON - BB: joins the Task Force off Guadalcanal -
command of Admiral Willis A. Lee, p. 229 ff.

WATCH DOG STATION: designated for DD duty with BBs bombarding
Japanese coast, p. 324 ff.

WEEMS, Captain P. V. H.: p. 72.

WILEY, Comdr. H. V.: skipper of the MACON when she was lost,
p. 101; p. 110.

WILLIWAWS: (Alaska), p. 300-1.

WORTHINGTON, RADM Joseph Muse: personal data, p. 1-3; lacked aptitude for law - sent to Executive Department, USNA, p. 117; his tennis prowess puts him in touch with senior officers in Hawaii, p. 145-6; his marriage while on duty at the Naval War College (Oct. 1943), p. 264; Adm. Pye delays his detachment in Dec. 1943, p. 264-5; his lectures to the Advanced Intelligence School at the Henry Hudson Hotel, p. 266-7; retirement, p. 397; post retirement activities, p. 398.

YAMAMOTO, Fleet Admiral I.: p. 209-10.

YAMATO - Japanese Super Battleship: U. S. fleet units train to meet her in Alaskan waters, p. 306-8.

YANGTZE River: see references under gunboat TUTUILA.

USS YORKTOWN: for participation in Battle of MIDWAY - see entries under MIDWAY.

Appendix

1. Exercises against submarines and aircraft on 14 and 15 November 1928: observations and comment on,

2. Diary of a Trip Up the Yangtze March 1929.

3. Total Losses and Wrecks Yangtze River 1900 - 1929

4. History of USS TUTUILLA commissioning until 8 December, 1930.

5. C. O. PALOS letter dated 1 November, 1930 Subject: Interference with Shipping on Yangtze River by unwarranted gunfire from shore by bandits or communists.

6. Despatch from USS GUAM to COMYANGPAT Feb 17th 1930 re TUTUILA armed guard action mileage 181-186 Brigadier General Dai Tien-min embarked in CHIOHUEN.

7. Despatches from TUTUILA to COMYANGPAT 8 Sept 1930 re TUTUILA action 81 miles above Chengling at Beacon 21 and TUTUILA War Diary 8 - 9 September 1930.

8. Japanese plan and brief 3 - 4 June 1942.

9. A Destroyer at Midway.

10. Opposing Forces Midway.

11. Industrial College of the Armed Forces-Letters.

12. Industrial College of the Armed Forces-Charter.

13. Cruisers Atlantic Battle Efficiency 1949.

14. C. C. ROCHESTER (Duke) letter of 23 December, 1949.

15. Commander Cruisers Atlantic Fleet Letter of December 24, 1949. (Rear Admiral Allan E. Smith.)

Appendix

1. Exercises against submarines and aircraft on 14 and 15 November 1928: observations and comment on,

2. Diary of a Trip Up the Yangtze March 1929.

3. Total Losses and Wrecks Yangtze River 1900 -1929.

4. History of USS TUTUILA commissioning until 8 December, 1930.

5. C. O. PALOS letter dated 1 November, 1930 Subject: Interference with Shipping on Yangtze River by unwarranted gunfire from shore by bandits or communists.

6. Despatch from USS GUAM to COMYANGPAT Feb 17th 1930 re TUTUILA armed guard action mileage 181-186 Brigadier General Dai Tien-min embarked in CHICHUEN.

7. Despatches from TUTUILA to COMYANGPAT 8 Sept 1930 re TUTUILA action 81 miles above Chengling at Beacon 21 and TUTUILA War Diary 8 - 9 September 1930.

8. Japanese plan and brief 3 - 4 June 1942.

9. A Destroyer at Midway.

10. Opposing Forces Midway.

11. Industrial College of the Armed Forces Letters.

12. Industrial College of the Armed Forces Charter.

13. Cruisers Atlantic Battle Efficiency 1949.

14. C. C. ROCHESTER (Duke) letter of 23 December, 1949.

15. Commander Cruisers Atlantic Fleet Letter of December 24, 1949. (Rear Admiral Allan E. Smith.)

CL15/A16-3 U.S.S. MEMPHIS

Manila, P. I.

From: Lieutenant (jg) J.M. Worthington, USN.
To : Commanding Officer.

Subject: Exercises against submarines and aircraft on 14 and 15 November, 1928; observations and comment on.

Reference: Your memorandum of 19 November, 1928.

    1.   On 14 November, 1928, I observed one submarine about 0700 and a second one at 1400. Both were on the surface and well outside our anti-submarine screen. Our main battery fired upon them. In time of war this might not be practicable, but vessels of the screen should be able to drive them off successfully.

    2.   During the air attack on 15 November, 1928; the diving - straffing attack of the pursuit planes appeared to be the most effective. The excessive speeds of these planes would make them difficult to hit with our present anti-aircraft battery. It is a question whether or not their machine gun fire would do much damage during the short interval of the attack. Anti-aircraft crews could take cover, then bring down the planes when they began to climb. The bombers and torpedo planes, due to their slow speeds and low altitudes, afforded excellent targets for our anti-aircraft battery. One torpedo plane appeared to be the best target of them all.

    3.   Under war conditions the zigzagging would have to be done at high speeds to be effective.

    4.   Our main battery with present type of shell would be almost useless against aircraft. Fitted with fused and supersensitive projectiles it should be effective against torpedo planes; also other planes at long range; were it possible to divert it from its main objective, enemy surface ships. A modern five-inch anti-aircraft battery should be able to prevent such an air attack as was made on 15 November from reaching its objective.

                                            J.M. WORTHINGTON

DIARY OF A TRIP UP THE YANGTZE MARCH 1929.

S.S. KUNGWO 9 March

Sailing from Shanghai at eight a.m. we soon passed Woosung and commenced the thirteen hundred mile voyage up the Yangtze River. The larger steamboats only make the docks at the most important cities, but at other places passengers are embarked or disembarked in the following manner. Some distance, up or down river as the case may be, from where it is desired the ship to stop; a flag of the steamboat company is hoisted in a conspicuous place. A large sampan puts out from the shore, the ship stopping only long enough to pass a line to it, then proceeds towing the sampan alongside. The passengers scramble in and out, their baggage is tossed after them; and the sampan cast off to work its way back to the village often some distance away. Josh sticks are set off to insure safe passage to those departing on the steamer.

Nanking 10 March

From the river the Nationalists' capital of China is a most unimpressive sight. Several government buildings are in view displaying the Nationalist flag quite prominently. British, French, Japanese and Chinese warships are anchored in the harbor. Considerable troops movements are in evidence. All day long soldiers of Chiang Kai Shek's army were embarking on tenders and transports. These ships had recently been commandeered from the China Merchant Steamship Navigation Company and are apparently bound up river. The troops appear well clothed and equipped, fairly well disciplined but very young looking.

The writer was informed that these guns were of Japanese make, of very inferior quality and could not last firing a hundred rounds. Also that the bullets which they used were made of compressed paper and not dangerous over fifty yards.

Nganking 11 March

The waterfront here is lined for miles with tooops; some are marching to the westward along the road on the North bank of the river, others lined up in ranks and the remainder bivouaced. One of the recently commandeered China Merchant ships, Ning Shah, lies moored to the docks still loaded to capacity with troops. These were embarked at Nanking yesterday. At least ten thousand troops are in view along the river bank.

Wu Chang Hien 12 March

This is one of the more important industrial cities of China. There are extensive Japanese interests here in iron ore, coal and limestone. No Chinese soldiers are in sight but considerable peacetime activities.

The mile after mile of mudflats of the lower Yangtze are a very unattractive sight as are the mud and straw huts on the river banks which house millions of Chinas people. The rice paddies form the greater part of the green crops which are everywhere at this season. Further up the river, nearer Hankow, the banks become higher, hills appear back from them; and/all kinds of crops are flourishing on the intervening ground. Not only the level ground is cultivated but the hillsides are terraced and thus made productive. The houses in this area are batter most of them being built of wood and many of brick or stone. The proximity of armies does not appear to have stopped the normal activities of the people.

S.S. Siang Tan, Hankow 13 March

This city appears peacefully outwardly but there is an undercurrent of feeling that trouble might be anticipated at any time. American, British, French, and Japanese men of war are present; the last named being far the greater number. The Japanese concession is well barricaded and defended by three thousand marines ashore, in addition to their warships afloat. The Chinese had just celebrated the second month of the Japanese boycott. Regardless of expected trouble the docks bore evidence of much work going on in loading and unloading cargoes. All ships flying foreign flags, excepting Japanese, are loading to the maximum draft permitted by the depth of water at the present time, for up and down river ports. There seem to be much more cargo than available ships.

The uncertainties of river transportation are illustrated by the apparent inability of shipping agencies in one port to give information as to sailings in the next port. Cook's representative in Shanghai sold a ticket to Hankow with a permit to obtain a ticket on any one of four steamship companies (Two British, one American, one Chinese) which might be operating between Hankow, Ichang, and Chunking. Meanwhile the Chinese ships had been taken over by the soldiers and were not handling passengers. Shipping agencies in Hankow would give no assurance as to when the next ship might be expected to leave Ichang for Chungking, or that there would be one sailing soon.

This trip of the S.S. Kung Wo from Shanghai was her first one without an armed guard of British Bluejackets on board. This is also the first trip of the Siang Tan without one. The latter has considerable armor plate placed around her bridge, and still bears marks of previous meetings with bandits. They seem to delight in firing at foreign merchant ships whether or not they also attempt to rob them.

Cheng Ling   14 March

This town is situated at the point where the Yangtze branches off, one branch continueing on known as the middle Yangtze, the other leading to Lake Tung Ting. This ship was required to stop here to clear the customs before proceeding up river. Although Yo Chau a large city lies on the lake but five miles distant, all their goods must pass through the customs authorities here. Yo Chau has repeatedly attempted to have their own customs officials, but with no success. The only foreigner regularly living here is a Frenchman who is in charge of surveying the middle river.

15 March

Late yesterday the U.S.S. Palos passed us standing down river. The American Flag and the old gunboat were both welcome sights. The SiangTan anchored for the night one hundred and eighty miles above Hankow, while the Captain and the Chief Officer kept watch on the bridge in case of trouble. This is the part of the river where one has to steam eightyfour miles to cover twenty in a straight line.

Sha Sze   16 March

While passing Temple Hill, mileage one hundred and twenty-five from Cheng Ling about dusk last evening, we were fired on from shore. Two shots struck the water about twenty yards ahead of the ship, causing the coolies forward to stampede aft and the Chinese pilot to stop the ship. The Captain reached the bridge immediately and rang up full speed ahead . It was necessary to anchor the ship for the night about an hour later.

Shipping on this part of the river has experienced considerable trouble from bandits in the last two years. Only in December a ship of this company was pirated from within. This latter danger readily exhists , where in a ship of six hundred tons there are several hundred coolie passengers, with the Captain and his Chief Officer the only foreigners on board.

We arrived here this afternoon discharging many passengers and considerable cargo. A squad of soldiers thoroughly inspected every piece of personal baggage taken ashore. It seemed to be a rather unusual sight to an American, to see a private soldier inspect a Chinese Army Officer's baggage the latter being in full uniform) in the same manner as the coolies'. A Japanese gunboat is the only foreign man of war present. There are few foreigners here.

Ichang 17 March

Anchored last night thirty miles above Sha Sze, continued at dawn and reached here early this afternoon. The upper part of the Middle Yangtze River is far more interesting and attractive to see than the lower. Farms are everywhere and crops of many kinds flourishing. Many fruit trees are in full bloom.

S.S. Kang Ting

Upon arrival here transferred to this ship which had been scheduled to sail at eleven this morning. An opium raid had just been made and considerable quantities found on board. The ship had recently been laid up at Chungking due to low water, which time had been taken advantage of by the coolies to smuggle some aboard. The leading Chinese fireman had been arrested and the others went ashore on a strike in sympathy.

The Captain, Chief Officer, and two engineers are the only foreigners regularly on the ship. For the present there is a British Bluejacket Guard of one petty officer and three men, which make travelling on these ships safer. They are armed with a Lewis machine gun, which is kept mounted during the day, and four rifles. The guard keep a continuous watch day and night. The general opinion is that ships without armed guards are often fired at, while those with them are usually left alone. There is a British and a Japanese gunboat here. The U.S.S. Palos had just left for overhaul at Shanghai. The U.S.S. Monocacy is due to arrive shortly.

18 March

The Head fireman was bailed out of jail for a thousand dollars, the compredore for five hundred, the striking firemen returned and the ship sailed at three p.m., an hour later entering the gorges. These Gorges of the Yangtze certainly are one of the wonders of the world. A swift current varying from four to fourteen knots, rocks of all kinds some awash but the most dangerous ones concealed beneath the surface of the muddy water, and a constantly changing depth of water, are some of the worst of the dangers to navigation encountered in the passage through them.

It is next to impossible for a foreigner to navigate them properly. Almost super sense of these waters by the Chinese pilots bring ships safely through. They have spent their lives in this work, starting with junks, and their ancestors have done the same for centuries before them. It is fascinating to watch them guide the ship by amotion of the hand to the native quartermaster at the wheel.

About sixthirty pm. we passed through a particularly dangerous place in the Kung Ling Tan rapids, when the water is at this level. In the last two months five ships have struck here, two are total wrecks, one cost several hundred lives, the others had to be sent to Shanghai for repairs. We struck our starboard propellor and were headed for another rock, when the Captain by fine shiphandling took the conn from the pilot and brought the ship to a safe anchorage above the rapids.

Kwei Fou 19 March.

The ship received a pirating this morning of a kind the armed guards were helpless to prevent. With our four thousand horsepower in this two hundred/ton ship, we backed up all possible steam for an attempt at the Hsin Tin Rapids. In a distance of two hundred feet there is a rise of several feet in elevation at this stage of the water. We swung back and forth balanced in the rapids with both engines steaming full speed ahead, and called for the Chinese trackers (men who make their living hauling ships over) to take our line. Seeing our perilous position they refused to take our line until promised a thousand dollars, the usual price being a hundred and seventyfive. The wire line was lead to a rock ahead on the beach and our capstan soon pulled us over. When the trackers came aboard they were bargained down to threehundred and twenty dollars and a promise that the next trip would cost the regular price. The trackers presented the Captains with some fresh fish and left the ship the best of friends.

A little farther on a Chinese ship was being hauled over the rapids by a hundred or so trackers. We held back as long as possible but were forced to pass them in the rapids, a dangerous undertaking. We missed them with few feet to spare, as our stern swung across their bow.

In the afternoon passed through Wind-box gorge with the water at its lowest level. At high level it rises to a hundred and eighty feet and the current becomes very strong. This water rises as much as forty feet in a few hours. The sides of the gorge rise almost perpendicular, two to three thousand feet. It is a most interesting sight. Up river from the gorge is a large salt settlement in the bed of the river. The houses are all of bamboo and it is often necessarry to abandon the village on a few hours notice, sometimes with considerable loss of life. Everywhere along the river the Chinamen build houses and plant their crops as fast as the water drops.

Wansien 20 March

Anchored last night above Kwei Fou and worked our way over Hsin Lung Tan rapids this morning. We did this in a different manner from the others. Having stuck at the top the passengers were moved forward and the ship slid over. Just below here the U.S.S. Oahu and the H.M.S. Tern are anchored to protect foreign interests. The latter reports that taxes are becoming more and severe all the time, even to the extent of taxing an individual duck purchased ashore for the officers mess.

The ship was stopped here to be inspected by the custom's officials. At the present time Wansien considers herself neither in Ah Hui nor Sze Cuan Province, hence claims the right to tax all goods passing up or down river. Our small cargo was taxed to the extent of four hundred dollars. The inspection was made by a group of about forty men dressed in anything from rags to uniforms. They carried flashlights, sticks, and iron pokers digging into every possible place on the ship for an hour. They even attempted to inspect the foreigners baggage, but were not permitted to do so.

Fou Chou   21 March

During the day passed six ships of the Yangtze Rapids Company, flying the American Flag and standing down river. These ships are painted white and have large American Flags painted conspicuously in about six different places. Their shallow draft and high power permit operating on the upper river in the low water season, when nearly all other ships are stopped. At present they are not carrying armed guards.

Chunking   22 March

Arrived here this afternoon thirteen hundred and thirty miles from Shanghai. Foreign men of war present are; U.S.S. Tutuila, H.M.S. Gannet, French, Japanese and Chinese gunboats. There is a large foreign community here.

Little mention has been made in these notes of the great beauty of the upper river. That is a large subject of which much has already been written. The gorges are wonderful, and the scenery from Wansien here particularly fine at this season.

TOTAL LOSSES
AND
WRECKS.

1900 Paddle steamer "Suihsiang"	Wrecked at Kunglingtan. T. L.	
1915 S.S. "Lichuan"	" at Yehtan T. L.	
1919 " "Chuchuen"	" Lanchupa, in fairway, blown up April 1920 T. L.	
1921 " "Meishun"	Wrecked at Moukoutan; made fast; submerged all summer; salved Feb/March 1922	
1923 " "Anning"	Wrecked below Fouchou; made fast, submerged all summer; salved Feb/March 1924.	
1924 " "Robert $"	Wrecked at Chaipantze, made fast, submerged all summer; boilers. deck fittings and 60 feet of fore and of vessel salved.	
" " "Pakiang"	Wrecked at Yehtan T. L.	
1925 " "Hanhuo"	" at Tatungtan. T. L.	
" " "Anlan"	" at Changshou. T. L.	
1926 " "Tehyang"	" at Hsiangchi. T. L.	
" " "Chiyung"	" at Shipaochai. T. L.	
" M.V. "Chiayang"	" at Yehtan T. L.	
1928 S.S. "Fooklai"	" at Kunglingtan. T. L.	
" M.V. "Pinghuo"	" at Miaochitze, made fast. submerged all summer salved Feb/March 1929; ready to float on rising river.	
1929 S.S. "Pingfu"	Wrecked at Kunglingtan; in fairway, blown up. T. L.	
" M.V. "Chunan"	Wrecked at Yaochanho. T.L.	
" S.S. "Chuhuo"	" at Hsintan. T.L.	

HISTORY OF THE U.S.S. TUTUILA

The U.S.S. TUTUILA class of gunboat was designed to answer the long felt need for a type of vessel capable of steaming in any section of the Yangtze River, from its mouth to Chungking, at any water level. This type of ship was particularly designed to operate in the upper river between Ichang and Chungking, during the dangerous low water season. Her construction was begun by Kiangnan Dock and Engineering Works, Shanghai China, in 1926, under the direct supervision of United States naval officers. In her trials held off Woosung, China, 17/ 20 February, 1928, she made 15.6 knots, 360 revolutions per minute. Her maximum designed speed was 14.5 knots, 322 revolutions per minute.

The TUTUILAS main propelling machinery consists of two vertical triple expansion reciprocating engines, built by Kiangnan Dock and Engineering Works, Shanghai, similar to those engines installed in upper river merchantmen of the I'PING type, having a combined horsepower of 1950. Steam is supplied by two Thornycroft boilers of the watertube express type, located in a single fireroom. Two large reciprocating blowers supply forced draft. Electricity is generated by two 25 kilowatt turbo generators (Westinghouse) and a 10 kilowatt auxiliary kerosene generator. Refrigeration is supplied by a York one ton carbon dioxide ice machine. There is installed a rugged steam steering engine to operate the three rudders simultaneously, and an ingenuous device for rapidly shifting to hand steering in an emergency. The ground tackle is very heavy and designed especially for upper river duty. The anchor engine drives the capstane either for handling chain, or wire cables used to heave the rapids should that be necessary. The radio equipment consists of a low and a high frequency transmitter, one each low, intermediate and high frequency receiver.

The TUTUILA armament consists of two 3" 23 caliber guns, firing high explosives and shrapnell, and eight mounted Lewis machineguns. In addition there are Lewis machine guns, Thompson subcaliber 45s, light Browning automatic rifles, Army riot shotguns and Springfield rifles, for use as may be required in equipping armed guards or a landing force. The bridge and radio room are well protected with special bullet proof armor, while the mounted guns also have shields.

The TUTUILA was commissioned 2 March, 1928, in Shanghai and commanded by Lieutenant Commander Frederic Baltzly, U.S. Navy. Her complement then was three line and one medical officer; fiftyfive enlisted men and five native boatmen. She departed upriver 13 March and spent three months convoying merchantmen in the upper Yangtze River, returned to Shanghai for post commissioning repairs in June, resumed convoying in July steaming 4859 miles during the next three months. This is the greatest mileage ever steamed by a river gunboat in a like period of time, and most of it was steamed in the upper river during the high water season when the current is very swift. She returned to Shanghai again for repairs on 16 October and proceeded upriver again on 3 December. On 29 December while convoying two Yangtze R Rapid ships the TUTUILA had her first engagement, and was required to silence fire from troops ashore at Lochi with machine gun fire. She arrived at Chungking the same day and from 3 January to 16 February was engaged in arduous convoy duty in the upper river between Chungking and Ichang during the dangerous low water season.

The following data is taken from an analysis of accidents in the upper Yangtze River since steamer operation commenced: total losses thirteen, submerged for the summer and subsequently salvaged at low water level four, salvaged ten, salvage pumps in operation 1925 29 fortytwo. In the year 1929 there were : seventy vessels operating, fortyseven accidents, eighteen ships suffering minor hull damage, fourteen extensively damaged necessitating vessel being repaired in Shanghai seven accidents to propellors and rudders, three damaged shafting, and three total losses.

On 8 February 1929 the TUTUILA proceeded to the assistance of the S.S.Chita, which ship had struck at mileage 206.6 above Ichang, beached to effect repairs, to her badly damaged forehold, and was attacked by bandits. On 22 March the ships motor sampan turned over in a rapid at Lungminho off Chungking and sank immediately. No trace was ever found of this motorpan. On 24 March the TUTUILA received Priority orders to Hankow and proceeded at once, altho the water was known to be dangerously low.

At 1052 on 26 March, 1929, while steaming downriver the TUTUILA struck a submerged rock at mileage 102.5 above Ichang. Two of her five large compartments and twofuel oil tanks were taking water fast and at 1055 the ship was successfully beached at mileage 102. The ship was rapidly sinking and at the instant of beaching her main deck forward on both sides was going under, and she was drawing nine feet while her normal draft fully loaded is six feet. In order to lighten the ship forward: anchors and chain, gunone 3" with shields, wire cables with reels, ammunition and all accessible gear forward: were removed. The oil bunkers were pumped out and holes cemented up. The following day, H.M.S. TERN, Lieutenant Commander MacKenzie, Royal Navy Commanding, arrived from Wanhsien with cement and other necessary salvage gear, and stood bye the TUTUILA until this vessel was afloat and Yangtze Rapid Ships IPing and L'Ling stood in from down river. The Masters of these ships Captains J.Harris and Jollidon respectively assisted in effecting temporary repairs with all the facilities at their command. There was great danger of a sudden rise in the river at this low water level submerging the ship. The ChiPing, Captain J.Anderson, carrying salvage gear, pulled out her windlass attempting to heave the Hsin Tan rapid. The little Chi Nan, Captain Opperman, finally succeeded in getting over this rapid with a large salvage pump and cement.

The compartments were pumped down, holes in the bottom plugged and cemented, nine tons of dry cement being required, and on 1 April the ship proceeded to Shanghai under her own power for extensive repairs.

On 15 April, 1929, Lieutenant Commander S.D. Truesdell, U.S. Navy assumed command. Two great improvements in design resulted from this accident to the ship. Two double bottom compartments were installed forward, and later an eleven inch main drain connection was made to the fire room and engineroom and the main circulator capable of pumping the ships displacement in water overboard in an hour. On 6 July the TUTUILA proceeded upriver again visiting various ports in the lower and middle river reaching Ichang 22 September. From that date until 28 April 1930 the TUTUILA was based on Ichang, Chungking and Wanhsien, and operating entirely in the upper river.

On 20 January, 1930, the TUTUILA steamed past the wreck of the S.S. Shuhuo in the Hsintan rapid making extra flank speed, by bypassing high pressure steam to the intermediate pressure cylinders, sixteen knots, four hundred revolutions per minute. The previous winter this vessel steamed the same rapid at the lowest level it has ever been steamed, but that was not as dangerous as passing the wreck of the Shuhuo in the rapid at a slightly (0.4 foot) higher local (Hsintan) water level. Altho well equipped for heaving rapids with steel wires, capstans, rolling chocks and anchor engine, the TUTUILA has always had sufficient power to steam the worst rapids at the lowest water levels.

After the S.S. ChiPing, Captain Opperman, (Lieutenant U.S. Naval Reserve) was heavily fired upon, and Lieut. (J.G.) Winslow U.S.N. commander of the armed guard was wounded, the TUTUILA was ordered down river and steamed to Ichang on 15 March, returning upriver the following daylight with Yangtze Rapid ships I8Ling, I'Ping, ChiChuen and ChiNan in convoy. On 17 April, 1930, the TUTUILA proceeded to Ichang again, embarked Commander Yangtze Patrol, Rear Admiral T.T. Craven U.S.N., and carried him on an inspection trip to Chungking and return. In the summer this ship visited Hankow, Kiukiang and Shanghai. At the latter place on 17 July Lieut. Comdr. L.P. Bischoff U.S.N. assumed command.

On 8 September, while proceeding upriver mileage 210 above Hankow, the TUTUILA had her first main battery action, being fired on by a trench mortar ashore, and promptly destroying its emplacement with three inch high explosives. The following day she was fired on by rifle fire at Kwai Yin Dzo, 8 miles below Shasi, and silenced this fire with three inch and machine guns. On 17 November the TUTUILA was fired on by field guns on Temple Hill and replied with twenty four rounds of three inch, dislodging one gun. Twentyfour minutes later, four miles downriver two trench mortars fired at fifty yards range. Fire was returned with five three inch and machine gun fire. On 18 November this ship was fired on by rifle fire mileage 156 above Hankow, where S.S. Kiating was aground. The TUTUILA returned fire with twentyseven three inch and machine guns.

During the winter 1929 30 the TUTUILA furnished armed guards consisting of an officer and six men, on merchant ships. These guards were resumed again in September, 1930, and engaged in numerous accidents with the Communists, who maliciously fired on American Merchantmen in the middle river. These guards protected the lives of our nationals and their property.

U.S.S. PALOS

Chengling, China
1 November, 1930.

MEMORANDUM:

From: Commanding Officer, U.S.S. PALOS.
To: Masters, American Merchant Ships operating on Yangtze River.
Officers and Petty Officers of Armed Guards.

Subject: Interference with Shipping on Yangtze River by unwarranted gunfire from shore by bandits or Communists.

1. There is listed below a summary of recent localities where firing has occurred on merchant and Naval vessels from shore.

Places of Danger on Middle River.

Miles above Cheng-ling	Rifle - R Mortor muzzle- } - M Loader Fieldgun - G		Mileage Hankow to Chengling Bluff = 128.3 Details	Who & When reported.
-13	M		1 miles below Yanglachi - left bank	Luzon 25/10/30 Br.G.Boat 25/10/30
-12	M		Yanglachi - left bank.	
-8.9	R-M		- Left bank.	SS Siangtan 23/10/30
-6.5	M		Polachi - left bank	
3	M		Polachi - left bank.	YR #2 23/10/30 H.K.K.Stmr. 23/10/30
4	R		Tungting village - left bank	
6	R-M-G	1A	#2 Crossing - left bank	B&S steamer 24/10/30
6	R	2A	#2 Crossing - left bank	B&S steamer 24/10/30
9	R-M-G	3B	#3 Crossing - left bank	
12	R-M-G	4C	#4 Crossing - left bank	
12	M		#4 Crossing - left bank	Widgeon 24/10/30
14	R		#7 Crossing - left bank	
19	R	8	#8 Crossing - left bank	
37	G	9A	Hsia Chi Wan	Luzon 27/10/3
40	R	10B	Shang Chi Wan - Headquarters.	
56	R	11A	#15 Crossing - left bank	
58	R		#16 Crossing - Kienli, left bank	Aphis 30/10/3
64	R		- left bank	
69	R		- left bank	
71	R		#18,#19 Crossings, both banks	
72	M		#18,#19 Crossings, left bank	YR #2 24/10/30 LKK Stmr. 24/10/30
76	R		#20A Beacon - left bank.	
	R		#23 Crossing - left bank.	
79.5	R		Bedwell's reach - right bank	Oahu 15/9/30
124	R		Temple Hill - Right bank	
140	M		4 miles below Hosueh	YR #2 24/10/30
144	R		Hosueh - left bank	SS Poyang 12/9/30
164	R		9 miles below Shasi - left bank.	
164	R		9 miles below Shasi - left bank.	S/S Wuhu 28/10/30

R.D. Tisdale,
Lieutenant Commander, U.S.Navy,
Commanding, U.S.S. PALOS.

U.S.S. TUTUILA

TO: COMYANGPAT
FROM: USS GUAM
INFO: USS TUTUILA, PANAY, OAHU

FEB 18TH 1930

DATE
Release
System RADIO

1017 TUTUILA ARMED GUARD REPORTS 30 SHOTS FIRED AT CHINAN AND CHICHUEN MILEAGE ONE EIGHT ONE RIGHT BANK BY FIVE CHINESE SOLDIERS BELIEVED TO BE STRAGGLERS FROM ONE THOUSAND TROOPS ON MARCH MILEAGE ONE EIGHT TO ONE EIGHT SIX REPORTED TO BE REVOLTED YANG SEN SOLDIERS ENROUTE TO FENGTU TO JOIN LIU HSIANG FORCES FIRE SILENCED BY THREE MACHINE BURSTS TOTAL ROUNDS TWENTY THREE NO CASUALTIES BRIGADIER GENERAL DAI TIEN MIN IN CIVILIAN CLOTHES TOOK PASSAGE ON CHICHUEN WANHSIEN TO FENGTU 1200

YANGTZE PATROL, U. S. ASIATIC FLEET

FROM	TUTUILA	Date **8 SEPT**
TO	COMYANGPAT	Rec'd by
INFORMATION	CINC ASIATIC	System
HEADING:	~~(CONFIDENTIAL)~~	TFC / TOB

0008 FIRED ON AT FIFTEEN TEN BY TRENCH MORTAR FROM RIGHT BANK EIGHTY ONE MILES ABOVE CHENGLING AT BEACON TWENTYONE PERIOD ONE SHOT FIRED FROM SHORE PERIOD SILENCED THE FIRE WITH FOUR HUNDRED ROUNDS MACHINE GUN AND FOUR THREE INCH PERIOD NO CASULTIES ON BOARD PERIOD BELIEVE SHORE GUN DESTROYED 1610

YANGTZE PATROL, U. S. ASIATIC FLEET

FROM	TUTUILA	Date **8 SEPT 30**
TO	COMYANGPAT	Rec'd by
INFORMATION		System
HEADING:	~~(CONFIDENTIAL)~~	TFC / TOB

0008 SHORE GUN FIRED AT RANGE SEVENTYFIVE YARDS ON PORT QUARTER PERIOD RED FLAG WAS HOISTED OVER LOCATION OF FIRING IMMEDIATELY AFTER SHOT AND TWO MEN APPEARED OVER BANK PERIOD ALL SHOTS FROM THREE INCH GUNS MADE DIRECT HITS ON EMPLACEMENT AND MACHINE GUN FIRE EFFECTIVE PERIOD RED FLAGS ARE DISPLAYED AT MOST TOWNS ALONG THIS SECTION OF RIVER 2030

YANGTZE PATROL, U. S. ASIATIC FLEET

FROM	TUTUILA	Date 9 SEPT
TO	CYP	Rec'd by
INFORMATION	OAHU CINC	System
HEADING:	(CONFIDENTIAL)	TFC / TOR

0009 AT THIRTEEN FIFTY FIRED ON BY RIFLE FIRE LEFT BANK EIGHT MILES BELOW SHASI AT KWAI YIN DZO PERIOD ABOUT THIRTY RIFLE SHOTS XXXXXX FIRED FROM SHORE PERIOD SILENCED FIRE WITH TWO HUNDRED ROUNDS MACHINE GUN AND TWO ROUNDS THREE INCH PERIOD NO CASUALTIES ON BOARD PERIOD CASUALTIES ASHORE UNDETERMINED 1445

YANGTZE PATROL, U. S. ASIATIC FLEET

FROM	TUTUILA	Date 9 SEPT 30
TO	COMYANGPAT	Rec'd by
INFORMATION		System
HEADING:	(CONFIDENTIAL CODE)	TFC / TOR

0009 NO HITS FOUND ON SHIP PERIOD RIFLE FIRE WAS DESULTORY AND COMMENCED UPON OUR APPROACH TO THE SOLDIER APPARENT HAVING HIS WAY AT SPOT WHERE RED FLAG WAS HOISTED PERIOD MADE TWO DIRECT HITS ON THIS PLACE WITH THREE INCH HIGH EXPLOSIVE SHELLS AT RANGE TWO HUNDRED YARDS PERIOD XXXX MACHINE GUN FIRE ALSO EFFECTIVE PERIOD THIS PLACE SCENE OF THE LADYBIRDS ACTION REPORTED BY OAHU PERIOD MADE REPORTS OF OUR ACTION TO COMMANDING OFFICER FASHIN AT SHASI 1810

(CODE K)

ENROUTE HANKOW TO ICHANG, CHINA
8 SEPTEMBER, 1930

~~CONFIDENTIAL~~

COMMANDING OFFICER'S DIARY OF DAILY EVENTS.

MONDAY, 8 SEPTEMBER, 1930

AT 5:74 UNDERWAY UPRIVER. THE MOON WAS UP SO WE WERE ABLE TO GET GOING EARLY. THE CURRENT IS RUNNING STRONG IN THE RIVER SO PROGRESS HAS BEEN VERY SLOW.

COMMENCING AT BRINDS BEND RED FLAGS WERE DISPLAYED AT MOST OF THE VILLAGES.

AT 1510 JUST AFTER PASSING CLOSE TO A SMALL VILLAGE ON RIGHT BANK AT BEACON 21- EIGHTY ONE MILES ABOVE CHENGLING A TRENCH MORTAR WAS FIRED AT US AT CLOSE RANGE, DISTANCE ABOUT SEVENTY-FIVE YARDS. ONLY ONE SHOT WAS FIRED. IMMEDIATELY THEREAFTER TWO MEN APPEARED OVER TOP OF EMPLACEMENT AND PLACED A RED FLAG. THEY DROPPED WHEN FIRED AT BY RIFLES FROM BRIDGE. THE SHORE GUN FIRED ON OUR PORT QUARTER. ONE MACHINE GUN COULD OPEN FIRE SO TURNED SHIP AND OPENED FIRE WITH STARBOARD MACHINE GUNS AND THREE INCH GUNS. FIRED PORT BATTERY AS PROCEEDED UPRIVER. FIRE WAS VERY EFFECTIVE, ALL SHOTS FROM THREE INCH MAKING DIRECT HITS ON GUN EMPLACEMENT DESTROYING IT. IT IS NOT KNOWN WHETHER THE GUN CREW ESCAPED OR NOT. THE VILLAGE ITSELF WAS NOT SHOT UP BUT MAY HAVE RECEIVED RICHOCHETS. SOME WOMEN AND CHILDREN WERE LEAVING THE VILLAGE MOST CASUALLY AS WE APPROACHED. THIS SHOULD BE AN INDICATION IN THE FUTURE THAT THERE MAY BE ACTION. THE OCCUPANTS FLED TO THE WOODS ABOUT HALF MILE AWAY WHEN WE OPENED FIRE.

THE CREW BEHAVED VERY WELL AND PERFORMED THEIR DUTIES WITHOUT ANY UNDUE DISPLAY OF EXCITEMENT.

OUR NEXT TOWN WAS CHOW CHING KOU. IT WAS RESPLENDENT WITH RED FLAGS AND A GROUP OF PRESUMABLY SOLDIERS WERE WEARING RED SLEEVE BANDS. THE WHOLE TOWN WHICH WAS QUITE LARGE TURNED OUT AND WATCHED US PASS. NO INDICATIONS OF ANY ACTION WERE OBSERVED HERE. THEY HAD PROBABLY HEARD OUR FIRING SEVEN MILES AWAY NOR HAD GOT WORK.

WE HAD TO SPEED UP A BIT TO MAKE A SUITABLE ANCHORAGE JUST ABOVE KWAI YINZO

HELD MOVIES AS USUAL THE AUDIENCE BEING INCREASED BY INSECTS OF ALL DESCRIPTIONS.

~~CONFIDENTIAL~~

COMMANDING OFFICER'S DIARY OF DAILY EVENTS.

TUESDAY, 9 SEPTEMBER, 1930.

    BEGAN TO BELIEVE THEY WERE CONVINCED THAT GUNBOATS WERE NOT TARGETS. WHEN WE APPROACHED KWAI YIN DZO 9 MILES BELOW SHASI, A RIFLE SHOT RANG OUT OVERHEAD AND A SMALL PUFF OF SMOKE WAS SEEN ON BANK TO LEFT OF CITY. A LITTLE LATER ANOTHER BUT DIDN'T SEE THE PUFF. A RED FLAG WAS PERCHED ON BANK WHERE FIRST SHOT APPEARED. COMMENCED SENDING RANGES TO GUNS. A SOLDIER APPEARED ON THE BANK WAVING A RED RAG AND THEN FIRED AT US. SHIP THEN COMMENCED FIRING WITH STARBOARD BATTERY RANGE 200 YARDS. AFTER THREE INCH PUT ONE SHOT IN BANK NEAR RED FLAG. IN MIDST OF FIRING SOLDIER AGAIN APPEARED WITH RED RAG, AND AS HE DISAPPEARED THREE INCH HIGH EXPLOSIVE SHELL MADE A BEAUTIFUL HIT TEARING A BIG HOLE IN THE DIKE AND STRUCK THE RED FLAG AND I BELIEVE DESTROYED THOSE BEHIND IT. THE MACHINE GUNS WERE THROWING A BARAGE. CEASED FIRING SEEING NOTHING FURTHER TO SHOOT AT. THERE WERE NO MORE RIFLE SHOTS SO I CONCLUDED THAT THE RIFLE FIRING WAS THE WORK OF POSSIBLY THREE OR FOUR SOLDIERS. THE CAPTAIN OF THE H.M.S. LADYBIRD INFORMED ME THAT THEY CAME UNDER HEAVY FIRE AT THIS TOWN AND WAS OBLIGED TO BOMBARD IT ON SATURDAY, 6 SEPTEMBER WITH HIS ENTIRE BATTERY OF THREE INCH AND SIX INCH GUNS INFLICTING HEAVY CASUALTIES AND DRIVING THE COMMUNISTS TO THE HILLS. AT THAT TIME THE MAIN COMMUNIST ATTACKING FORCE WAS LOCATED HERE. IT WAS SAID ASHORE THAT THE RED COMMANDER WAS KILLED BY THE BOMBARDMENT. WE PROBABLY CAUGHT A FEW REMNANTS WHO WISHED TO BE CALLED "BRAVOS" DONT BELIEVE ANY SHIP WILL BE FIRED ON IN THE FUTURE AT KWAI YIN DZO.

    AS IN THE PREVIOUS ACTION THE OFFICERS AND CREW WERE NOT EXCITED. AMPLE PREPARATIONS HAD BEEN MADE TO MEET ALL EMERGENCIES.

    ANCHORED AT SHASI, ASTERN OF THE H.M.S. LADYBIRD AND BRITISH BOARDING OFFICER CALLED IMMEDIATELY. THE DOCTOR AND I CALLED ON THE LADYBIRD AND THE CAPTAIN GAVE ME ALL THE NEWS. HE ASKED ME TO TAKE AN ACUTE CASE OF APPENDICITIS TO ICHANG AS HE HAD NO DOCTOR, TO WHICH REQUEST I GLADLY CONSENTED. A BRITISH PHARMACIST'S MATE ACCOMPANIED HIM ON THE TRIP.

Brief 3 - 4 June 1942

In brief the Japanese plan was to strike our northern forces and bombard Dutch Harbor on 3 June, and divert our other forces in that direction. The carrier striking force was to soften up Midway the following day, and then strike our Pacific Fleet. The landing force was to take Midway on 6 June. The Aleutian Support Force was to take station half way between Midway and the Aleutians. The Main Body cruised several hundred miles to the rear of the striking force.

First action on 3 June was the attack on Dutch Harbor. Next, our patrol plane sighted Jap occupation force southwest of Midway, and B 17s launched unsuccessful attack, but night patrol pines damaged enemy tanker.

Early on 4 June many planes reported approaching Midway. Simard launched every flyable plane to intercept, and directed fighters to stay clear at first, then attack approaching bombers. The first enemy wave was intercepted, some damage was inflicted on Midway, but the airfield remained operational, and the Japs ordered a second attack. Meanwhile, Simard ordered his planes to land and refuel.

In the next couple of hours there were eight successive attacks by Midway based planes upon the Jap carrier task forces. First, dive bombers and B-26s; second, high level B-17s; third, glide bombers; fourth most obsolete of our planes. Although no hits were scored by these courageous attacks, those making them contributed much to the ultimate success of this battle. The Japanese were confused, their aircraft operations were seriously hampered, and their forces became scattered. About the time of the fourth attack our submarine appeared, and caused further confusion, and unwittingly let our planes to the target. The valliant torpedo plane attacks, while suffering terrible losses, added greatly to the confusion of battle. All these earlier attacks contributed to final victory.

UNITED STATES SHIP BENHAM

A DESTROYER AT MIDWAY

A 1,500 Tonner and 925 Survivors.

A Record Rescue?

by RAdm. Joseph M. Worthington, USN (Ret.)

ON THE MORNING OF JUNE 4, 1942 I was in command of the United States Destroyer BENHAM, DD-397, 1,500 tons, stationed in the screen of the carriers ENTERPRISE and HORNET. Our aircraft were then engaged in intensive offensive operations against the large Japanese forces approaching Midway. Shortly after noon, orders were received from our task force commander, Admiral Raymond A. Spruance, to join the heavy cruisers PENSACOLA and VINCENNES and the destroyer squadron flagship BALCH, and to proceed at maximum speed to reinforce the cruiser-destroyer screen of the aircraft carrier YORKTOWN, which was under heavy attack by Japanese carrier aircraft. Our small group had no sooner started in the direction of the YORKTOWN task force than we sighted dead ahead a huge column of smoke over the horizon, which was pouring skyward from YORKTOWN's first battle damage of the day.

After joining, about 1335, the YORKTOWN task force which had stopped while repairs were being made to the carrier, our ships took their stations in the screen, and as soon as possible all ships increased speed to the maximum the damaged carrier could attain, at first 5 knots, but 17 knots by the time that the Japanese torpedo attack reached the launch point.

At about 1432 the planes had been reported approaching the formation from a radar bearing 200 degrees true distant 30 miles, and about three minutes later BENHAM opened fire on the enemy planes at maximum range bearing 270 degrees. The torpedo planes flew so low that they appeared to be dipping between the masts of the ships in the screen. Every anti-aircraft gun in the task force which could be brought to bear was firing on the attacking planes. Some cruiser eight-inch guns were also firing into the sea in advance of the torpedo planes in the hope that the shell splashes would interfere with the accuracy of the torpedo fire.

During this attack Ensign Walter E. Pierce of BENHAM was mortally wounded and four others also were wounded by fragments of an anti-aircraft shell which struck the stack, and severely damaged our only lifeboat. All the enemy planes were shot down, most of them by anti-aircraft fire from our ships. I remember radically maneuvering the BENHAM to avoid being struck by falling flaming planes which hit the water close aboard. Some flaming aircraft narrowly missed other vessels in the screen as they crashed into the sea. The BENHAM was credited with assisting in shooting down five planes. Nevertheless, two torpedoes struck the YORKTOWN, and she quickly took a list toward the damaged side.

That famous aircraft carrier had been structurally weakened by battle damage in the Coral Sea engagement, and had had only hurried twenty-four-hour emergency repairs at Pearl Harbor enroute to Midway. She had already sustained bomb hits from enemy carrier planes in the first attack of the day and she now received severe underwater damage from torpedoes. Extensive damage control measures were attempted, but the ship lay dead in the water, and took a severe list, which steadily increased from progressive flooding. Capsizing appeared likely, another air attack was imminent, and enemy submarines were known to be present in the area; the order was given to abandon ship.

About 1500, 4 June the officers and men of the YORKTOWN climbed down cargo nets and ropes and slid into the sea, while several destroyers closed in to effect the rescue of some 2,300 men in the water. Life rafts were dropped into the ocean by all the ships in the vicinity. The one damaged lifeboat of the BENHAM was launched immediately and did splendid service both in rescuing personnel from the sea, and in towing heavily loaded life rafts to the destroyer.

One near tragedy occurred when another air attack was reported. The destroyers were ordered to cease rescue operations, and resume their anti-aircraft stations in the screen of the now crippled carrier, which still lay dead in the water. The BENHAM interrupted rescue operations momentarily. But her position near the stern of the carrier, in the middle of hundreds of men close aboard awaiting rescue, made it impossible to turn over the propellers without the great danger of injuring some of those struggling in the ocean to keep afloat.

Fortunately, this air attack was unable to penetrate the surface screen, and rescue operations were quickly resumed. When the first rescuing destroyers were loaded, they returned promptly to stations in the screen as ordered, and other destroyers relieved them in the lifesaving operations. Because of the BENHAM's position in the middle of the floating mass of

The YORKTOWN takes a direct hit from an enemy bomber despite the intensity of anti-aircraft fire.

Joe Worthington is a Marylander, born and bred; in fact he's from "Crabtown-on-the-Bay" and now lives in retirement at Gibson Island, Maryland. In addition to command of the BENHAM during World War II he was on the staff of Commander-in-Chief, U. S. Atlantic Fleet and in the last year of the war commander DesRon 57 in the Western Pacific. He's a member of the class of '24 and a mighty tennis player.

humanity in the sea she did not follow the prescribed procedure, but continued rescue operations. We took aboard, in all, 725 survivors of the aircraft carrier, by cargo nets, lifelines, rafts, stretchers and our damaged lifeboat.

The task of caring for such a large number of survivors in so small a ship, with such limited facilities, was a stupendous one. All those taken aboard who were able to walk were directed aft to the fantail, where oil-soaked clothing was removed and thrown in a pile. Several hoses were led out to enable survivors to wash off as much oil as possible. Then the rescued were directed in groups as large as could be accommodated to the boiler and engine rooms, steering engine room and to every available compartment below decks, where they could dry off and warm up. These groups were followed by successive groups until all had been taken care of as well as possible.

Officers and men of the BENHAM supplied the naked men with clean and dry clothing from their personal wardrobes. The large number of rescued were crowded into every possible space in the ship for the night. Some forty officers were squeezed into the commodore's small stateroom and day cabin which I used as my in port cabin. They took turns throughout the time they were aboard standing and sitting, and they left behind them oil smudges on the bulkheads.

One unusual incident occurred when the crew started to throw overboard the pile of oil-soaked clothing, which had reached such proportions as to seriously impede service to weapons in the fantail area. (BENHAM mounted four five-inch 38's. One five-inch, the depth charge racks; four K-gun throwers and 20 mm. were aft.) A survivor suddenly remembered having left a large sum of money in the pockets of his discarded dungarees. An inspection not only resulted in recovering this money, but much more money and many valuables from the clothing. Money and personal possessions were returned to their owners, who had been much more concerned with the safety of their shipmates than in recovering their valuables.

The final rescue on June 4 by the BENHAM was that of a fighter pilot, a tall Texan, who was spotted on his little raft at sunset by an alert lookout. His shouted comment, as the BENHAM approached him, is worth quoting:

"Take your time Captain—I'm in no hurry. This raft won't run out of gas."

Subsequently one of his shipmates revealed that this same pilot had been forced down three times recently in flight operations because he had a habit of chasing Japanese aircraft to the limit of his own gasoline supply.

The rescuing destroyers and the cruisers were ordered to retire eastward during the night. Every effort was made by all hands to render first aid to the injured, and to feed and care for the survivors.

The more seriously injured were attended in the destroyer wardroom where the ship's doctor, Lieutenant (jg) Seymour Brown (MC), had set up an operating room. Later, when the urgent work of attending the injured was completed, the young doctor learned that among able assistants in the wardroom were the medical and dental officers of the carrier recently rescued from the sea. They had been far too busy caring for those needing attention to identify themselves. Dr. Brown's comment afterwards was:

"I thought those volunteer assistants seemed well qualified in rendering first aid."

The task of feeding so many from so small a galley was quite an operation. Soup, coffee, beans and other foods were quickly broken out from the storerooms, and the galley was operating to capacity on an around the clock basis, with the galley force ably augmented by all the cooks among the YORKTOWN survivors.

Shortly after sunrise the following morning June 5, Ensign Pierce was buried at sea. Chaplain Hamilton, recently rescued from the YORKTOWN, conducted the service, and shipmates acted as pallbearers.

The next task on the 5th was the transfer of 7 officers and 16 men, selected damage control personnel from the YORKTOWN survivors, to the ASTORIA for subsequent salvage work. The remainder of the 725 rescued were then transferred to the heavy cruiser PORTLAND, while both ships were underway at sea. Five breeches buoys were used simultaneously to transfer personnel, and the airplane crane of the cruiser was employed to handle stretcher cases, the entire operation lasting nearly four hours. The transfer by means of breeches buoys seemed a comparatively smooth and simple operation from the destroyer viewpoint. PORTLAND personnel controlled all lines, had more space to work from than the destroyer, and her men were well trained and proficient in this work. Handling stretcher cases was a much slower operation, and required considerable care, since for each transfer the destroyer had to move in very close to the cruiser to enable the airplane crane to reach over to the smaller ship's well deck, and then sheer out as soon as the stretcher was lifted.

About midpoint during this transfer operation, in response to an inquiry from the PORTLAND, the writer estimated total transfers would reach a figure of about 400. The executive officer of the cruiser, Commander T. R. Wirth, then advised that that number had already been received aboard his ship by actual count. When informed then that only about one-half of the survivors had been transferred his comment was:

"You must think this ship is the Grand Hotel."

With the crowded conditions then prevailing in the destroyer, it was difficult to obtain an accurate count, so we were happy to receive the PORTLAND figure as official. Among incidental operations concurrently conducted by the cruiser without interrupting breeches buoy activities were fueling the destroyer and catapulting and recovering scouting aircraft engaged in anti-submarine patrol.

The transfer was completed about 1223 June 5. Aboard BENHAM it had been standing room only for almost 20 hours.

Upon completion of the transfer operations the BALCH, BENHAM and HAMMANN were sent back some 150 miles to the YORKTOWN then drifting virtually derelict and severely damaged, in tow of the ancient tug, VIREO, a converted minesweeper. The destroyer HAMMANN took station alongside the YORKTOWN, put back on board volunteer members of the latter's crew, and also furnished auxiliary power for lighting and operating salvage pumps in the carrier. Salvage work was progressing favorably early on the afternoon of June 6th when torpedoes were reported approaching YORKTOWN from 195 degrees true from outside the screen. A little over two minutes later these struck the HAMMANN and the YORKTOWN at the same time. The destroyer disappeared beneath the sea in about three minutes, and suffered very heavy personnel casualties; the carrier still floated, listing heavily.

Destroyers undertake rescue operations around the damaged YORKTOWN.
OOR-W-NSSD - 6212313   Official U.S. Navy Photo

It is ironic that the HAMMANN, the only destroyer in the screen equipped to measure underwater sound conditions, had reported earlier in the day that sound conditions were very bad due to thermal layers prevailing in the area at that time, and as a result, destroyer underwater sound detection was reduced to almost zero.

For the second time in three days the officers and men of the BENHAM were engaged in rescue operations, although this time their task was to prove far more difficult. Many of those awaiting rescue were wounded, a large number severely. The one life boat and life rafts, all badly damaged, had had to be abandoned upon completion of rescue operations two days previously, and there were few medical supplies, or spare clothing left in the ship.

The BENHAM eased into the sea area of struggling survivors and floating debris. Some 18 of BENHAM's crew jumped into the oily water swimming with life lines to the aid of those in urgent need of help. The rescued were pulled back to the ship, and a great many seriously wounded were lifted aboard in stretchers which had been lowered to the water's edge. First aid for the lightly wounded was administered by members of the crew, for Lt. Brown, the ship's doctor, and his several medical assistants were fully occupied caring for the severely injured.

Too much praise cannot be given to all those officers and men who displayed such selfless devotion to duty in very dangerous waters in order to save others: swimming to the aid of the severely wounded, resuscitating the apparently drowned, and attending the severely injured, who filled nearly every bunk in the ship until the BENHAM reached Pearl Harbor.

The BENHAM rescued some 200 officers and men on June 6, most of whom were survivors of the destroyer HAMMANN, herself at the time engaged in aiding the crippled carrier YORKTOWN. The other survivors were from the YORKTOWN, a number of these having been rescued from the same ship by the same destroyer for the second time in three days. When I recognized several of the YORKTOWN rescued from their previous "cruise" aboard BENHAM, I could not resist remarking:

"The next time you get rescued by a good ship, be sure to stay aboard and don't repeat the ordeal."

The only engineering casualty suffered by the BENHAM occurred early during operations in the debris filled sea, when the starboard main circulator became clogged, and went out of commission. Thereafter there was no backing power on the starboard engine until repairs were effected at Pearl Harbor. Most fortunately full power ahead was available, and that was of vital importance toward completing this rescue mission of delivering wounded to hospitals at Pearl Harbor.

While the wounded were being cared for as well as could be done with the destroyer's limited medical personnel and facilities, funeral services were conducted by the commanding officer for the 26 who died; 16 late on June 6 and the remainder on the next two days. The bodies were sewn in canvas and weighted with drill shells until BENHAM's allowance was gone; then we used live ammunition.

As Captain I conducted most of the services from the forecastle reading extracts from the burial service for the dead at sea from the Episcopal Book of Common Prayer. Lieut. Sloat, the exec, conducted some of the services. BENHAM slowed when the bodies were committed to the deep—but did not stop; we were in submarine waters.

At dawn on the 7th the small salvage group still stood by the YORKTOWN in the hope that with additional help reported enroute to the area, it might still be possible to save her. But the carrier settled to starboard, and soon went under as the ships present rendered honors. Aboard BENHAM we stood at attention facing the great dying ship and half-masted our colors.

The BENHAM was directed to transfer all wounded to a submarine tender cruising in a rear area as an emergency hospital, but I reported that many of the wounded were too severely injured to risk transfer at sea at that time. We were then ordered to Pearl Harbor where the best medical attention and adequate hospital facilities were available.

On departure from the area the BENHAM received from Commander Destroyer Squadron Six, Captain E. P. Sauer, a "Well Done," always most welcome by all hands. Fortunately, a calm sea enabled the ship to proceed at 27 knots, and we arrived at Pearl Harbor early in the afternoon of June 9, the first combatant ship returning from the Battle of Midway. At Merry Point the ship was met by Admiral Nimitz, members of his staff, and a large number of medical personnel and ambulances. Approximately 50 stretcher cases, and 25 ambulatory cases were transferred to the Naval Hospital at Pearl Harbor, and U. S. Mobile Hospital Number 2. All other survivors were transferred to the jurisdiction of their respective type commanders based at Pearl Harbor.

The performance of duty of all officers and men during the brief action against enemy planes on June 4, and again during rescue operations on that date and on June 6, was of such high standard as to make it difficult to single out individuals for especial noteworthy performance. But these men and others reflected the highest traditions of the naval service:

Lieutenant Frank P. Sloat, Executive Officer, for work at his battle station, and general supervision of all rescue operations, and attention to survivors after rescue.

Lieutenant Robert B. Crowell, Gunnery Officer, for controlling the main battery during air attacks, and maintaining the battery alert for expected additional attacks.

Lieutenant (j. g.) Almer P. Colvin, Chief Engineer, for indefatigable efforts in giving first aid to the injured, and resuscitating the apparently drowned.

Lieutenant (j. g.) Russell Merrill, Communications Officer, as officer-of-the-deck during action and both rescue operations.

Ensigns Oliver D. Compton and James V. Heddell, for assisting injured personnel out of the water, caring for them on deck, and finding places for them in the ship.

Lieutenant (j. g.) Seymour Brown (M.C.) first attended a number of wounded from the action on June 4. For the first two hours after the torpedo attack on June 6, he was the only medical officer attending 82 seriously wounded, and a large number of more lightly wounded patients. Later in the day, Lieutenant (j. g.) Edward A. Lee (M.C.) was borrowed from the BALCH. He remained overnight and rendered most valuable service. Also, Lieutenant (j. g.) J. J. Peterson (M.C.) was rescued from the HAMMANN, and after recovering from shock was able to help out.

Pharmacist Mate First Class Kenelm Dyches most ably assisted the medical officer day and night from June 4 until arrival in Pearl Harbor on June 9.

Many others were untiring in helping the medical personnel throughout this trying period among them:

Pharmacist Mate David Walker, Fireman Jackie Spieler, Mess Attendants Alonza Crawford and Leroy Spiller.

The point in this story, which is as vivid today to the writer as it was when observed at close hand over twenty years ago, is the extreme danger to which man will expose himself to save his fellow man. There were a great many examples of personal heroism in the rescue operations carried out by BENHAM. Every officer and man did his utmost, seemingly with no thought of the personal danger that was always present from the enemy in the air, and under the sea. This personal heroism may best be described by quotations from two citations (chosen from among many) for awards submitted subsequently:

... "On 4 June 1942, in the Battle of Midway, during rescue operations of YORKTOWN personnel, Coxswain Hughes, Seaman 2nd Class Callon, Fireman 1st Class Sims and Fireman 3rd Class Horton voluntarily manned the BENHAM's only available whaleboat, well knowing it to be in dangerous condition with falls cut, engine and hull holed by shell fragments, and that another air attack was imminent, fearlessly launched the boat, and by valiant efforts to keep it afloat and running, succeeded in rescuing a great many YORKTOWN personnel, particularly the more seriously wounded in urgent need of assistance. Their courage and devotion to duty contributed much to the success of the rescue operations and was at all times in keeping with the highest traditions of the Naval Service."

... "For distinguishing himself by gallantry and conspicuous devotion to duty while serving in the USS BENHAM (DD-397) in the Battle of Midway on 6 June 1942. With utter disregard for his own personal safety, Chief Boatswain's Mate Webb plunged overboard from the USS BENHAM immediately after the HAMMANN and YORKTOWN were torpedoed, and for more than an hour swam in sea strewn with debris and thick with oil to the aid of seriously injured personnel of those ships. By his great courage, personal daring and determination, he personally towed at least twenty injured men to safety. His leadership, courage, and devotion to duty contributed largely to the success of the rescue operations, and was in keeping with the highest traditions of the Naval Service."

* * * *

Editor's Note.

Never before or since as far as *Shipmate* knows has any destroyer rescued more survivors than did BENHAM during the Battle of Midway. The editor has not combed all the after-action reports (or ship's logs) of World War II but history probably offers no statistically comparable rescue operations, with the possible exception of the British destroyers that rescued the survivors of the PRINCE OF WALES and REPULSE off Malaya.

U.S.N.A. REGISTER OF ALUMNI FOR 1965

The NEW EDITION with address changes as reported to 15 Nov. 1964 can be obtained by filling in this coupon and mailing it with your check to

ALUMNI HOUSE
ANNAPOLIS, MD.

Check or money order should be for $4 plus postage (75¢ east of Mississippi; $1.25 west of Mississippi).

Enclosed is my check (M. O.) for $_____

Name _____

Address _____

appendix 10

BATTLE OF MIDWAY

Opposing Forces (Approximate) 3 - 6 June 1942

U. S.	Type	Jap.
3	CV	4
0	CVL-CVS	3
0	BB	11
8	CA-CL	17
17	DD	45
19	SS	16
	Air	
106	VF	105
139	SB	97
48	TPD	101
32	PBY VO	28
19	B-17	
4	B-26 (T)	
	Totals	
		71 in CVs for Midway
348		402

Midway Defense

6th Marine 2nd Raider 3rd Marine
2881 men

Losses (Approximate)

92 officers		3600
215 men		
1	CV	4 (2220 men)
0	CA	1 (1000) men
1	DD	1 (200 men)
23	VF	
50	SBD	
47	TPD	
1	PBY	
121 planes	Total	332 planes 180 pilots
27 pilots rescued		

BATTLE OF MIDWAY

Japanese Forces

Main Body	Yamamoto	3BB	1CVL	1CL	13 DD
Aleutian Screening (Support Force)	Takaso	4BB	2CL		
Second Fleet	Kondo	2BB	9 CA-CL	1CVL	9DD
Striking Force	Nagumo	2BB	4CV	3 CA-CL	12DD
Occupation Force	Tanaka		2CVS	1CL	11DD
Advance Exped."	Komatsu			1CL	16SS

Totals

- 11 BB
- 4 CV — 17 CA-CL
- 2 CVS — 45 DD
- 1 CVL — 16 SS

At 1220 June 4 Yamamoto ordered Support Force and Second Fleet to join Main Body by noon next day.

THE ARMY INDUSTRIAL COLLEGE
WASHINGTON, D. C.

25 June 1946

Dear Captain Worthington:

Your contribution to The Industrial College of the Armed Forces has been of such value that as the date of my departure draws near I want to leave with you a record of my appreciation. Your handling of the difficult assignment as Director of the Department of Instruction has shown ingenuity and energy of the highest order. You have been an outstanding example of Army-Navy cooperation and your unusual intellectual capacity and broad experience have combined to make you an outstanding member of the staff of the Industrial College. I think I can best indicate my estimate of your character and ability by telling you that I have recommended that on Captain Henning's departure you be promoted to become the Assistant Commandant of the College.

I regret that this letter does not add another ribbon to your unusual collection. Nevertheless, you have the consciousness of duty performed with exceptional skill and ability and that, it seems to me, is worth more than any decoration.

With thanks to you for your loyal cooperation, I am

Sincerely yours,

D. ARMSTRONG,
Brig. General, U. S. Army,
Commandant.

Captain Joseph M. Worthington, USN,
Director, Department of Instruction,
The Industrial College of the Armed Forces,
Washington 25, D. C.

McKINLEY/lh

27 September 1946

To: The Honorable W. John Kenney
Assistant Secretary of the Navy
Washington 25, D. C.

Subj: Promotion of Captain Joseph M. WORTHINGTON, 58719.

Ref: (a) BuPers ltr to Captain Joseph M. Worthington dtd 27 July 1946, 58719, Pers-31521-RM-1C.

1. It is recommended that Captain Joseph M. Worthington be promoted to the rank of Commodore.

2. This officer has done outstanding work in this institution as the Director of the Department of Instruction. Upon the recommendation of the College he was, by Reference (a), assigned as Deputy Commandant, effective 1 September 1946.

3. It is desired that the Navy Deputy Commandant at this College be in the grade of Commodore at this time in order that the Navy may not be at a disadvantage when the Air Forces finalizes the present tentative assignment of a Brigadier General as the Army Deputy Commandant.

4. Eventually, it is proposed that the Industrial College maintain a senior staff made up of a Rear Admiral of the Navy and a Major General and a Brigadier General, one from the Ground and Service Forces and one from the Air Forces of the Army. The Major General and the Rear Admiral will alternate as Commandant and Deputy Commandant and the junior Army representative will, of course, be the additional Deputy Commandant. The recommendation for promotion contained herein is a step in this direction and will complete the presence of three Flag or General Officers from the Services concerned.

E. B. McKINLEY
Brig. General, U. S. Army
Commandant

Pers-32151-ed

14 JAN 1947

Brigadier General E. B. McKinley, U.S. Army,
Commandant, Industrial College of the Armed Forces,
Washington, D.C.

Dear General McKinley:

The Honorable W. John Kenney has referred to me for reply your letter of 27 September 1946 wherein the promotion of Captain Joseph M. Worthington, U.S. Navy, is recommended.

While fully appreciating your interest and the intent of your letter, it is not considered advisable to recommend the promotion of Captain Worthington to the rank of Commodore at this time. In compliance with the desires of the President, it is the present policy of the Navy Department to effect a reduction in the overall number of officers serving in flag rank, and accordingly, it is contemplated to discontinue further spot promotions to the rank of Commodore.

It is regretted that favorable action cannot be taken on your recommendation for the promotion of Captain Worthington, however, your letter will be made a part of his official record.

Sincerely,

Louis Denfeld
Vice Admiral, U.S.N.
The Chief of Naval Personnel

COMMISSION ON ORGANIZATION
OF THE
EXECUTIVE BRANCH OF THE GOVERNMENT

1626 K STREET NW.
WASHINGTON 25, D. C.

September 24, 1948

Captain Joseph M. Worthington, USN
Deputy Commandant
Industrial College of the Armed Forces
Washington, D. C.

Dear Captain Worthington:

    The members of the Committee on the National Security Organization have asked me to express to you their appreciation and thanks for your kindness in appearing before them this week.

    Your comments constituted a material contribution to the appreciation and understanding of some of the serious problems that lie before the Committee.

    May I add my personal thanks to those of the other Committee members.

Sincerely yours,

F. Eberstadt, Chairman
Committee on the National
Security Organization

24 NOV 1948

From: Vice Admiral R. B. Carney, USN, Deputy Chief of
Naval Operations (Logistics).
To: The Chief of Naval Personnel.
Via: The Commandant, Industrial College of the Armed Forces.

Subject: Observation of Captain Joseph W. Worthington, USN
(5_718), performance of duty.

1. On the occasion of Captain Worthington's impending detachment from the Industrial College of the Armed Forces, I wish to record the high regard in which I have come to hold his professional and personal qualifications.

2. Through the Op-4L2 Section of my office, I maintain continual liaison with the Munitions Board, Industrial College of the Armed Forces, and similar activities concerned with the broader phases of producer logistics and, consequently, have had frequent opportunity to size up Captain Worthington's judgment and attainments in those fields.

3. Captain Worthington has been extremely helpful in voluntarily furnishing essential information to this office, in addition to his response to specific queries. He has furnished valuable counsel and assistance in furthering the project of broadening the Navy's logistic education base; and finally, he has been very largely instrumental in maintaining the Department's continuing interest in the objectives and potentialities of the Industrial College.

4. I appreciate the services he has rendered to the Department, and his interest in broader nautical departmental matters associated with the work of the Industrial College. He has shown himself to be a broad-gauge officer of cultural interests considerably beyond the average.

5. It is requested that a copy of this letter be placed in Captain Worthington's official record.

ROBT B. CARNEY

Originated by V. Adm. R.B.Carney, USN (Op-04)
at BUPERS, 24 Nov 48, W.Trowson.

THE INDUSTRIAL COLLEGE OF THE ARMED FORCES

The Industrial College of the Armed Forces is reconstituted as a joint educational institution operating under the direction of the Joint Chiefs of Staff. This institution is recognized as being on the highest level in the educational field within the National Military Establishment.

MISSION

The mission of the Industrial College of the Armed Forces is—

a. To prepare selected officers of the Armed Forces for important command, staff, and planning assignments in the National Military Establishment and to prepare selected civilians for important industrial mobilization planning assignments in any governmental agency by—

(1) Conducting a course of study in all phases of our national economy and interrelating the economic factors with political, military, and psychological factors.

(2) Conducting a course of study in all aspects of joint logistic planning and the interrelation of this planning to joint strategic planning and to the national policy planning.

(3) Conducting a course of study of peacetime and potential wartime governmental organizations and the most effective wartime controls.

FACULTY

a. The Office of the Commandant will be rotated from time to time between Army, Navy, and Air Force officers as directed by the Joint Chiefs of Staff.

b. There will be two Deputy Commandants of flag or general officer rank, one appointed from each service other than that of the Commandant.

c. The faculty and staff will be composed of approximately equal Army, Navy, and Air Force representation, plus such civilian associates as are required, the total number to be determined by the Commandant.

COURSES

The regular course of instruction will be approximately 10 months' duration with classes commencing annually about 1 September. The College also will conduct courses for officers of the National Guard, Reserve officers of the Army, Navy, and Air Force, and selected executives of industry, educators, and prominent citizens. This will consist of a condensed version of the regular course and will be conducted either at the College or in cities throughout the country by members of the faculty of the College.

STUDENT ENROLLMENT

The total student enrollment and the allocation of student vacancies to the services, and to the National Security Resources Board for selected civilians, shall be determined annually by the Joint Chiefs of Staff acting on recommendations of the Commandant. Qualifications of civilian students nominated by the Chairman of the National Security Resources Board shall be subject to the approval of the Commandant.

CRUISERS ATLANTIC FLEET
FINAL RESULTS BATTLE EFFICIENCY COMPETITION
COMPETITIVE 1949

SECTION	WT.	ALBANY CA-123	ROCHESTER CA-124	FARGO CL-106	DES MOINES CA-134	WORCESTER CL-144	MACON CA-132	MISSOURI BB-63	MISSISSIPPI EAG-128	COLUMBUS CA-74	HUNTINGTON CL-107	LITTLE ROCK CL-92	PROVIDENCE CL-82	PORTSMOUTH CL-102	MANCHESTER CL-83
C.I.C.	8	343	432	687	252	261	315	800	136	489	484	531	380	309	138
COMMUNICATIONS	11	622	826	910	315	689	1083	1100	477	931	679	977	939	800	758
DAMAGE CONTROL	12	869	1200	1138	140	455	1089	1057	115	634	841	920	980	777	99
ENGINEERING	24	2350	2393	2400	852	1613	2100	2383	1435	2306	2369	2270	2398	2393	1848
GUNNERY	24	1327	1610	1752	240	298	374	2400	362	686	1654	542	492	737	1301
MEDICAL & DENTAL	3	210	212	241	—	300	209	226	177	196	192	228	182	246	191
SEAMANSHIP	8	774	735	600	—	—	247	683	—	361	800	462	390	440	48
SHIP ADMINISTRATION	6	492	570	432	453	538	568	547	600	504	362	442	512	482	449
SUPPLY	4	360	400	269	—	315	346	340	316	371	291	164	56	309	231
TOTAL		7347	8378	8429	2252	4469	6331	9536	3618	6478	7672	6536	6329	6493	5063
FINAL STANDING		5	3	2	1 MONTH IN COMPETITION	12	9	1	13	8	4	6	10	7	11

NOTE: 1. NEWPORT NEWS, ROANOKE, SALEM & DAYTON IN COMPETITIVE STATUS LESS THAN 3 MONTHS.
2. WORCESTER IN COMPETITIVE STATUS LESS THAN 10 MONTHS.
3. HUNTINGTON, LITTLE ROCK, PROVIDENCE, & PORTSMOUTH IN COMPETITIVE STATUS LESS THAN 9 MONTHS.

ENCLOSURE (J)

U. S. S. ROCHESTER (CA-124)
CARE OF FLEET POST OFFICE
NEW YORK, N. Y.

23 December

Dear Joe,

The enclosed squib from the Newport Bugle will be of interest to you. I understand we made the Providence paper also.

I wish to tell you again how much I thank you for an efficient, easy turnover. You made it a pleasant operation all around, and, as I said Wednesday night, any success I may have during the next year will be in large measure because you gave me something good to work with. You should have a nice sense of "job satisfaction" as a result of your work in this fine ship.

All the officers and men would join me in Christmas greetings to the Worthington family if they knew I was writing you.

Sincerely,

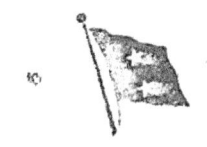

Commander Cruisers
United States Atlantic Fleet

U. S. Naval Base
Norfolk 11, Virginia
December 27, 1949

Captain J. L. WORTHINGTON, USN
Commanding, USS ROCHESTER (CA124)
c/o Fleet Post Office
New York, New York

Dear Worthington:

Thank you for your letter of 21 December, and a Happy New Year to you.

A cruise of a Captain these days is so short that each one of them is up against a very difficult and individual situation if he is to obtain worthwhile results.

Most of the reports I have received concerning the ROCHESTER have been in the area of Excellence.

It is pleasing to see that you consider the ROCHESTER in such fine shape to report to ComCruDesPac.

With kindest regards, and a happy and successful cruise in your new assignment.

Sincerely,

Allan E. Smith

ALLAN E. SMITH
Rear Admiral, USN

www.ingramcontent.com/pod-product-compliance
Lightning Source LLC
Chambersburg PA
CBHW080624170426
43209CB00007B/1511